African Studies
History, Politics, Economics, and Culture

Edited by
Molefi Asante
Temple University

A Routledge Series

AFRICAN STUDIES
HISTORY, POLITICS, ECONOMICS, AND CULTURE
MOLEFI ASANTE, *General Editor*

THE EXPERIENCE OF ECONOMIC REDISTRIBUTION

The Growth, Employment and Redistribution Strategy in South Africa

Clarence Tshitereke

Routledge
New York & London

Routledge
Taylor & Francis Group
270 Madison Avenue
New York, NY 10016

Routledge
Taylor & Francis Group
2 Park Square
Milton Park, Abingdon
Oxon OX14 4RN

© 2006 by Taylor & Francis Group, LLC
Routledge is an imprint of Taylor & Francis Group, an Informa business

Printed in the United States of America on acid-free paper
10 9 8 7 6 5 4 3 2 1

International Standard Book Number-10: 0-415-98014-3 (Hardcover)
International Standard Book Number-13: 978-0-415-98014-2 (Hardcover)

Library of Congress Cataloging-in-Publication Data

Tshitereke, Clarence, 1975-
    The experience of economic redistribution : the growth, employment and redistribution strategy in South Africa / Clarence Tshitereke.
        p. cm. -- (African studies : history, politics, economics, and culture)
    Includes bibliographical references and index.
    ISBN 0-415-98014-3 (alk. paper)
        1. Gold industry--South Africa. 2. Gold mines and mining--South Africa. 3. Industrial relations--South Africa. 4. South Africa--Economic conditions--1991- 5. South Africa--Politics and government--1994- I. Title.

HD9536.S62T77 2006
338.2'7410968--dc22   2006019785

Visit the Taylor & Francis Web site at
http://www.taylorandfrancis.com

and the Routledge Web site at
http://www.routledge-ny.com

Contents

List of Tables

List of Figures

List of Acronyms

ACSA	Airports Company South Africa
ANC	African National Congress
BCM	Black Consciousness Movement
BEE	Black Economic Empowerment
CMLIA	Chamber of Mines Labor Importation Agency
CODESA	Convention for a Democratic South Africa
COSATU	Congress of South African Trade Unions
CSIR	Council for Scientific and Industrial Research
DBSA	Development Bank of Southern Africa
DRD	Durban Rodepoort Deep
EEC	European Economic Community
FDI	Foreign Direct Investment
FEDUSA	Federation of Unions of South Africa
FRELIMO	Frente de Lebarticao de Mozambique
GATT	General Agreement of Tariff and Trade
GDP	Gross Domestic Product

GEAR	Growth, Employment and Redistribution
GENCOR	General Mining Union Corporation
GNP	Gross National Product
IDASA	Institute for Democratic Alternative in South Africa
IDC	Industrial Development Corporation
IFI	International Financial Institutions
IMF	International Monetary Fund
JCI	Johannesburg Consolidated Investment
JSE	Johannesburg Securities Exchange
MERG	Macro-economic Research Group
NEDLAC	National Economic Development and Labor Council
NRC	Native Recruiting Corporation
NUFCOR	Nuclear Fuels Corporation
NUM	National Union of Mineworkers
PAC	Pan-African Congress
RDP	Reconstruction and Development Programme
SABS	South African Bureau of Standards
SACOB	South African Chamber of Business
SACP	South African Communist Party
SANLAM	South African National Life Assurance Company
SAP	South African Police
SAP	Structural Adjustment Program
SAR	South African Republic
SARB	South African Reserve Bank
SASOL	South African Coal, Oil and Gas Corporation Ltd

SETA	Sector Education and Training Authority
SWAPO	South West Africa People's Organization
TEBA	The Employment Bureau of Africa
UDF	United Democratic Front
WNLA	Witwatersrand Native Labor Association

Foreword

South Africa's mineral industries have powerfully shaped our social arrangements for well over 100 years. Southern Africans who made up anonymous pools of cheap migrant labor came to the Witwatersrand to mine our gold and uranium, extract our vast quantities of seemingly inexhaustible supplies of coal and, once done, were spat back to their area of origin, only to resume the cycle of return migration all over again.

At their work, they lived in single-sex quarters called compounds, could not legally join trade unions and were subject to an extraordinary level of regimentation we have come to associate with apartheid. A color bar regulated which categories of work they were permitted to undertake.

Still, the mineral industry provided thousands—close to a million at one time—of Africans with work, income and benefits they had come to grudgingly value. They were exploited certainly, but they had jobs. The coming of democracy in 1994 promised them an even better life and the question is whether it did or not.

A number of monographs that documented the (partial) breakdown of the labor system were published in the 1980s and 1990s, of which mine titled *Our Precious Metal* was one.[1] We then saw the erosion of the color bar in employment, the rise of African trade unionism, improvements in income and conditions of work. We speculated about what the introduction of democratic and constitutional rights for all under the leadership of President Nelson Mandela might mean for the social organization of the mining industries.

Clarence Tshitereke's wonderful work brings a longstanding tradition of research on the mining industry to the present. There is of course an irony in the fact that the start of democracy in South Africa was accompanied by an acceleration of economic globalization. As this work shows, we began in 1994 by abandoning the idea of nationalizing our mines, proceeded to adopt a package of budgetary interventions called the *Reconstruction and Development Programme* or RDP and finally settled into the *Growth, Employment and Redistribution Strategy* or GEAR which Clarence Tshitereke describes as a 'macroeconomic policy and as ideology' driving 'South Africa's post-apartheid reconstruction.'

He examines GEAR's consequences by way of a case study of the labor dynamics in the gold mines over the last twenty or so years, picking up where I and others left off. He interrogates what he calls 'neo-liberal economics' and what that do for economic redistribution and meeting the expectations for social justice. He assesses the extent to which GEAR has met its intended outcomes, particularly in creating employment and the overall objective of achieving 'a better life for all.' He searches for a balanced assessment of GEAR's performance as macroeconomic policy measured against job gains and losses, class mobility and immiserisation and poverty reduction or it's deepening.

Does he find the balance? I think he does—but read on and decide for yourself. It is perhaps striking but not entirely unexpected to find that, notwithstanding all of the extraordinary changes that have occurred, the fundamental elements of the migrant labor system remains. Yes, workers have rights, but foreign workers have fewer rights than South African ones, so check out the mix. African workers now rise up the ranks and make good wages, but entry level is hard to access and pays little. South African workers may bring their families with them, but who in their right minds would want to do that to them.

This is a valuable and welcome contribution to the academic and public understanding of the limits and possibilities of South Africa's democratic transformation. The dollar price of gold is currently breaking all known records and who knows how in the end it will challenge Clarence Tshitereke's assumptions and conclusions. Typically, the higher the price of gold the more low-grade ore can be profitably mined. The more miners penetrate the low-grade parts of the ore body, the more jobs are created. As Clarence Tshitereke shows, the age of globalization presents constraints and opportunities for South Africa, as it does for every other country.

Dr. Wilmot James
Chief Executive of the Africa Genome Education Institute

Preface

South Africa's political transition from white minority rule to black majority rule closed an agonizing chapter of colonialism on the African continent. However, South Africa is still a traumatized society trying to overcome its bleak past. There have been many analyses that sought to dissect South Africa's transition, especially the African National Congress' change from socialist leanings to neo-liberalism. These analyses stemmed from the African National Congress' adoption of the Growth, Employment and Redistribution Strategy (GEAR) in 1996 and the rejection of a largely socialist developmental blueprint in the form of the Reconstruction and Development Program (RDP). Since then, there have been robust criticisms of GEAR and neo-liberal economics in general, as responsible for job loses and undermining economic redistribution and inevitably, the African National Congress' promise of a "better life for all."

The analysis presented in this book seeks to assess the degree to which the correlation between GEAR and job losses is necessarily true. This is accomplished through a case study on labor trends in the Chamber of Mines affiliated gold mines. For a more nuanced understanding, it presents a historical analysis of the evolution of South Africa's "cheap labor" system and the challenges and constraints that faced the gold mining industry within the context of South Africa's transition. Overall, it demonstrates how the legacy of "cheap labor" has come to undermine South Africa's reconstruction project. Essentially, this study is an evaluation of GEAR in terms of the need for optimal equilibrium between financial and macroeconomic stability against the need for social justice, amongst others, employment and economic redistribution. The analysis also challenges some of the hypotheses on the discourse of South Africa's transition. It focuses on the political establishment in the post GEAR period, the alliance between the African National Congress, the South African Communist Party and the Congress of South African Trade Unions.

Dr. Clarence Tshitereke,
May 2006, Pretoria

Acknowledgments

The successful completion of an academic exercise of this magnitude cannot be achieved single handedly. In this respect, I wish to express my deepest and sincere gratitude to my parents Muthundinne Tshitereke and Thambatshira Tshitereke and my siblings, Christopher, Mpfunzeni, Nthanyiseni, Mashudu, and Priscilla Tshitereke. Gratitude also goes to my grand parents, Mukatshelwa Khumela, Nyawalitsheni Tshitereke. Gratitude also goes to my extended family, Mr. Denga Mphigalale, Ms. Thikhathali Maselesele, Mr. Ntsengeni Matodzi, Mr. Matodzi Khumela, Ms. Sophie Demana, Ms. Pauline Ramulwela and all my teachers.

Special thank goes to Professor Bruce J. Berman at the Department of Politics, Queen's University at Kingston, Canada, who has gone beyond his call of duty to help me strengthen my arguments, provided unfailing support and guidance. I would also like to thank Professor Jonathan Crush of Queen's Southern African Migration Project for his influence, motivation and assistance provided towards this research, also Professor Alan Jeeves and Dr. Bruce Frayne. I would also like to thank the Queen's community, Professor David Haglund, Professor Michael Hawes, Professor Charles Pentland, Professor Kim Nossal, Professor Mark Epprecht, Professor David McDonald, Ms. Barbara Murphy, Ms. Shirley Frazer, Ms. Evelyn McCaugherty and Ms. Frances Shepherd. Gratitude also goes to Dr. Peter Henshaw, Dr. Belinda Dodson for their friendship and support during this exercise. I would also like to thank Ms. Maria Salamone and Ms. Christina Decarie of the Southern African Migration Project for her assistance in the course of writing.

Gratitude also goes to friends who have been there to help me keep my sanity, Dr. Khaukanani Mavhungu, Dr. Alhaji Bah, Dr. Peter Arthur, Dr. Kobena Hanson, Dr. Patrick Demana, Dr. Pandelani Mathoma, Mr. Keith Williams, Mrs. Janet Williams, Mr. Peter Williams, Mrs. Joan Corrigan, Mr.

Michael Heal, Dr. Tiffany Jones, Ms. Lydia Ntenga, Mr. Jonathan Sears, Mr. Nissim Mannathukaren, Dr. Chweya Ludeki, Ms. Christelle Esso.

In the Presidency in South Africa, I would like to thank Reverend Frank Chikane, Mr. Joel Netshitenzhe, Trevor Fowler, Dr. Vusi Gumede, Dr. Ellen Kornergay, Dr. Anne Letsebe, Mr. Alan Hirsch, and Ms. Mpho Thamage.

I would also like to thank the Chamber of Mines for their invaluable statistics; Mr. Roger Baxter, Mr. Johan Liebenberg, Mr. Peter Bunkell, Dr. Frans Barker, Mr. Vusi Mabena and Dr. Mike Gouws. At the National Union of Mineworkers, Mr. Gwede Manthashe, Mr. Humbulani Tshikalange, Mr. Archie Palane and the co-operation of mineworkers. At the Congress of South African Trade Unions, I would like to thank Dr. Neva Makgetla and Mr. Wolfe Bande. I would also like to thank Dr. Robert Davies, and Mr. Jeremy Cronin of the African National Congress and the South African Communist Party respectively. Gratitude also goes to Professor Guy Mhone, Professor Hennie Kotze, Professor Estian Calitz and Dr. Patrick Matlou.

Special thanks to the Routledge editorial team in New York for their diligence. Gratitude goes to Dr. Molefi Asante, Mr. Benjamin Holtzman, Mr. Michael Davidson, Ms. Eleanor Chan and Ms. Alicia Solsman.

This research was made possible through the generous financial support of the South African National Research Foundation.

Setting the Scene: An Introduction

BACKGROUND

When the African National Congress took over government in 1994, it was confronted by the challenge of addressing apartheid social inequities. Most importantly, it had to meet the expectations of its overwhelming black political constituency by addressing demands for social justice. By 1994, an estimated housing backlog ranged from 1.4 million to 3 million units and people living in shacks or informal settlements numbered between 5–8 million. Sixty percent of the population had no access to electricity while 6 million had no access to water. Furthermore, 22 million people did not have access to adequate sanitation. There were 17 fragmented departments of education with a disproportionate high allocation of resources to "white" schools. To be addressed in the shortest period possible, all these required radical policy approaches.

This critical analysis of South Africa's political economy of transition examines the effects of the Growth, Employment and Redistribution Strategy (GEAR) both as macroeconomic policy and as ideology on South Africa's post-apartheid reconstruction. The analysis of GEAR's effects is two fold, first through a case study on labor in the Chamber of Mines affiliated gold mines, 1987–2005, and second, as an analysis of neo-liberal economics and their constraints on economic redistribution and meeting the expectations for social justice. While the gold mining industry has been shedding jobs since 1987, in the post-GEAR period (1996 onwards) job losses in the gold industry have been attributed to the introduction, of GEAR, just as they have been in other sectors, usually government owned that have borne the brunt of retrenchments.

This analysis seeks to assess the extent to which there is correlation between GEAR and job losses through a case study of the Chamber of Mines affiliated gold mines. It also assesses the extent to which GEAR has met its intended outcomes, particularly in creating employment and the overall objective of achieving "a better life for all." This is important in challenging the conventional wisdom that holds GEAR as responsible for job losses. The performance of GEAR as macroeconomic policy should be assessed against the actual reduction of unemployment and the subsequent alleviation of poverty for the millions of South Africans who, since 1994 have heightened expectations for the future.

THE MINING INDUSTRY IN SOUTH AFRICA'S ECONOMY

After a century of mining activity, South Africa remains the world's pre-eminent mining nation. By 2003, the total number of mines stood at 749 producing from aluminium to zinc; over 60 minerals are mined and exported to over 100 countries around the world.[1] The structure of mineral production and South Africa's position in the world is as follows:

The largest of all the industries both in terms of scale and production has been the gold mining industry. As a result of both over a century of mining and the economic value of gold itself to South Africa's economy, gold mining remains the largest sector, despite its waning importance as an economic stimulus. Overall, the mining industry remains one of the largest employer and one of the dominant industries in the South African economy. What is interesting is that the industry has been controlled by a cartel of

Table 0.1. South Africa's Mineral Reserves and Production, 2004[2]

Mineral	Reserve (thousand tons)	% of world Production	World Rank
Aluminium Silicates	50	37	1
Chrome Ore	5 500	72.4	1
Gold	36 000	40.7	1
Platinum Group Metals	70 000	87.7	1
Manganese Ore	4000	80	1
Vanadium	12 000	41.4	1
Vermiculite	14	40	1
Titanium Minerals	244	29	2
Zirconium Minerals	14	19.4	2
Fluorspar	80	17	2
Coal	33.8	3.6	7

Table 0.2. Total Capital Accumulation of Selected South African Mining Houses[3]

Anglo-American (R182.1 billion)	Anglo is one of the world's largest mining groups. Although mainly involved, through its subsidiaries, in gold, diamonds and platinum, it has extensive industrial minerals. It generates more than 51 percent of its revenue offshore. Listed on the London and JSE bourses.
BHP Billiton (R103.7 billion)	The merger of BHP and Billiton has created a global mining giant with interests in base metals, coal, steel, ferroalloys, coal, aluminium, titanium, nickel and copper. Well over 40 percent of revenue comes from Australia
AngloGold (R73.1 billion)	One of the World's foremost gold producers, AngloGold is controlled by Anglo American but has a high proportion of foreign shareholders. 30 percent of income now comes from offshore.
Anglo American Platinum (R70.7 billion)	AngloPlat is the world's largest producer of platinum and palladium. Gold, copper, nickel and cobalt are also recovered as by-products. Anglo-American controls the company. All revenues are derived from South Africa, but over 80 percent of production is sold offshore.
Gold Fields (R60.1 billion)	The country's second larges gold producer, with assets in Ghana and Australia.
Impala Platinum (37.8 billion)	The world's second biggest producer of platinum, Impala has a large number of international shareholders. Most revenues are generated within South Africa.

mining capitalists whose interests in other areas of the economy meant that they ultimately came to own a significant percentage of the South African economy in general. By January 2003, the total capital accumulation of selected South African mining houses was as follows:

In addition to these, there are other companies in the banking sector and the insurance groups that are under the control of mining houses. For instance, First Rand, the country's largest banking group, was formed in 1998 when Anglo-American and Rand Merchant Bank merged their financial services interests. In South Africa, mining capital wields such conspicuous power financially, ideologically and even politically. A combination of these powers has been the cornerstone of South Africa's mining industry's accumulation strategies for more than a century. For the gold mining industry in particular, one of the benefits of its corporate power, has been the ability to persuade—and if necessary, coerce—the state to implement favourable, but repressive labor practices to its benefit, not only in the gold mining industry, but also in the economy in general throughout the last century. However, it was in the gold mining industry where working conditions were most ruthlessly exploitative. This is because the Chamber of Mines was given monopolistic exploitation rights over the African workforce. The *Mail and Guardian* summed up the Chamber of Mines' record as follows:

> For many, many years the mining industry operated in South Africa almost as a law unto itself. It has milked untold riches from the country at the expense of the impoverished majority, been allowed to conduct iniquitous labor practices, and been given free reign to hoard mineral rights.[4]

This reality has been the hallmark of South Africa's corporate sector, both during apartheid and even in the post-apartheid democratic political dispensation. Corporate South Africa continues to shape and dominate the discourse (less so by the mining industry today) on how South Africa's society should be organized politically, economically and socially in the post-apartheid reconstruction. In the process of bargaining for policies favourable to its ends, corporate South Africa has legitimized its aggressive pursuit of capitalist interests through a series of myths popularized by its controlled media. Sampie Terreblanche summarized these myths as follows; "first has to do with the alleged capacity of the liberal (or free market) capitalist system to promote the interests of the population irrespective of whether or not the economic system in South Africa can credibly be described as such. Second is the contention that a high economic growth rate in South Africa will—despite deeply institutionalized inequalities—automatically 'trickle down' to the poor."[5] While the capitalist propaganda of corporate South Africa asserts that South Africa is a free market capitalist economic system, it hides the fact that it is simply monopoly capitalism that was driven by the subjugation of black South Africans into a captive labor force. This subjugation has left such a legacy of inequality that requires robust redistributive policies to address the imbalance.

MINE LABOR IN SOUTH AFRICA

For over a century (1886–1987), South Africa's gold mining industry recruited largely unskilled labor from within and throughout the southern African sub-continent. During this period, the overwhelming demand

for labor—"cheap labor," to be precise, required that the mining industry collude with the state in implementing statutory provisions that pushed
the African peasantry into the capitalist wage labor system. Indeed, it was
largely with state assistance that the gold mining industry successfully
established and consolidated labor recruitment networks that ensured a
sufficient supply of "cheap labor." It is important to emphasise that the
industry did not always get what it wanted from the state, especially before
the Boer War and sometimes during apartheid, 1948–1994. However, what
is equally important to note during this period 1948–1994, is that the necessary statutes that ensured steady supply of "cheap labor" were already
in place. In the racial capitalist system that was rapidly emerging, African
peasants were systematically forced to sell their labor. Their traditional
mode of production was disrupted and they essentially became a captive
labor force subject to the whims and dictates of mining capitalists.

Capitalists (mining in particular) also largely drove South Africa's political and economic transition so that they could escape apartheid's economic
confinement under sanctions and globalize their business. Their awareness
of the constraints that could arise under a black government necessitated
seeking avenues for global expansion. In the changing environment of international political economy, efficiency and productivity rendered the labor
recruitment apparatus that existed for almost a century irrelevant. The challenge was to have a small well-paid labor force of professional career miners. In reality, the industry had to reduce its labor force by more than two
thirds in the face of competition at the international level, this time without enjoying a privileged status from the government. This reality bestows
an opportunity to study the political economy on South Africa's transition,
how it impacts on labor, employment and redistributive justice.

In the post-apartheid period, the industry was plagued with and even
constrained by a labor surplus and was battling to reduce the number of
existing miners to save escalating costs following the rise of black union
power. Balancing its capitalist drive for profits required reducing production costs which were largely and still remain labor. What was once
"cheap labor" was increasingly becoming expensive as the National Union
of Mineworkers bargained for better working conditions and better wages
throughout the 1980s. By 2001, labor alone accounted for 56 percent of
the total cash operating costs in the gold mines.

In 1994, the mining industry as a whole employed 610,026 miners,
representing approximately 4.3 percent of the total economically active
population or 6.3 percent of all those formally employed in the economy.
Two years later in 1996, gold mines affiliated to the Chamber of Mines
employed 309,011 workers. In 1997, the need for gold producers to press

ahead with restructuring and re-organization, coupled with the consequences of the fall in the gold price, led to the average number of miners
in gold mines declining by 39,611 workers, to end the year at 269,400.[6]
One of the findings of this research is that although this was in the post
GEAR period, the retrenchments cannot be solely attributed to GEAR,
but instead to the restructuring imperative in the South African economy
in general and the need for competitiveness with other gold producers at
the international level. However, unsubstantiated acrimonious debates
over GEAR, either in the media or labor forums makes it a convenient
scapegoat.

By 1998, the labor force employed in gold mines affiliated to the
Chamber slid by 23 percent, and in 1999, the figure for the whole mining
sector had dropped to 436,500 employees as a consequence of the continued restructuring required for competition at the international level.[7]
In addition to retrenchments in other industries, that were taking place at
the same time, according to the government's household survey of October
1997, about 22 percent of South Africa's economically active population
was unemployed.[8] By September 2000 the South African Reserve Bank officially estimated unemployment to be 25.8 percent. The result has been an
increase in the number of people living in poverty, that is, people living in
households with an income below the poverty line.[9]

SOUTH AFRICA'S TRANSITION IN RETROSPECT

South Africa's history since the discovery of gold can be divided into four
periods. The first period, 1886–1902, saw the discovery of gold and the
emergence of a capitalist industry. This period was characterised by statutory African subjugation into bonded labor in the midst of the struggle
of mining capitalists to establish the conditions necessary for the mining
industry to function optimally, namely the need for "cheap labor." Industry's efforts were frustrated by the political administration of Paul Kruger
that was not interested in mining's demand for "cheap labor." Favourable
policies for the gold mines to access "cheap labor" meant competition with
farmers who made up a political constituency, Kruger was not prepared to
alienate. These differences were only reconciled through the Boer War and
its aftermath from 1902. Through the Boer War, capital was able to overcome the obstacles to satisfactory accumulation during the first 16 years
after gold was discovered, 1886–1902. Capital had successfully solicited
military assistance from the British to overcome its political problems. The
British for their part committed as much as 450,000 troops in South Africa
to protect their investments to the tune of £700 million.

The second period, 1902–1948, saw the emergence of an imperial political administrative system crafted by the British to support the capitalist interests of the mining industry. It was during this period that state-capital alliance was forged that eventually provided the necessary statutory requirements for a "cheap labor" system. Industry's needs for "cheap labor" were met, at the expense of Africans who were turned into a captive labor force through forcible incorporation into the capitalist system. Afrikaner nationalism was initially at its lowest level because the political system that emerged was designed to limit that spirit to avoid it undermining the capitalist system that was rapidly emerging. It is important to note that it was during this period that South Africa's industrial revolution took place and capitalism in general was consolidated. Within the scheme of things, Africans featured only as far as "cheap labor" was concerned. The political system crafted by the British appeared to wane in the late 1940s, because it focused more on capital accumulation while neglecting Afrikaners' deep feelings of patriotic nationalism. The reason Prime Minister Jan Smuts lost the vote in 1948 was that he appeared to champion the British cause more than Afrikaner nationalism. Besides, he was presiding over a British crafted political system, under which Afrikaner nationalists could not realize their aspirations.

The third period, 1948–1994, saw the reversal of the British-crafted political system with the rise of Afrikaner nationalism and the triumph of the Afrikaner National Party. However, there is an interesting coincidence as the Afrikaner National Party managed to hold on to power for the same 46 years before yielding to African pressure. After the end of the Boer War in 1902, Afrikaners had to wait for 46 years to realize their nationalist dream. At the same time, blacks had been waiting for their political freedom long before that. What dominated this period was Afrikaners' fascination with racial purity and its application through apartheid. The system refused to allow Africans permanent residence status in the cities where they were needed the most to sell their labor. Coercive push-pull measures ensured labor was abundant where it was needed. Blacks bore the brunt of it. For the first 25 years until 1973, apartheid repression literally silenced African political voices and the system appeared to work. However, discontent with racial policies and their neglect of 75 percent of the population contradicted the logic of capitalist accumulation. Pass laws were overtly violated and, increasingly, the state could not intimidate Africans by violent means, thus weakening its regulatory responsibility.

The fourth period, 1994-, saw Africans realizing their dream of freedom 342 years after the first white settlers arrived in South Africa. For the first time, an all-inclusive new democratic political system was negotiated. The new African National Congress (ANC) led government was confronted with severe challenges: first, extreme poverty and inequality, an outcome of centuries of racism and social exclusion. Second, an economy in regression augmented by severe unemployment—which was and still remains—one of South Africa's social, economic and political problems. The challenge was how to redistribute wealth and income to meet people's expectations when the economy was in shambles. So, igniting the economy became the main emphasis of government policies, although it was in the reverse order initially. As President Nelson Mandela put it in his Presidential inauguration speech, May 10, 1994:

> The time for the healing of the wounds has come. The moment to bridge the chasms that divide us has come. The time to build is upon us. We have, at last, achieved our political emancipation. We pledged ourselves to liberate all our people from the continuing bondage of poverty, deprivation, suffering, gender, and other discrimination . . . we enter into a covenant that we shall build the society in which all South Africans, both black and white, will be able to walk tall, without any fear in their hearts, assured of their inalienable right to human dignity—rainbow nation at peace with itself and the world.[10]

While the challenge for redistribution to address apartheid imbalances remained daunting, the ANC had to tread carefully to maintain optimal equilibrium between the need for social justice and the interests of corporate South Africa. More importantly, what was to be redistributed and from where? How was the economy to become an instrument of policy towards meeting the needs of the disadvantaged Africans without antagonising the whims and interests of corporate South Africa? In addition to these, replacing racial capitalism and consolidating institutions for democratic participation based on reconciliation, nation building and respect for human dignity became the central goals along with economic emancipation. Essentially, non-racial democratic principles guided the transition. In the first 10 years of democracy (1994–2004), there have been remarkable successes in addressing apartheid's social imbalances. In the process, the economy became an instrument of policy to meet the needs of the disadvantaged Africans. However, there was a contradiction immediately when the need for maintaining fiscal discipline transcended objectives of achieving social justice.

For, the adoption of neo-liberal policies has had unintended consequences as it shut the most vulnerable sectors of the population out of the job market. Understanding the circumstances that led to the adoption of neo-liberalism requires an analysis of South Africa's history and the development of capitalism in the periods outlined above. While GEAR is an outcome of the prevailing restrictive international economic system, the moral debate over its adoption is still useful for a nuanced understanding of South Africa's transition. It needs to be acknowledged "that the economy could not afford the luxury of an extended debate on macroeconomic policy before essential stabilisation measures were put in place."[11] Seeking consensus would have harnessed the energies and expertise of the ANC and its alliance partners, while simultaneously compromising the economy by delaying the implementation of essential polices for growth and redistribution.

* * * * *

Chapter One is a theoretical account of the analytical approaches employed. It reviews South Africa's political economy of transition and focuses on the relationship between macroeconomic policies and job losses. It sets out the theoretical background necessary for a nuanced dissection of the complex relationship between capital and the state and how they imposed a system of racial capitalism.

Chapter Two summarizes the historical discovery of gold and the origins of the Chamber of Mines, an umbrella body that represents the interest of mining houses with both government and labor. The analysis focuses more on how the Chamber in its drive to acquire "cheap labor" struggled against and colluded with successive South African governments to its cause, even leading to the Anglo-Boer War, 1899–1902. The outcome of the War served the interests of the gold mining industry and government support facilitated the establishment of labor recruitment apparatuses, the consequences of which undermine South Africa's reconstruction efforts. It traces the successes of a state-capital alliance regarding gold mining's access to "cheap labor" that was forged after the Boer War and lasted until the early 1970s. The analysis also shows the extent to which "cheap labor" policy was central to apartheid in the post 1948 period and how apartheid repression eventually undermined it in the period 1974 to 1987.

Chapter Three assess the extent to which labor retrenchments in the Chamber of Mines affiliated gold mines were caused by GEAR or by other imperatives. It analyses the gold mining industry from the perspective of its relative importance to the South African economy. This chapter argues that new challenges to "cheap labor" forced the industry to restructure itself. First, was the increasing union power that ultimately led to the 1987 NUM strike; second was the declining gold price; third was the need to compete with other gold producers in preparation for offshore investments; fourth was the introduction of new labor laws (post-apartheid) that effectively removed the "cheap labor" system with a new labor market. In response to these imperatives, the industry restructured itself into a globally competitive industry. South African mining companies have globalized their operations, and the industry has become more efficient. The restructuring process preceded GEAR by more than a decade and therefore job losses in the gold mining industry cannot solely be attributed to it.

Chapter Four approaches the political economy of transition and the shift in macroeconomic policies from the macro-economic populism of the Reconstruction and Development Program (RDP) to the neo-liberal Growth, Employment and Redistribution Strategy (GEAR). It presents a critical analysis of competing development perspectives through an assessment of the premise of GEAR as neo-liberal macroeconomic policy and how it has performed in relation to labor retention and the economy's performance. The analysis also demonstrate how South Africa's transition was largely driven by capital and the extent to which it has succeeded in doing so by coercing government to permit it to globalize its business.

Chapter Five analyzes South Africa's gold mining industry after the transition and the post GEAR period. A comparison with other major gold producers, Australia, Canada and the USA show challenges that continue to confront the gold mining industry. It also analyses the relationship between the gold industry and the ANC government and the relative position of labor in the restructuring process. It also presents some of the political challenges facing the ANC-SACP and Cosatu alliance after GEAR. More importantly, it reveals the economic outcomes of GEAR and the challenge of economic redistribution.

In conclusion, it is the central argument of this analysis that, contrary to common assumptions about GEAR, and its negative impact on the South African working class, it is not a cause, but rather an effect of global restructuring. It is in the context of the interface of global restructuring and increased competition within the mining sector globally, that we can understand the impact democratization and neo-liberalism have had on a unique system of racialized labor exploitation in the South Africa.

Chapter One
Theoretical Approaches: Modes of Regulation and Accumulation

INTRODUCTION

The political economy of South Africa's transition presents profound challenges and opportunities to dissect problems that confront the post-apartheid economic and social reconstruction. In the post-apartheid era, there have been tectonic shifts in the state-capital alliance that formed the bedrock of the gold mining industry's exclusive position in the development of the economy. Simultaneously, the adoption of neo-liberal macroeconomic policies undermined economic redistribution and the "cheap labor" access monopoly the gold mining industry had with an intentionally unbiased labor market system that applies evenly for all companies. In the post-apartheid political economy, issues of productivity and efficiency confront those industries that, for decades, appeared productive as a consequence of the abundance of a substantially docile and exploitable labor force.

This research analyzes labor trends in the post-apartheid reconstruction under a neo-liberal economic development paradigm. It also assesses the extent to which neo-liberalism undermines economic redistribution and its globalization imperative provides new lenses for analyzing the gold mining industry and the effect it has had in the post-apartheid South Africa. This is important because the gold mining industry has reaped the benefits of exceptional entitlement to its operating procedures that were not extended to any other industry. This reality has made it one of the most vulnerable industries once the political system changed. Conversely, it has also presented new opportunities for the industry to conduct its business differently.

THEORETICAL APPROACHES

The political economy of South Africa's apartheid state, its relation to capital and ways in which it could be dismantled puzzled scholars throughout the 1970s and 1980s. These complexities stemmed from the alliance between the two that can be attributed to the discovery of gold and the emergence and growth of capitalism in South Africa since the arrival of Europeans in the 17th century. It is important to note at the outset that unlike the development of capitalism elsewhere, its development in South Africa was of a special type as it took the form of apartheid into what Stephen Gelb aptly refers to as "racial Fordism," the productive model typified by Henry Ford's car plans in which workers on a production line, perform specialized tasks repetitively.[1]

Marxist theoretical explanations of the state may not adequately explain South Africa's "racial Fordism," and the interplay between the state and capital in installing the building blocks of the system. The two most popular Marxist theories of the state, the *"instrumentalist"* and the *"structuralist"*: "share a preoccupation with the relative autonomy of the state (with little consideration of why, how and to what it is relative)."[2] The *instrumentalist* approach of the state-capital relationship:

> Stresses the common class origins, ideology and social ties that give the bourgeoisie a predominant influence over state activities, but then insists that the state authorities can and do act 'autonomously' on behalf of the maintenance of capitalism rather than at the direct behest of particular capitalist interests.[3]

The relative autonomy of the state in relation to other structural levels of the capitalist *mode of production*, as Berman argues, "is determined by the specificity of its function within the whole, subordinate to the general requirement of maintaining the unity of social formations."[4] While it is true, that "the state cannot be seen simply as the pliant servant of capital," in the case of South Africa, the state (South African Republic under Kruger) seems to have existed independent of capital. After the Boer War, (1899–1902) throughout apartheid, and at least until the early 1970s, successive South African governments acted as compliant servants of capital, "rarely questioning the mining industry's arguments, ever-responsive to the claim that South Africans were 'unsuited' for mine work and that without foreign labor (and special treatment) the mines and the country would collapse."[5] The state, however, possessed the legitimate use of force, which capital could call to its rescue. Although not every state action served capitalist interests, the determination of the state to crush rebellion and industrial protests (both black and white) when called upon demonstrated the cooperative relationship between the two. For instance, the Smuts government put down the Rand Revolt of 1922 with military force. It was a systematic state-capital relationship that commodified the African proletariat.

The structuralist theory comes closer to explaining the relationship between capital and the state. From the structuralist lenses, "the state possess the political sphere as an 'objective relation' within the structure of the capitalist mode of production; as one of three specific and relatively autonomous levels or instances within capitalism, along with the economic and the ideological."[6] The role of the state is to "serve as a factor of cohesion between the levels of a social formation . . . and as the regulatory factor of its global equilibrium as a system."[7] As this analysis progresses, the essence of state-capital alliance in formulating a mode of regulation under which capital accumulated profits between 1900 and 1994 becomes relevant. Mode or regime of regulation refers to the written and unwritten laws of society which control the regime of accumulation and define its form—it is therefore the political superstructure.

In the contemporary analysis of the interplay between the state and capital in South Africa's transition, most analysts have employed the same structuralist/regulation theory in asserting the weight of capital in pursuing political objectives that facilitated its business imperatives.[8] In his analysis of the state and the politics of the National Party between 1948 and 1994, Dan O'Meara presents competing paradigms of analysing political change/ transition in the context of South Africa.[9] It is not necessary to outline the details of each paradigm here. Instead, this analysis focus on one that comes close to the "regulatory factor" that Berman discusses. O'Meara refers to this as the "functionalist/regulationist" paradigm.

The regulation theoretical framework, which emerged in the 1980s, "sought to avoid the class reductionism and economic determinism for which much of the earlier South African Marxist literature had been rightfully criticised."[10] Regulation theory rests on the assumption that long waves in capital accumulation can be explained as a consequence of the successive creation and collapse of supportive socio-institutional structures. Writers in this tradition, argue that institutional structures (such as the welfare state) and state intervention (income policies and Keynesian full employment strategies) allowed a balance between growth in output (aided by techniques of mass production) and purchasing power.[11]

A form of industrialization through import substitution was achieved "through the 'Fordist' integration of white workers and white population in general, and the peripheral—'Fordist' integration of only a section of the black majority, and the exclusion of the rest."[12] Put simply, the state became an instrument of redistribution and employment for whites (who would have otherwise remained unemployed). Large state-owned enterprises absorbed unemployed whites including, amongst others, Telkom, Eskom, and Iscor. The bureaucracy, the railway, the military/police and the post office also served to alleviate the white unemployment crisis. While these initiatives effectively solved the poor white problem and reinforced a sense of Afrikaner nationalism, they excluded Africans.

The regulation theory presents a critical analysis of the apartheid state. Its distinctive feature in the analysis of political economy is that "it explains not only the working of the market mechanism, but the long-term dynamics of the capitalist economy from a broad social and political perspective."[13] It fuses Afrikaner nationalism and largely English controlled capital's demands for a system of racial capitalism to argue that the two were intrinsically linked. The mines got their "cheap labor," while government's *pork-barrel* apartheid policies succeeded in creating a better life for its minority white political constituency. However, successes of the two, the state and capital, were at the expense of the black majority who were forcibly incorporated into the rapidly emerging capitalist system. Essentially, as Francis Wilson pointed out, the story revolves around the way in which mining entrepreneurs and the state resolved the difficulties they faced in securing the labor needed to dig for gold at the lowest possible cost.[14] Ralph Miliband argues that: "the state is seen as the instrument, the 'guiding intelligence' of the capitalist system, able by its relative detachment to take a broader view and coordinate reforms and other strategies that ensure the continuing survival of the system.[15]

Arguments presented in this analysis demonstrate that, since the end of the Boer-War, the state-capital alliance that ensued put the Afrikaners back into political power, but they had to implement policies that were favorable to the aspirations of the gold mining industry. For the Afrikaners, the bitter lesson of the Boer War was that capitalists had no interest in assuming direct political power, but if necessary, they would intervene (even militarily—for *regime change*), if the bureaucrats in Pretoria (the seat of government) pursued policies incompatible with their overall objectives of maximizing profits. Eventually a system was laid out that forcibly incorporated Africans into the capitalist system as subservient "cheap labor."

This analysis applies a modified version of the regulation theory to argue that the state-capital alliance ensured that the state provide a mode of regulation (that is, the integration of the role of political and social relations in structuring the reproduction of the capitalist system[16]) under which capital accumulation (that occurs with the stabilisation of a specific mode of regulation with a particular pattern of production and consumption[17]) could take place. Therefore, the construction of a stable framework means that the political and social forces are managed in such a way that capital is able to accumulate and invest on profitable terms.[18]

With the discovery of gold, the Chamber of Mines of South Africa was the first body formed by mining capitalists to confront the government on policy matters that affected the gold mining industry's operations. In David Yudelman's study of this relationship since 1902, the *modus vivendi*, as he puts it, reveals increased state intervention to satisfy the needs of a rapidly expanding industry in the transition to the deep level phase of production.[19] While acknowledging the power that capitalists had, he argues that the state-capital relations forged were on equal terms. As he puts it:

> The state-capital relationship in South Africa, then, was not characterized by the dominance of Afrikaner nationalism, as the liberal, nationalist and pluralist schools of thought have all argued. Nor was it characterized by the dominance of capital, as the Marxists and neo-Marxists suggest. Rather, it was characterized by symbiosis. Individually, neither the state nor big business could attain hegemony in South Africa; combined, they very early established an effective dominance. The dominance has endured until the present, surviving important changes in the composition of both the state and capital.[20]

It is important to point out that the two existed as separate entities. The state was not simply an instrument of the bourgeoisies but state and capital nevertheless needed each other for their mutual benefit. Indeed, the state-capital alliance forged after the Boer War persisted well until the 1970s, an indication that the state fulfilled its regulatory responsibility for efficient capital accumulation. The analysis presented throughout the following chapters indicates the successes of state-capital alliance in assisting the gold mining industry's mode of accumulation, through access to "cheap labor." Mode or regime of accumulation refers to the systems of production and consumption such as "racial Fordism" for apartheid as Stephen Gelb calls it. The determination on the part of the state to ensure that the gold mining industry's mode of accumulation was efficient even went so far as granting the industry permission to recruit indentured "cheap labor" as far as China (1904–1907) and from the Southern African hinterland (1920s onwards). As a result of the successes that mining capitalists had in accessing "cheap labor" it can be argued that the South Africa state, although remaining separate from capital, historically served the interest of mining industries. This mode of regulation was premised on racial domination, which would later undermine its functionality.

In the 68-year period (1902–1970), various South African governments successfully passed statutory provisions that ensured the gold mines had the "cheap labor" they wanted. Overall, while acknowledging that sometimes the state support faltered, Crush *et al* argue that the trend in industry-state relations was toward more cooperation and interdependence.[21] There was an overwhelming element of reciprocity. The gold industry depended on sympathetic government policies to mine gold profitably, while the efficient extraction of gold and subsequent increase in production output meant increases in state revenue from taxation.

After Union in 1910, a series of legislative instruments were enacted to ensure that the mines got the "cheap labor" they wanted. The Land Act of 1913 formed the pillar of these policies of dispossession. In addition, the Pact Government was swept to power campaigning on "common suspicion of the dominance of mining capital, and a determination to protect the interests of white labor by intensifying discrimination against blacks."[22] It introduced other laws governing social relations and labor transactions. For instance, the "civilized labor policy"[23] preserved the privileges of white miners in the gold mining industry, even reinforcing them with the Apprenticeship Act of 1922, Colour Bar Act, the Urban Areas Act (1923), the Industrial Conciliation Act (1924) and the Wage Act of 1925. Throughout, the Chamber occasionally solicited the action of the state's security apparatus when necessary to crush industrial action by miners. Ultimately, in its report in 1998, the Truth and Reconciliation Commission (TRC) acknowledged that the Chamber of Mines' actions in shaping the migrant labor system was the clear example of business working closely with the (minority) white government to create the conditions for capital accumulation based on cheap African labor. Indeed, "there is no doubt that the mining industry harnessed the services of the state to shape labor supply conditions to its advantage."[24]

Afrikaners' enforcement of more racist legal instruments, amongst others, Prohibition of Mixed Marriages Act, 1949; Immorality Act, 1950; Population Registration Act, 1950; Group Areas Act, 1950 and the Reservation of Separate Amenities Act, 1953, in the apartheid project from 1948 to the 1970s strengthened the mode of accumulation. The enactment of these racist legal instruments resulted in the golden age of rapid economic growth 1960 and 1973—grand apartheid. During this period, the economy grew by as much as six percent per annum. It was during this period that the Bantustan policy, which effectively severed citizenship of as many as eight million black South Africans, was implemented. However, the repression of this period, in addition to lack of African representation, began to undermine the mode of regulation, as African protests against apartheid, both industrial and political, turned violent. The inevitable outcome of these protests was a fundamental disequilibrium, in the configuration of social relations which undermined the foundations of the mode of accumulation. Some of the details of this disequilibrium are presented throughout the chapters of this analysis. O'Meara argues that from the 1970s onwards, the growing African discontent with "racial Fordism," together with key changes in South Africa's integration into and role in the world economy, brought apartheid's racial capitalist accumulation model into crisis. Any control achieved remained temporary and incomplete. Apartheid's mode of domination had exceeded the limit required by the mode of accumulation as it now came to rely increasingly on coercive brutality. Anthony Giddens notes:

> All strategies of control employed by superordinate individuals or groups call forth counter-strategies on the part of subordinates . . . No matter how great the scope of intensity of control superordinates posses, since their power presumes the active compliance of others, those others can bring to bear strategies of their own and apply particular types of sanctions.[25]

In the same vein, Bruce Berman argues that "a state based solely on the continuous resort to compulsion is revealed as an obvious instrument of class domination, generates diverse forms of resistance rather than compliance, and becomes the focus of costly, disruptive and unpredictable struggles."[26] In South Africa, crisis occurred because the institutional forms of response were tuned to respond to certain sets of external elements (the ANC's armed wing), and turned out to be unable to cope with unexpected internal uprising (African discontent with apartheid). The state could neither secure nor guarantee conditions for capital accumulation beyond the capabilities of individual capitalists. This made efficient accumulation of capital impossible without resort to open compulsion.[27] In his analysis of crisis and control in colonial Kenya, Bruce Berman's analysis also mirrored South Africa's realities. As he put it:

> However, impressive the achievements of corporate planners and state managers, however elaborate the analytic schemes and policy innovation produced by their academic auxiliaries, unforeseen events and unintended consequences disrupt conscious efforts to reproduce a stable equilibrium and predictable control that a contradictory and recalcitrant system perversely refuses to produce automatically.[28]

Continuing low wages in the face of increasing inflation led to industrial action. In the gold mining industry, this forced Anglo-American to increase the basic pay for African mineworkers by 70 percent between 1972 and 1973. African discontent was triggered by the very functioning of the then existing mode of regulation (political exclusion and apartheid repression), which triggered, in turn economic, financial and social events that destabilized the coherence of the institutional forms of accumulation at the core of the regulation mode.

Until the 1970s, collective bargaining for Africans was still governed by industrial councils for various trades or by conciliation boards where no industrial councils existed, such as in the mining industry. Indeed, African workers "could not take part in the structured negotiations, nor could they legally strike without certain complex conditions having been met."[29] After all, Africans were *foreigners.* Furthermore, "only white trade unions could be formally recognised by the Industrial Registrar—which left black grievances outside the formal bargaining process."[30] The exclusion of Africans from South African citizenship, political suffrage and the economic benefits of racial capitalist accumulation became the *Achilles' heel* of the apartheid state's mode of regulation. African political representation instead of armed repression was the logical answer to the accumulation crisis. With this crisis, "the key to a new mode of regulation was a new hegemonic project to solve the national question and elaborate a new definition of the nation-people."[31]

African discontent played itself through industrial action in the workplace, becoming an expression of political frustration and demands for equitable working conditions. When put in context, the emerging Black Consciousness Movement in the early 1970s, the Soweto uprising in 1976, and the nationwide industrial action could not be dealt with through the prevailing fascination with racial segregation and the securitization of non-existential threats. It required a comprehensive overhaul of the system, which Prime Ministers B.J. Vorster and P.W. Botha could achieve, but were unwilling to acknowledge. The state needed "to elaborate a new regime of accumulation and mode of regulation."[32] Change is viewed as a consequence of a 'crisis,' which later is itself conceived as a new terrain of contradictions in which the regime of accumulation of capital is no longer "guaranteed" by the mode of regulation.

Because of his fascination with racial purity and the determination to retain political power, P.W. Botha could not read through this logic of capitalism. Instead of crafting a new mode of accumulation and mode of regulation, the largely militarised state sought to contain the violent discontent using increasing levels of force. However, in Botha's convoluted logic, this was understandable, as the new mode of regulation required giving blacks the vote, unless Afrikaners were willing to just give up political power. Berman points that "efforts to restructure capitalist social structures can threaten to destroy the reified appearance of social relations and undermine the autonomy and legitimacy of the state, thus revealing the reality of exploitation and domination."[33]

Instead of focusing on what needed to be done, that is, creating a new mode of regulation for capital accumulation, and to accommodate African political aspirations, the apartheid regime focused on "total strategy" against the "total onslaught" from black resistance movements infiltrating South Africa from the neighbouring countries. Essentially, the enemy was externalized, a rather convenient form of displacement. This led to the militarization of South African politics, which ultimately delayed the crafting of a new mode of regulation by an additional 15 years from the Soweto uprisings in 1976 to the release of Nelson Mandela and other political prisoners in 1990. During his much anticipated speech on August 15, 1985 (Rubicon speech) which was expected to outline new political reforms, with his wagging finger, Botha told black South Africans and the international community not to "push us (Afrikaners) too far," and that he was not "prepared to lead white South Africans and other minority groups to abdication and suicide."[34]

During this 15-year period, 1976–1990, meaningful political reforms, progressive Afrikaner intellectuals and businessmen understood, required negotiating with the ANC's exiled representatives in defiance of the government's professed will in an attempt to dissipate fears of a prospective black government. The message from business South Africa to the ANC, apart from being a *mea culpa*, was simply: "we are prepared to work together in solving our common problems." As the state was getting more absorbed into controlling the bourgeoning African militant protests, the intensity of the mass democratic movement threatened the mode of accumulation further. This spawned a crisis, which prompted capital to intervene on the political sphere.

For instance, in 1981, Harry Oppenheimer, chairman of De Beers Consolidated Mines and the Anglo-American Corporation publicly attacked P.W. Botha's "total strategy" as a threat to the country. Oppenheimer believed that Botha's "total onslaught" was being waged against South Africa from external and internal Marxism, Western pressure, rising black-nationalism and arch conservatives within the National Party, and that Botha's beliefs prevented him from carrying out reforms.[35] It is important to note that the formation of the National Union of Mineworkers in 1982 and the cosmetic constitutional reforms that gave coloureds and Indians political representation in separate chambers of Parliament was an attempt to address the growing political discontent and therefore ease the crisis of the mode of regulation. Co-opting coloureds and Indians through what Bruce Berman aptly calls "an illusion of access to the state," became one of the strategies for sustaining the "autonomy and legitimacy" of the apartheid state.[36]

However, the fact that blacks were still left out of the new constitutional representation antagonised them further. Crisis management took the form of trial and error. The countrywide protests following black exclusion from the new constitutional settlement further widened the gap between the mode of accumulation and the mode of regulation. As violence spun out of control, Botha responded with a declaration of the state of emergency in 1985. As South African politics became militarised and the crisis of accumulation deepened, expenditure (including, in addition to the cost of military entanglements in Angola and continued harassment of the Front Line States) augmented by African rent boycotts crippled the economy. The military budget exceeded four percent of the GDP in the late 1980s, something the economy could not sustain. In addition to all these factors, incremental advances of African unionization and its bargaining for better working conditions inevitably meant that the gold mining industry was no longer mining gold cheaply. The mode of accumulation was further destabilised by the international sanctions campaign and industrial protests of the 1980s that were becoming more violent following the state of emergency.[37] Thus, from the 1970s, Afrikaner nationalism was in conflict with the capitalist accumulation regime forged at the turn of the century.

It was indeed the crisis of capital accumulation spawned by the crisis of regulation that forced capital to demand the dismantling of apartheid. The political strategies of P.W. Botha, especially "total strategy," were not solving the pressing problem of capital: rising African political discontent, which threatened the margins for profit. Instead, Botha's policies deepened the structural crisis of regulation and accumulation. Consequently, the question regarding the long-term viability of the regulation mode remained unanswered.

REGULATION/ACCUMULATION CRISIS: A CAPITALIST RESPONSE

Aware of international economic trends, it was important for capital (mining in particular) to exert pressure on the apartheid government into a negotiated settlement, if it valued its investments and prospects for continuing business in the future. This marked the turning point in South Africa's capitalist evolution. It brought a realization that unless a new mode of regulation was worked out, both blacks and whites stood to lose. There was hope for institutional transformation when F.W. De Klerk assumed presidential power in

1989. On February 2, 1990, President De Klerk announced the un-banning of political parties: the ANC, the Pan Africanist Congress (PAC) and the South African Communist Party (SACP).

Throughout the 1980s, corporate South Africa had come to understand that apartheid was a system that could not and did not work and eventually broke down as its own contradictions revealed themselves. With this insight, capital responded in a classical capitalist way by forcefully interfering in the political arena for a favourable regulation and accumulation regime. Eventually, a new mode of regulation was negotiated as a compromise (non-racial multiparty democracy) and a new mode of accumulation (neo-liberalism), were adopted for post-apartheid reconstruction. The basic institutional forms of regulation were redesigned within a new democratic order, which amply rewarded the mode of accumulation. Greenberg argues that the outcome of the transition reflected the balance of forces, as they were found at the time of the negotiated settlement in the early 1990s.[38]

For mining capital, the option that appeared more attractive and workable was to get rid of apartheid and have multiracial capitalism. Capital contributed to getting rid of apartheid, especially through various treks to negotiate with the ANC in exile and through the subsequent adoption of GEAR as the new mode of accumulation in the post-apartheid South Africa. Foresighted and calculating, capital needed to design strategies that would make industries competitive in the post-apartheid international economic system, and as this analysis argues, in the gold mining industry that has been so dependent on "cheap labor," this was achieved through a radical restructuring, the details of which are presented in chapters three and five below. With remarkable success during the negotiations period, capital pressed its position for the liberalization of trade as a way of expanding its operational base.

In this vein, Hein Marais argues that a plethora of much more capital-friendly corporate planning scenarios, unleashed after 1990, inundated the ANC's economic thinking. These explain why in 1993 the ANC effectively rejected the policy findings of the Macro-Economic Research Group (MERG), which it had set up to formulate a post-1994 economic policy. MERG called for a program of fiscal expansion directed towards social and physical infrastructure, a balanced monetary policy, and a more active role for the state in the economy.[39] The first of the corporate scenario-planning exercises was Nedcor/Old Mutual's prospects for a *Successful Transition*, launched in late 1990 and completed in 1993. The insurance conglomerate Sanlam's *Platform for Investment* scenario and the social-democratic *Mont Fleur Scenarios* followed. In addition, other documents such as the South African Chamber of Business (SACOB) *Economic Options for South Africa* were also wheeled into the main fray.[40]

However, there were drawbacks in these scenario exercises. Sampie Terreblanche argues that whenever the corporate sector becomes too closely and too prescriptively involved in formulating economic policy, there are always four dangers that need to be kept in mind. First, the corporate sector will only provide advice that will advance its own interests. Second, the corporate sector—with its often-myopic vision—could be inclined to twist the trade-offs involved in favor of its own short-term profitability, to the detriment of the long-term interests of all the other interest groups in a society. Third, the corporate sector cannot be held responsible by an electorate for erroneous policy advice, while the government of the day has no option—in a well functioning democratic system—but to take responsibility for that advice. Fourth, in many countries—including South Africa—the media are controlled by the corporate sector and as a result, tends to portray the latter's activities in a more sympathetic light than those of the political sector.[41]

Within a relatively short period of time, the ANC came to understand the capitalist rationale and radical rhetoric of nationalization was dropped. The aggressive pursuit of Black Economic Empowerment is a reflection of the ANC's understating that real power is economic, not political. However, capital has succeeded in buying-off into its fold disillusioned recalcitrant Marxists through Black Economic Empowerment. While there may have been successes on the part of capital through the neo-liberal ideology that informed GEAR, initially the ANC pressed on with the privatization of the very state enterprises that once employed millions during apartheid. The job losses that ensued have largely brought back the poor whites problem in the post-apartheid South Africa. For instance, Telkom, the state-owned telephones company once employed 60,000 employees in 1994. Today, 30,000 have lost their jobs with the partial privatization.[42] Iscor's Vanderbijlpark plant has shed 16,000 jobs in the past 10 years and it is the source of most white poverty in the Vaal Triangle.[43] Making it worse, the legacy of Hertzog's "civilized labor policy" makes it hard for unemployed whites to do "uncivilized work." Ironically, the Apprenticeship Act of 1922 is the downfall of many poor whites today as contemporary realities have reversed its original purpose. It stipulated a standard six (Grade Eight) pass as a minimum qualification for apprenticeship in 41 trades, including the giant iron and steel industries. In addition, minimum wage laws that insulated semi-skilled whites from competition by unskilled blacks have been scrapped, leaving unemployed whites vulnerable.

This analysis uses a diffusion of aspects of the regulation theory's approaches to state-capital relations, notably the mode of accumulation and the mode of regulation. It uses a historical perspective in analyzing South Africa's shift from a "cheap labor" system to the subsequent embrace of neo-liberalism. The analysis employs the hegemony of neo-liberalism (in the post-cold war period) to explain realities that undermined the ANC's pursuit of socialist policies in light of the dominance of corporate South Africa, its demands for a neo-liberal capitalist economic system, contrary to the ANC's socialist agenda. Even under the new democracy (new mode of regulation) it is important as Berman points out that:

> The autonomy and legitimacy of the state, the fundamental separation of economic and political spheres, require constant efforts to renew and maintain them in the face of the actual involvement of states in accumulation and class struggle, ranging from the high levels of coercion during the period of primitive accumulation to the continually expanding and ever-more complex forms of state management in contemporary capitalist societies.[44]

This analysis provides detailed empirical analysis of the ANC's changes in macroeconomic policies and how the hegemonic forces of neo-liberalism fettered its socialist ideological commitment, eventually undermining the project of economic redistribution. As Martin Andrews has argued, "the distribution of power among states shapes the political structure of transactional markets, as it does inter-state politics generally."[45] Before the analysis begins, it is important to summarize the hegemony of neo-liberalism in the post-cold war international political economy, under which South Africa's transition took place.

POST COLD-WAR NEO-LIBERAL HEGEMONY AND SOUTH AFRICA'S TRANSITION

The dominant post-World War II development theory was Keynesianism named after British economist, John Maynard Keynes (1883–1946). The Keynesian economic formula revolutionized economics and swiftly became the mantra of government development policies. Keynesianism outlined how governments could control and manipulate the economy to avoid the worst slumps and inflationary booms. This involved the idea of using budget deficits or surpluses to counter trends in the economy by pumping money to the economy during a slump, thus increasing purchasing power and raising demand out of the economy. Its emphasis was the notion that developed and underdeveloped economies were characterized by pervasive market failures.

Keynesian formula was contrary to orthodox view that under competitive conditions each resource will be fully employed, as did his argument that economists need two economic models, one for analyzing economies operating at full employment, and one for those operating below full employment.[46] In his *General Theory of Employment, Interest and Money* (1936), Keynes declared that in a depression, there was no wage so low that it could eliminate unemployment. It was therefore unrealistic to blame the unemployed for their predicament. Furthermore, he emphasized that aggregate demand, that is, the total spending of consumers, investors and public enterprises—which, when low, sales and jobs suffered. Conversely, when it was high, optimal equilibrium is achieved.

The *naïve* conception of the state and its clumsy interventions in the economy formed many of the weaknesses that neo-liberals effectively exploited to their advantage from the 1970s onwards. The benevolence Keynesian economics bestowed on the state began to wane as international market forces increasingly affected countries' domestic economy and political apparatus. With this reality, economic and political requirements of countries that industrialized early when they had few competitors and low capital technology were different from those such as South Africa that are industrializing when there is intense competition on the launch pad to economic prosperity. In retrospect, Keynesianism benefited today's developed world since they mostly industrialized in the era of direct state intervention.

Today, the more advanced the world economy, the greater are the entry costs for the late industrializing countries, especially those that have been internationally isolated from it such as South Africa—whatever level of isolation. On the other hand, it is also acknowledged that developing nations like South Africa cannot go individually through stages of economic development when they are merely a part of a world capitalist system that fundamentally conditions the path of economic change. In essence, globalization and neo-liberal policies have come to undermine the accord upon which social democracy had developed in the post-1945 period.[47] With no prospects for successful alternative development paths (after the collapse of the Soviet socialist model), neo-liberalism has consolidated itself as the dominant economic development model. It is from this perspective that the ANC's shift from a largely socialist developmental blueprint to full-blown neo-liberalism should be understood.

The structural tenets of neo-liberalism challenge the very essence of Keynesian paradigm that sees the state as an agent of development. Helen Milner notes that in the aftermath of the two world wars, government intervention in the economy became accepted practice at both micro- and macro-levels for eliminating the bust cycles in the economy.[48] Indeed, the twentieth century has witnessed the greatest growth in government interventions in the economy ever seen. Globalization and the spread of more "orthodox" economic ideals, however, have undermined confidence in such interventions in many areas. These interventions were born out of an acknowledgement that free markets are not self-regulating; but are inherently volatile institutions, prone to speculative booms and busts.

Joseph Schumpeter understood capitalist development and business cycles better than most other twentieth century economists.[49] In his analysis of the development of analytic methods in economics, he saw that capitalism did not work to preserve the cohesion of society. Capitalism requires constant surveillance, in the absence of which it becomes a ferocious juggernaut that once left people queuing for a cup of soup at the height of the Great Depression of the 1930s. As capitalism flourish, he predicted that it would eventually perish of its own success, thus giving way to public control of its apparatus or socialism—maybe not as envisaged my Karl Marx.

Throughout the period in which Keynes's thought was a dominant influence, it was recognized that free markets are highly imperfect institutions. To work well, they need not only regulation, but also active management, and empirical evidence reveals that governments have performed this function diligently than other institutions.[50] There is no doubt that for some time, Keynesian-oriented development policies protected the state from the vagaries of capitalism as a chaotic and unstable economic system. Using Walt Rostow's airplane metaphor, those countries whose economies *took-off* during the era of Keynesian political economy did so owing to a strong state that directed and allocated resources.[51] Thus, the cold war ideological divide provided the environment in which countries could pursue state-led development policies. However, the dramatic suddenness with which the conflict ended meant that those who are eager to pursue state-led development policies find themselves swimming against the impervious tides of globalization and the international financial institutions, which wield such conspicuous power and wealth that even eternal realists, are now convinced that they rival or surpass the power of the state.[52]

Today, the global expansion and operations of economic and technological agencies require active promotion by political processes, particularly the actions of governments to create national and international conditions conducive to their needs.[53] The opening up of all countries and all economic sectors to the global operations of such industrial, financial and technological agencies has required the removal of unacceptable regulatory terms and conditions, identified as barriers to business in the functioning of market forces. Contrary to empirical evidence that demonstrate remarkable achievements of the state as an agent of development, markets are believed to be the efficient magical elixir, while government intervention in the economy is seen as distorting and inefficient. However, minimal government intervention in the provision of infrastructure and education can be undertaken provided that such intervention is functional, or "market friendly."[54]

Overall, the greatest currency of neo-liberalism is its undeviating insistence on limiting the power of government. Therefore, the main principle of neo-liberalism regarding the economy is that the less governments' destructive interference with economic life of the community, and in obstructing the flow of trade, the better.[55] Simplified, government must not do for the individual what he is able to do for himself/herself. This view and the prevailing neo-liberal orthodoxy were best spelled out by Thomas Jefferson in his advice that government is best that governs least. In the United States, this has had an axiomatic grip on the psyches of generations of Americans who have almost ritualistically believed and acquired a conviction premised on this notion of state. However, the contemporary variant of liberalism is even more amorphous and Jefferson's advice has today acquired new meaning.

Central to the neo-liberal thesis, the key to making the state more efficient is to open it up—in terms of both its internal organizational structure and the regulatory and policy constrains it imposed on the market—to wider global market forces.[56] The imperative here, as Razeen Sally puts it, is " . . . to pave the way for the unfettered play of market forces."[57] Thus, "rolling back the state" and "unleashing the market" became the key objectives of the political and economic reform agenda. Despite decades of socialist rhetoric, the ANC was to embrace these dogmatic approaches after assuming political power. The real meaning of neo-liberal globalization and the rollback of social democracy is that governments that were once capable of protecting their own citizens are now called upon to sacrifice their sovereignty and their citizens to the interests of maximum shareholder value. Still, the East Asian Tigers are acclaimed for the provision of conducive environment for capital investment that ultimately facilitated growth. What is simply forgotten is that governments have been deeply involved in the economies of all the East Asian countries.[58]

*   *   *   *   *

Despite these apparent contradictions, the neo-liberal message to the late industrializing countries of the south, Africa in particular, is loud and clear: governments should let the market forces of capitalism play unfettered if development is to be realized. Notwithstanding the experiences of the Newly Industrializing Countries, and their state-centered development, neo-liberals advocate that growth is easy, provided governments do not act to obstruct the natural growth-inducing process of a capitalist economy. Susan George reminds us that in 1945 or 1950, if one had seriously proposed any of the ideas and policies in today's standard contemporary neo-liberal tool-kit, one would have been laughed off the stage at or sent off to the insane asylum.[59] At least in the Western countries, at that time, most people were Keynesians, social democrats or social-Christian democrats, or some shade of Marxists. The idea that the market should be allowed to make major social and political decisions, the idea that the state should voluntarily reduce its role in the economy, or that corporations should be given total freedom, trade unions should be curbed and citizens given much less rather than more social protection—such ideas were largely foreign to the spirit of the time.[60]

In the past few decades, however, Keynesian ideas steadily got relegated to the museum of antiquity, resulting in the state and its intervention in the economy being seen, rather, as the major obstacle to development. Everything must be left to the market forces of capitalism for development to be realized, so the litany goes. Susan George argues that the rationale for redistribution of wealth to the best-off as opposed to the worst-off is that increased incomes for the rich and higher returns to capital will lead to more investment, more efficient allocation of resources and will consequently provide more employment and greater welfare for everyone. Rich people's money is thus assumed to have a higher "multiplier effect," but in reality, people at the top end of the scale already have most of the goods they need. The bulk of their wealth [technically known as "savings"] heads straight for financial markets, with much of it placed in speculative financial instruments.[61]

The barriers to development, Western economists argue, reside primarily with the countries themselves; these include such social and cultural phenomena as the extended family, religious practices, patterns of land-holding and lack of capital, [i]rational economic decision-making, as well as political obstacles such as corruption, regime instability, and ineffectual bureaucracies.[62] Whether these obstacles can be countered by giving markets the upper hand remains vehemently contested. Be that as it may, neo-liberalism has invariably become the "major world religion with its dogmatic doctrine, its priesthood, its law-giving institutions and perhaps most important of all, its hell for heathens and sinners who dare to contest the revealed truth."[63] Socialism—it is widely averred, has, despite achievements in the field of social services and equality, failed the Third World economically. Conversely, the same verdict must apply to neo-liberal capitalism. The basic tenets of neo-liberalism are best summed up in the so-called Washington Consensus, which outlines "the lowest common denominator of policy advice addressed by the Washington-based institutions to Latin American countries as of 1989."[64] The Washington Consensus is premised on the following ten points:

Table 1.1. Washington Consensus[65]

Fiscal Discipline Large and sustained fiscal deficits contribute to inflation and capital flight. Therefore, governments should keep them to a minimum.	**Trade Liberalization** Tariffs should be minimized and should never be applied toward intermediate goods needed to produce exports.
Public Expenditure Priorities Subsidies need to be reduced or eliminated. Government spending should be redirected toward education, health, and infrastructure development.	**Foreign Direct Investment** Foreign investment can bring needed capital and skills and, therefore, should be encouraged.
Tax Reform The tax base "should be broad," and marginal tax rates "should be moderate."	**Privatization** Private industry operates more efficiently because managers either have a "direct personal stake in the profits of an enterprise or are accountable to those who do." State-owned enterprises ought to be privatized.
Interest Rates Domestic financial markets should determine a country's interest rates. Positive real interest rates discourage capital flight and increase savings.	**Exchange Rates** Developing countries must adopt a "competitive" exchange rate that will bolster exports by making them cheaper abroad.
Property Rights Property rights must be enforced. Weak laws and poor judicial systems reduce incentives to save and accumulate wealth.	**Deregulation** Excessive government regulation can promote corruption and discrimination against smaller enterprises that have minimal access to the higher reaches of the bureaucracy. Governments have to deregulate the economy.

This blueprint was to dictate singular practices that developing countries had to adopt as theirs if ever they wished to escape from their *underdeveloped* condition.[66] These prescriptions presented a new formula to organize economic policies, but they nevertheless inadvertently influence a particular way of life, culture and behavior necessary for the prescribed economic system to function. Thus, from the perspective of the *underdeveloped*, development has come to be seen as an ethnocentric top-down imposition of alien cultural values, norms, sets of belief systems of one particular society. Therefore, to call this lowest common denominator of policy advice a "consensus" implies that developing countries also gave consent for the implementation of such destructive policies in their countries. Judging by the magnitude of discontent with these policies, it becomes clear that prescriptions are nowhere close to a consensus, than they are to coercion.

CONCLUDING REMARKS

This analysis seeks to dissect South Africa's transition using the regulation theory's key concepts outlined above, the mode of regulation and the regime of accumulation. In the prevailing development orthodoxy, there exists little disagreement on the causes of the problem but also little consensus about what needs to be done. From the perspective of the *developer*, "the essential is to press on with structural reforms, or so the litany goes, people can be bracketed for a while, even if hundreds of thousands might die, hail the market!"[67] Unfortunately, for the *developed*, using Gilbert Rist's language, the promise of a better life "appears to recede like a horizon just as they think they are approaching it."[68]

This reality has led some scholars to question the logic and origins of development as a universal remedy. Rist's tracing of the origins of the discourse concluded that the notion is undoubtedly Western. He argues that the idea of development as natural and necessary always existed in Western thought since Aristotle, through the Enlightenment and the triumph of social evolutionism. In the same vein, owing to its origins in the West, in the history of capitalism, in modernity and the globalization of Western state institutions, cultures and mechanisms of exploitation, Jonathan Crush concluded that the development discourse is to that extent ethnocentric.[69] The ethnocentric bias has been a source of discontent for some time.

Whatever the concerns, if Rostow's stages of economic growth are anything to go by, it becomes clear that even if South Africa's economy is to *take-off*, it would be under the auspices or influence of foreign development blueprints. But are there no alternative development models at all or the arrogance of neo-liberals will simply not tolerate competitive alternative models, contrary to their vigorous encouragement of competition in the market place? Answers certainly contradict the extent to which there is genuine commitment to principles of fairness, competition, choice and the highly acclaimed self-regulation of the market system. A modified version of socialism may still remain an alternative, but it is not viable under the current dominance of neo-liberalism in the international economic system.

Chapter Two

Chamber of Mines and Labor: The Political Economy of South Africa's Gold Mining Industry, 1886–1987

INTRODUCTION

The history of South Africa is the story of conquests, gold, apartheid and more recently democratic transition. It was the discovery of gold which attracted foreign attention and marks the beginning of an era that saw the lives of ordinary whites and blacks change. As the mining of gold was labor intensive, it was the beginning of African subjugation to a system of wage labor. "We must have labor," declared the president of the Chamber of Mines in 1912. He further added: "the mining industry without labor is as bricks would be without straw, or as it would be to imagine you could get milk without cows."[1] As labor was central to the success of gold mining in the pre-industrial period of South Africa, the priority of the mining industry was to secure its access for the mines, and this was achieved primarily through coercing Africans to sell their labor.[2]

This chapter briefly examines the origins of the "cheap labor" system in the South African gold mining industry, and its centrality to the development of capitalism and its relationship with the state for successful gold extraction in the period 1886–1987. It demonstrates the extent to which the Chamber of Mines' recruitment campaign succeeded in accessing labor through statutory measures imposed by the state. It also examines factors that eventually undermined that "cheap labor" policy with the re-emergence of African unionization in the gold mining industry after a long period of repression.

ORIGINS OF THE CHAMBER OF MINES

Soon after gold was discovered in Johannesburg, the system of mining groups in which each mining house had its own family of subsidiary mining companies that operated the mines was actively evolving.[3] It became clear that the mines could not be run by individual entrepreneurs, because the mining of ore from great depths—though the great depths of those days seems as nothing to us now—had to be done by companies with substantial capital, as it required an investment of millions which no individual mine by itself could raise. For this purpose in 1887 the Diggers Committee was formed with the sole mandate of protecting common interests of the mining industry.[4] By 1889, the Diggers Committee was dissolved and substituted by the Chamber of Mines.[5] With this development, South Africa's mining industry was taking shape in a manner that distinguished it from mining industries elsewhere. At that time, the Chamber had no administrative or managerial authority, but its representative standing was due to the general recognition of the value of consultation and co-operation in matters of mutual concern. These matters included European and Native labor issues; technical questions such as those connected with mining regulations, legislation, and health conditions on the mines, patent applications, taxation, and the collection of statistics.[6]

It was the Group System, which shaped the basic structure of the South African mining industry making it the force it was. By 1892 there were 95 members of the Chamber of Mines representing 59 companies on the Witwatersrand and eight members representing four companies in other districts of the Transvaal.[7] By the end of the Boer War, more appropriately, South African War (1899–1902), there were as many as nine such groups, controlling 114 gold mines between them.[8] This initiative reduced many overhead costs. Through the Group System, independent individual mines had administrative and financial ties with major mining finance houses. Some of these conglomerates have moved to new areas of business such as banking and insurance. In the process, they have become an economic power block that also wields considerable political influence. Generally, the object of the Chamber was to watch over and promote the interests of the member mines as well as those of the industry. In the pre-1900 period, the industry was by no means as well regulated as it is today. Before the Johannesburg Stock Exchange came into being in 1887, the Chamber regulated market share prices and was also responsible for speculation. In addition to dealing with technical questions outlined above that were common to the industry, the Chamber acted and still acts as managing secretary to certain subsidiaries that are key to the industry. These include, amongst others, the Rand Gold

Refinery, miners' training school for novices and the Rand Mutual Assurance, an accident insurance company for miners.

In the past 100 years, however, the Chamber's role and functions have undergone substantial changes in view of developments unfolding in the external environment. A redirection of the organization has been undertaken: first, with a view to refocus the Chamber to position it as the principal advocate to government of major policy positions endorsed by mining employers; second, to end the Chamber's direct involvement in (and financial subsidization of) various industry services; and third, to expand the membership base of the organization. Consequently, the Chamber exists today primarily to provide strategic support and advisory input to its members. It facilitates interaction among mine employers to examine policy issues and other matters of mutual concern to define desirable industry-level stances. Consultation and co-operation within the Chamber system occur on a voluntary basis and does not encroach on the managerial powers or prerogatives of individual member mines and mining groups.

The Chamber provides a range of professional services to its members in numerous areas; these include mining health and safety, education and training, communication, environmental management, economics and industrial relations. Chamber influence over member affairs is, however, regulated by an approach to industry policy direction and formulation that is founded on the striking of consensus among members, all of whom associate within the Chamber system on a voluntary basis. Consensus is defined via the deliberations of a number of Chamber principal committees, headed by an Executive Council.

STATE-CAPITAL COLLUSION AND THE LABOR SACRIFICE

"Private enterprise has repeatedly failed in attempting to organize and maintain an adequate supply of *Kaffirs*. The task must be undertaken by the public authorities and the Chamber trusts that the government will lend it their indispensable assistance," wrote the Chamber of Mines to Kruger's government in 1890.[9]

In the post-Boer-War period, the mining corporations informed Alfred Milner that Africans could not be coerced into a wage-earning proletariat without the co-operation of his administration.[10] Efficient delivery of "cheap labor" had been facilitated enormously with the formation of labor recruiting institutions, which subsequently eliminated a labor market arrangement developed earlier by independent labor contractors. A developmental chronology of the mining industry since its early days leaves no uncertainty that the mining industry, at least with the complicity of the government of the day, exploited labor to its advantage. The industry's request to establish labor depots along the major routes to protect recruits from extortion by criminals who sought to capitalize on the system was also implemented. Even though the establishment of the Chamber of Mines was a move by the gold mining industry to take the recruitment responsibilities under its control after initial setbacks in accessing "cheap labor," with Alfred Milner in charge after the Boer War, the government was soon on board, even passing laws designed to ensure the mines got the labor they wanted.

However, in the early 1890s, if the South African gold industry were to put itself competitively against the Australians and the Americans who were also producing gold, there was no way it could secure a leading position without a systematic overall battering of the African peasantry. In the unfolding racial puzzle, the fact that white miners, especially from England, still made up a significant percentage of overall labor engaged in the mines meant that separate policies had to apply between blacks and whites.[11] As white mineworkers brought with them the tradition of trade unionism, they swiftly organized themselves to defend their relative position and privileges. For instance, fortune hunters who came from as far afield as Australia, California, Cornwall, Cumberland, Lancashire and Scotland as early as August 1892 formed The Witwatersrand Mine Employees and Mechanics Union.

*   *   *   *   *

Apart from the African Minewokers Union, AMWU, in the 1940s, Blacks had to wait for almost a century before the state and the Chamber of Mines would allow them to unionize successfully. Africans were continually harassed and industrial protests in 1913 and 1920 were ruthlessly crushed by the state. Sometimes even white miners were crushed. For instance, in 1914, General Smuts mobilized 70,000 troops to crush strikes called by railway workers and the South African Federation of Trades. The police also crushed another major African industrial action in 1946.[12] These responses by the state in protecting the industry sent a clear message to Africans that they risked their lives by involving themselves in any form of organized resistance that challenged the overwhelming control of the industry. The logic was simple: if labor could not strike, production costs will be cheap and gold could be mined efficiently.

In addition to quelling industrial action, Levy argues that the use of the state's institutions on behalf of the industry's recruitment drive was indispensable for the successful operation of the Chamber's low-cost labor system.[13] This was further reinforced when Sir Godfrey Ladgen (preferred by the Chamber of Mines) was entrusted with the supervision of African affairs in the Transvaal. In response to his appointment, the Chamber noted that, "with the efficient organization established by Sir Godfrey Ladgen, the laws will be duly enforced and the evils from which we have suffered so much in the past will no longer exist."[14] The close working relationship that ensued between Ladgen and the Chamber marks the beginning of state-capital collusion—a labor battering ram for the subsequent maximization of profits. As Alan Jeeves aptly points out, "it would be easy to make a case that Lagden and his officials answered rather to the Chamber than to their superiors in government."[15] Occasionally, the officials of the Native Affairs Department used their positions to encourage the flow of African labor to the mines and to intervene on behalf of mining management during industrial disputes. One could argue that the officials were the Chamber's appointed representatives in government. As a senior Chamber representative put it in 1903: "we have a certain amount of representation which we could never say we had before."[16]

The intensification of African labor recruitment remained one of the Chamber of Mines' main aims. As the migrant labor system had already proved itself to be cost effective—for the Chamber of Mines—the way was now clear for the industry to go on full-scale recruitment on the African continent. However, the drop in wages frustrated many of the gold mining industry's recruitment efforts (even some of the coercive instruments that were in place) that the mining industry introduced as a way to bring down the cost of production for a speedy post-war recovery. It was of cause, impossible for mine owners to control the price of labor unless they could also control the supply side.[17] This was achieved by appealing to the state for support in securing control over the supply of labor to the mines. Towards this objective, Wilmot James points out that the South African state "provided a supportive political framework for the migrant labor system that was taking form."[18]

THE CHAMBER AND LABOR RECRUITMENT AGENCIES

There was a need to access cheap, reliable and docile labor so that the gold mining industry could curtail escalating costs. The need for "cheap labor," as Lionel Phillips, then Chamber of Mines' President, once put it was that, "*Kaffirs* work for a given sum and not a given time, so the less we pay, the longer they will stay each time and the more efficient they will become."[19] In contrast, white labor was considered impractical. As P.R. Frames put it:

You could not search them, and could not put them in a compound. You could not put them in detention houses at the end of the period of service, to see that they do not take any gold out. To be perfectly candid, you would have them on strike. You cannot have a big industry like that dependent upon labor that can any day go out.[20]

This need for cheap docile labor and the extent to which it was afford-able was facilitated by the fixed gold prices between 1935 and 1972 at US$36 per fine ounce. What the fixed gold price meant was that the mining industry could not pass on any increase in production costs to consumers, but had to absorb it internally. As Wilmot James put it, "in the context of South Africa's racial order, in which African workers were politically powerless and economically vulnerable, austerity measures were most eas-ily targeted at the most convenient variable, the wage rates."[21] Cheap Afri-can labor meant that more labor could be engaged for increased output. This explains why the gold mining industry managed to engage hundreds of thousands of mineworkers from 1930 onwards.

Francis Wilson explain that the 'traditional' society provided the social security for African men who migrated to the towns as they sought occupations where the least skill was demanded and carried the lowest sta-tus.[22] They bore the brunt of the risks inherent in economic growth. They demanded little in the way of employment insurance, accident compensa-tion, sickness benefits or old age pensions. They depended for their security on the extended family network. For this reason, if migrant workers were sick, they knew they would be cared for; if they were unemployed they would be fed; if they were old, their relatives and friends in the community where they come from would provide a roof for them.

As mentioned above, independent contractors had provided flexibil-ities for workers, since they could negotiate their wages and even chose the mines at which they wanted to work. This was an additional frustra-tion for mine owners in their quest for labor, as Africans chose those mines with least onerous working conditions and the best safety records. Gener-ally, there was a relatively sluggish response of Africans to wage employ-ment opportunities. Most of the mines they chose were relatively shallow outcrop mines where drilling was easy and conditions least dangerous.[23] South Africa's gold deposits were (and still are) of extremely low grades and therefore, the mines they avoided were the deep level, low-grade ore mines where the rock was hard and the seams were narrow and tortuous in their descent.[24]

The fact that South African gold is extracted from low-grade ore meant that large numbers of laborers are required to extract the tons of ore needed to produce an ounce of gold (31.1035 grammes). The low grade is reflected in the fact that the average ore mined on the Witwatersrand was about 6.5 pennyweights (dwt) per ton while that for Canadian gold mines was 10 dwt per ton and for Australian mines 13 dwt. A mine was therefore regarded as producing a high-grade ore if it recovered half an ounce of gold from every ton of gold-bearing ore. In addition to the gold-bearing ore that had to be removed from the ground, another half a ton of waste rock for every ton of gold-bearing ore also had to be removed from the ground. The low-grade ore and the internationally fixed gold price meant serious profitability problems and as the depth increased, production costs also increased exponentially.

In the face of these realities, the independent contractors' labor market arrangement certainly did not suit the wishes of the leading mining houses that wanted a cheap, docile and exploitable labor force. It was necessary, therefore, to crack the unyielding de facto monopoly that private contractors exercised over the supply of labor.[25] Simply put, labor recruiting agencies were established to cut the cost of African labor, which by 1896 amounted to 28.6 percent of working costs on the Rand.[26] In addition, Patrick Harries points out that whereas in England wages accounted for 32 percent of total costs, on the Rand they amounted to some 50 percent, split equally between African unskilled and European skilled labor.[27] To cut labor costs, mine owners wanted to eliminate the labor contractors' hiring practices. Indeed, as Alan Jeeves correctly points out, "the mine owners did not want a labor market at all. Instead, they wanted their own tightly controlled recruitment organization on which they could impose their terms. They sought, therefore, to undermine the power of the independent contractors and to put their own organization in their place."[28]

There was a need to establish a central recruitment agency to take charge of this responsibility. The idea, of cause, was that centralized recruiting institutions under industry control would reduce costs, stabilize wages at a low level, end wasteful labor competition among the mines, and forestall the emergence of an open labor market in which the chamber would have to compete with other employers and with the African rural economy for its requirements.[29] Eventually, in 1902, the Chamber of Mines formed the Witwatersrand Native Labor Association (WNLA), and in 1912, the Native Recruiting Corporation (NRC). For its part, the NRC operated in British South Africa and the British Protectorates. Its first challenge was to organize itself as a credible labor recruitment agency and to eventually phase out independent labor contractors. The struggle against independent contractors was an uneven one, as the Union government's Native Affairs Department and the Native Labor Bureau intervened on the side of the NRC. The operations of the NRC were not limited to the recruiting of natives for the mines, but also covered the general *interests* of the recruited natives through special organizations for their *benefit*.

While the NRC was the domestic labor recruitment arm of the Chamber, the WNLA was its foreign recruiting agency. The two were modeled on identical lines and operated in the same pattern, except that the NRC sourced labor within South Africa and the protectorates, while the WNLA sourced labor from Southern Africa as a region. The two agencies combined set in place a systematic base for the labor recruitment machinery that would last over one hundred years.

The reason for establishing the WNLA was that the Chamber of Mines had expressed its preference for foreign workers with longer contracts and greater *reliability*. It made several petitions to the government to have the ban on recruiting within the tropical countries removed and even went so far as to establish the South African Institute of Medical Research in 1913 with the task of researching the causes of pneumonia which had killed many mineworkers before colonial administrators imposed recruitment bans.[30] The reason for preferring foreign miners was that they were cheaper, easily disposable and "that they were working on the mines to supplement the real earnings derived from their peasant farming," which explains the short durations of their contracts.[31]

The Chamber often argued that black South Africans were not available at the price the industry could afford to pay, an argument they used successfully to keep wages lower. In Johannesburg as an emerging city, black South Africans were also affected by events in the locations and by the protests of other industrial workers. This made them more difficult to control within the compounds than the east coast and tropical mineworkers, thus confirming the mine owners' preference for foreign workers. The British pound used in South Africa at the time had more value than most currencies used in territories outside British control such as Mozambique. As a result, "the lure of the higher South African mine wages worked its magic."[32] This made foreign mine migrant workers willing to accept what South African miners regarded as pittance and thus further depressing the wage level.

It was also because of low wages and the fact that Africans refused to work at that level that the Chamber of Mines even went so far as China to access "cheap" enough labor for successful gold mining between 1904 and 1907. However, this was a temporary provision, until such time that more stringent statutory provisions were in place to force Africans to sell their labor in the gold mining industry. In 1898, the last full year of relative peace shortly before the South African War, the gold mining industry produced 118 tons of pure gold. From then onwards, production declined

Table 2.1. South Africa's Gold Production, 1900–1920[35]

Year	Kgs	Labor	Year	Kgs	Labor	Year	Kgs	Labor
1900	10,852	-	1907	200,685	-	1914	261,147	190,549
1901	8,041	-	1908	219,500	-	1915	282,930	217,506
1902	53,437	-	1909	226,957	-	1916	289,168	225,995
1903	92,422	-	1910	234,252	207,414	1917	280,503	205,779
1904	117,291	-	1911	256,642	214,883	1918	261,841	202,392
1905	152,665	-	1912	283,315	216,634	1919	259,143	194,505
1906	180,187	-	1913	273,671	207,991	1920	253,756	198,255

significantly to as low as 8,041 kilograms (8 tons) in the year 1901. With the importation of Chinese labor in 1904, a new production peak of 117 tons was attained in the same year. The Chinese doubled gold output from 118,923 kilograms in 1898 to 219,500 kilograms by 1908.[33] However, in 1907, a decision was taken to repatriate the 63,296 Chinese miners.[34] This did not bring down gold output in the subsequent years as the Chamber had succeeded in lowering African wages across the mines. With this development, the labor recruitment drive throughout the sub-region intensified. The table above shows the total amount of gold produced per year (please note that the Chamber does not have the total number of labor employed in the gold mines between 1900 and 1909).

Granting the Chamber of Mines the right to import Chinese labor is just one illustration of the close relationship between gold mining capital and the state. Thus, after the Boer War, the mining industry developed and natured a rather unique mutual relationship with the sympathetic government administrations that followed.

STATUTORILY CONSOLIDATED "PUSH-PULL": THE MIGRANT LABOR SYSTEM

There was a need for a fixed and reliable system that would ensure that the mines had the African labor they wanted, at the price they were willing to pay. The migrant labor system suited the industry's wishes due to certain specific advantages which enabled the Chamber to cut the cost of production by paying low wages to single migrants who lived austere lives in urban mining compounds and whose families in the rural regions subsidized the mines rather than were supported by them.[36] Thus, there were obvious reasons why the Chamber of Mines preferred the migrant labor system. To give the mining industry a helping hand, government devised mechanisms, from which Africans could not insulate themselves, eventually disturbing the tranquility of entire traditional societies by forcing them to respond to the dictates of capitalism. For instance, through tax laws, government demanded that taxes had to be paid with money and not with cattle, as was the case before. Taxation became a device to "spur the natives to labor."[37]

The state's establishment of the South African Native Affairs Commission (whose responsibility it was to investigate the native problem over the longer term) on the basis of whose recommendations future native policy in South Africa were to be made, dominated the period 1903–1905. The commission's recommendations eventually formed the foundations of the 1913 Land Act, which reduced Africans' economic subsistence through land ownership. The commission essentially argued that:

> Certain restrictions upon the purchase of land by natives are necessary, and recommend that purchase by natives should in future be limited to certain areas to be defined by legislative enactment; and that the purchase of land which may lead to tribal, communal or collective possession or occupation by natives should not be permitted.[38]

Commenting on the commission's findings, Duncan Innes argues that:

> Here was the conceptual framework for racial segregation on a national scale in South Africa—that is, for the essential political means through which a reserve army of labor could be created and reproduced in the rural areas as the prerequisite for capitalist expansion.[39]

The 1913 Land Act followed from the recommendations of the Commission and effectively legalized the theft of land, thus creating a huge marginal peasantry cut off from the source of subsistence with little option but to turn into a captive labor force, an industrialized native.[40] The Act legally confined Africans to live within 8.8 percent of South Africa's land space.[41] Although a panoply of other coercive laws were passed, such as the Native Labor Regulations Act of 1911, which criminalized African participation in labor stoppages, giving the Chamber substantial control of the labor market, the Land Act stands out as the cornerstone for African destabilization. Nkomo quotes an unnamed sympathetic observer who saw the logic of events in 1914:

The evils of depriving them of so much land . . . will, I fear, end in the [African] becoming a nation of degraded servants of their own soil . . . the separation of Africans from productive agricultural land is devastating to their economic dependence and becoming migrant laborers is the only alternative to starvation.[42]

The 1913 Land Act, together with the Masters and Servants Act simultaneously abolished African ownership on the most productive land and interned several hundred thousand Africans as contract laborers. The only land on which Africans could farm for themselves was the tribal land in the reserves, which were already overcrowded.[43] By 1913, about 1,600,000 Africans, out of the total population of 3,880,000 lived outside the reserves, either on European farms or on land owned by Europeans but not occupied by them.[44] Although other measures took place long before the Land Act, the Act, however, further put the traditional family support systems in dire straits, thus making Africans wanderers whose only salvation was through formal employment in the mines. Thus, the push-pull forces were consolidated to turn Africans into a captive labor force. According to the push-pull theory, the oscillatory behaviour of individuals is viewed as a voluntary rational act, an attempt by individuals to maximize benefits and minimize costs. The diagram below demonstrates how the system functioned:

The diagram shows the push-pull forces causing oscillation of labor between two areas A and B. Force 1 is the seasonal demand for labor in area B. Area A represents rural areas, which supply and B represents urban areas, which demand labor. Force 4 is the push, by employers, of labor away from the area at the end of the season, in the mining industry this would

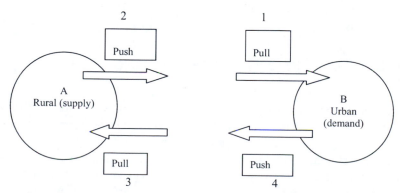

Figure 2.1. The Push-pull Model[45]

have been at the end of contracts, which were usually one year. Similarly forces 3 and 2 are the seasonal demand and push-pull, respectively, in area A and B. Where the areas A and B are sufficiently close for labor to be able to move between them and yet where the seasonal demands (forces 1 and 3) come at different times of the year, workers are able to maximize their earnings by oscillating backwards and forwards in response to the seasonal pulls and pushes.

Landless, unemployed and impoverished by forcible incorporation into the capitalist system, African peasants were pushed to sell their labor. The ethnocentric biases of development orthodoxy understood *underdevelopment* of the African peoples as an original state which the development of capitalist sector gradually eliminates. Thus, the development of capitalism emerged as an ultimately beneficial and rationalizing influence notwithstanding the fact that, over long periods, African workers and peasants derived little, if any, advantage from it.[46] As conditions in the reserves deteriorated due to long absenteeism and consumerism of African males, even the remaining young males were pulled to seek wage employment, leading to a structural disequilibrium in social order.

Although several deputations of African elites who were bitter over post Boer War political settlements went to London repeatedly to discuss their predicament and challenge the efficacy of the system with the masters of imperialism, it was to no avail. The British had betrayed their ideal of equality before the law at the expense of Africans. Eventually, the opposition to increasingly intransigent white rule and deliberate coercive measures exploded into outright resistance, becoming the spur to the formation of the first national organization devoted to opposing the white created racial order—the African Native National Congress—in 1912, which subsequently became the African National Congress (ANC). This was the beginning of a long protracted struggle to liberate Africans from the shackles of oppression and institutionalized inequality.

MIGRANT LABOR: CONSOLIDATION AND EXPANSION, 1920–1973

In the period between 1886 and 1920 the gold mining industry legitimized its operations and set up the essential institutions necessary for labor accumulation. A system of labor monopoly characterized by a single labor recruitment system owned by the Chamber of Mines emerged. The state-capital alliance that was forged after the Boer War facilitated the industry's consolidation of its accumulation strategy. Conversely, the period 1920–1973 was characterized by several developments. Amongst others, there was further consolidation and the opening up of new labor frontiers for the expansion of recruitment apparatus to the tropical countries.

This shift in geographical sources of labor supply between 1920 and 1950 saw the South African gold mining industry mounting a massive effort to beef up its access to labor in Bechuanaland (present day Botswana), Northern Rhodesia (present day Zambia) Nyasaland (present day Malawi) and Southern Rhodesia (present day Zimbabwe).[47] The expansion itself would not have been successful, had Africans throughout Southern Africa not been displaced and coerced through concealed forms of compulsion to earn a living and hard currency for their families through compulsory deferred payment. Although foreign labor was more expensive to obtain, it could be directed to dangerous mines that South Africans avoided. The rationale of this expansion, as Crush *et al* puts it, "was to remove the uncertainties that made the migrant labor supply liable to frequent unpredictable fluctuations."[48] By the 1940s, the WNLA was recruiting in almost every country in Southern Africa. As a result, whereas 58 percent of the black labor force originated in South Africa by 1936, the new recruitment in the north enabled the industry to reduce it to 20 percent by the late 1940s.

Accessing labor from these distant sources consolidated the cheap migrant labor system. The vulnerability of Africans allowed the Chamber of Mines to recruit aggressively not only within South Africa but expanded its recruitment apparatus throughout the sub-continent. This expansionist recruitment policy was prompted in 1936 when Hans Pirow, the Government Mining Engineer concluded that the mining industry would need at least 450,000 miners by the 1950s. This projection led the WNLA to commit vast sums of resources into the labor recruitment machinery. Transport networks were developed by both road and air, and in the process, the WNLA constructed over 1,200 km of roads in northern Bechuanaland alone and also established motor barge transport on the Zambezi and the Okavango. As Alan Jeeves put it, transporting miners by air "must have made it seem exotic, glamorous and possibly even supernaturally powerful."[49]

As a result of this expansion, whereas the gold mining industry employed a total of 174,402 workers in 1920, the number increased to almost 400,000 in 1961. More importantly, the outcome of intensified recruitment in the tropical areas was that from the 1950s onwards, foreign mineworkers dominated the mines making up over 70 percent of the labor force by the 1970s. The table below shows the number or miners by country of origin from 1920 to 1970 in five-year intervals. The table shows the increasing number of total miners from 174,492 in 1920 to 370,312 in 1970:

Table 2.2. Number of Mineworkers by Country of Origin, 1920–1970[50]

Year	Angola	Botswana	Lesotho	Malawi	Mozamb	Swazi	Tanzan	Zambia	Zimbab	RSA	Total
1920		2,112	10,439	354	77,921	3,449		12	179	74,542	174,492
1925		2,547	14,256	136	73,210	3,999		4	68	78,884	173,118
1930		3,151	22,306		77,828	4,345	183		44	92,772	200,634
1935		7,505	34,788	49	62,576	6,865	109	570	27	152,902	265,400
1940	698	14,427	52,044	8,037	74,693	7,152		2,725	8,112	179,708	347,766
1945	8,711	10,102	36,414	4,973	91,637	5,688	1,461	27	8,301	143,370	302,337
1950	9,767	12,390	34,467	7,831	86,246	6,619	5,495	3,102	2,073	121,609	294,425
1955	8,801	14,195	36,332	12,407	99,449	6,682	8,758	3,849	162	121,364	314,298
1960	12,364	21,404	48,842	21,934	101,733	6,623	14,025	5,292	747	141,806	375,614
1965	11,169	23,630	54,819	38,580	89,191	5,580	404	5,898	653	136,551	369,161
1970	4,125	20,461	63,988	78,492	93,203	6,269			3	105,169	370,312

When the Pact Government of Prime Minister J.B.M. Hertzog's National Party and Colonel F.H.P. Creswell's Labor Party came to power in 1924, it set itself the task of implementing what Hertzog called a "civilized labor" policy for whites and the "native labor" policy for Africans.[51] The Labor Party, which represented white miners, wanted to protect them against competition from black workers. In essence, the aim was to cement the foundations of the "cheap labor" system by introducing legislation that would protect white miners' privileges against harsh measures that were to be implemented against African miners. As Muller points out, in a circular, which Hertzog distributed to all government departments on October 31, 1924, he defined civilized labor as "all work done by people whose standard of living conforms to the standard of living generally recognized as decent from a white person's point of view." Uncivilized labor was defined as "work performed by persons whose goal is restricted to the mere necessities of life in accordance with the ideas of undeveloped and savage people."[52]

The "civilized labor" policy led to the systematic battering of the African proletariat while providing improved living conditions for thousands of poor whites who were absorbed *en masse* into other industries. To implement the civilized labor policy the pact government had to introduce harsh statutory provisions to make it work. The first of this legislative salvo was the Wages Act of 1925, which supplemented the Industrial Conciliation Act of 1924. The Industrial Conciliation Act of 1924 had led to the establishment of Industrial Councils with the powers to lay down minimum wages in the industry for which they were established. The Act protected unskilled white workers in all industries across the board. More importantly, it excluded domestic workers, farm workers and miners who were mostly non-white.

The Act empowered Industrial Councils to set working conditions for Africans, even though they were not represented in the Councils.[53] In addition, the Wage Act of 1925 enabled the government to set minimum wages directly for different grades in industries in which the "employees," as defined in the Act, were not organized into a trade union. Certainly, this Act was intentionally designed so that government could regulate minimum wages for Africans who were not unionized in such repressive industries as mining. This establishment was the beginning of the wage colour bar, in addition to the job reservation system, which restricted the employment of Europeans in unskilled work. These measures widened the gap in terms of wages and unskilled work that Africans could do against the skilled civilized labor policy for whites.

More statutes to encompass other areas of social life and not just coercion to the labor market further consolidated these policies. Africans faced a battery of laws that sought to undermine their chances of increasing their wages, to gather relevant job experience and to negotiate for better wages and working conditions.[54] It was through the enactment of racist native policy of subjugation that South Africa's industrialization took place in the period 1920 to 1973. For instance, the Native Urban Areas Act of 1923 had eliminated surplus unemployed Africans in the urban areas by defining urban Africans as temporary sojourners. It extended the Pass Laws to the whole of South Africa, thus further tightening the restrictions on Africans entering the 'white' cities.[55] The Urban Areas Act made it a crime for blacks to be unemployed and without a pass in South Africa's urban areas. Indeed, this was one of the Chamber of Mines' most potent weapons in its vast arsenal.

Amendments to the Act in 1937 enabled the government to mandate "influx controls" and separate African townships. Although African townships in the urban areas, or what Mamdani refers to as "the rural in the urban," consequences of the process of economic development, they contradicted the need for "cheap labor" to serve the very same economy.[56] Indeed, although blacks were needed for their labor in the urban areas, they were, however, not allowed to settle there permanently. As a result, numerous squatter camps that emerged within the vicinity of Johannesburg were bulldozed to make way for expanding industries and white urban areas. Ultimately, Pass Law related arrests reached 700,000 in 1968, which constituted approximately one arrest for every twenty economically active Africans.[57] What undermined the system was the need for labor without permanent residence in cities.

Iniquitous and repressive as these policies were, they enabled South Africa's industrial revolution and economic development to take place as they encouraged the emergence of local industries. There were at least two reasons for government's vigorous intervention in the work place, one social and the other economic. On the social front, the reason for encouraging industrial development was to solve the poor whites crisis by absorbing them into industries as wage earners. On the economic front, encouraging local factories would make the country economically self-supporting. With the imposition of import duties on certain commodities from overseas, except for raw materials needed by industries, this led to an industrial boom in the period 1924–1929. For instance, the number of factories grew from 6,009 to 6,238 and the value of GDP grew from £24 million to £33 million.[58] One such imposition of duties was aimed at promoting and protecting development in the agricultural sector. For instance, the Minister of Agriculture introduced a levy on the selling of imported butter and increased the import duty of sugar from £4.10s to £8 per ton in 1926. When the Great Depression set in, Africans bore the brunt of it.

South Africa also has large deposits of iron ore and the establishment of Iron and Steel Corporation (Iscor), in 1928 further stimulated industrial development. Industrialization was to further accelerate during World War II (1939–1945) and in the post-war period. The government founded the Industrial Development Corporation (IDC) in 1940, the Council for Scientific and Industrial Research (CSIR) and the South African Bureau of Standard (SABS) in 1945. The CSIR was to assist in solving problems frequently faced by industries, while the SABS was to test the quality of goods manufactured in South Africa's growing industries.

Afrikaner National Party and Apartheid

In 1948, the Afrikaner Nationalists came to power with a declared intention of introducing apartheid as the central compass guiding state policy aimed at facilitating the accumulation policies of racial capitalism. As Dan O'Meara puts it, "apartheid was designed to secure labor for all capitals, not to deprive any employer of it."[59] Despite this intention, the Afrikaners were further pressured by their own *Afrikaner Handelsinstituut* (Afrikaner commercial institute) and the farming community to implement policies to facilitate their economic advancement. In 1952, when Dr. Hendrik Verwoerd introduced influx control, it resulted in an institutionalized system that supplied cheap African labor to industries in the urban areas. This development further imposed the position of blacks as a docile subservient labor force serving both the mining and manufacturing industries. The strategy worked as the economy attained as much as a six percent growth rate per annum between 1950 and 1973.

The outcome of the Pact Government's polices that encouraged industrialization in the 1920s was increasing black urbanization. The apartheid regime wanted to consolidate Afrikaner nationalism while simultaneously encouraging industrial development without encouraging the increasing black urbanization. Discouraging black urbanization, however, contradicted the need to encourage industrial development. In addition to other pieces of legislation, it was the Group Areas Act (Act number 41 of 1950), which formed the cornerstone of segregated residential areas for all persons classified as white, coloured or black. Worse still, the amendment of the Native Urban Areas Act in 1955 was aimed at the "locations in the sky," that is the accommodation of non-white servants in flat premises. The Act provided that no more than five non-whites could be accommodated in a block of flats.

Apartheid operated at three essential levels. At macro level, "grand apartheid" tried to create black nation-states and to give them economic content by development of the homelands and the policy of industrial decentralization. The Bantustans were to become *national homes* to *problematic* blacks in the white urban areas. The strategy itself could work only if blacks could find jobs in these Bantustans, but the earlier policies, especially the Land Act of 1913 which sought to compel Africans to sell their labor, together with the statutorily consolidated push-pull forces discussed above, made it impossible. Interestingly, Dr. Verwoerd, the architect of apartheid and then Minister of Native Affairs, would not allow white business to invest in the Bantustans.

At the intermediate level or meso level, apartheid emphasized separation between race groups through influx control, urban settlement patterns, population removals and others. At the micro level, "petty apartheid" emphasized separation between individuals of different race groups through separate amenities and the prohibition of interracial marriages and sexual relations.[60]

*   *   *   *   *

What is important for this analysis is the extent to which the apartheid government managed to increase economic growth and industrialization. In the period between 1948 and 1961, the economy achieved remarkable growth. For instance, net national income increased from R2 billion in 1948 to more than R4 billion in 1961. The manufacturing sector, which contributed 17 percent to the GDP, increased to 21 percent by 1961. The highlights of the post-war industrial development include Iscor, which had been producing steel in its Pretoria plant, started production in its new steel plant in Vanderbijlpark in 1952, and Sasol's production of oil from coal at Sasolburg in the same year. Between 1948 and 1961, gold production doubled, and its value increased from R200 million in 1948 to R575 million in 1961.

There are three explanations for the remarkable increase of both production and the value of gold during this period. First, the Free State goldfields that were discovered in the 1940s started production in 1951. Second, the gold mining industry benefited from the devaluation of the South African pound in 1949, which caused the gold price to rise from R17.25 to R24.83 per fine ounce by today's exchange rate. The third explanation has more to do with the successes of labor recruitment methods that were strengthened since the 1920s onwards. The table below shows South Africa's gold production, 1921–1973 and the average labor employed.

Table 2.3. South Africa's Gold Production and Average Labor Employed, 1921–1973[1]

Year	Kgs	Labor	Year	Kgs	Labor	Year	Kgs	Labor	Year	Kgs	Labor
1921	252,831	170,930	1935	335,109	265,400	1948	360,329	271,399	1961	713,562	388,345
1922	218,031	159,298	1936	352,596	291,213	1949	364,068	286,076	1962	792,890	383,494
1923	284,568	175,976	1937	364,986	297,748	1950	361,849	294,425	1963	853,229	373,958
1924	297,817	176,729	1938	378,262	311,923	1951	358,202	286,688	1964	905,470	364,455
1925	298,519	173,118	1939	398,793	316,760	1952	367,602	286,329	1965	950,332	369,161
1926	309,628	180,307	1940	436,895	347,666	1953	371,395	278,327	1966	960,466	363,232
1927	314,845	185,421	1941	448,128	363,908	1954	411,720	301,298	1967	949,679	353,198
1928	322,054	195,161	1942	439,394	349,899	1955	454,154	314,298	1968	967,146	361,632
1929	323,860	192,127	1943	398,261	303,650	1956	494,442	323,514	1969	972,956	354,814
1930	333,316	200,634	1944	381,939	305,808	1957	529,715	324,581	1970	1,000,417	370,312
1931	338,337	208,359	1945	380,229	302,337	1958	549,177	329,951	1971	976,297	370,547
1932	359,511	216,372	1946	370,976	298,891	1959	624,107	370,026	1972	909,631	361,595
1933	342,565	228,045	1947	348,368	288,957	1960	665,086	375,614	1973	855,179	378,826
1934	325,960	245,159									

As the table indicates, from 1951 the total output of gold increased from 358,202 to 1,000,417 kilograms in 1970. This remarkable increase, at the height of apartheid repression, was made possible by the increasing number of mineworkers during the same period.[62] Simultaneously, the "cheap labor" system was extended to other sectors of the entire economy, facilitating the development of industrialization and capitalism in general.

The "cheap labor" system had successfully supplied the necessary labor to the urban areas, but their sheer numbers overwhelmed the control mechanisms of keeping African laborers out of urban areas. Blacks could not be removed faster than the rate at which they were coerced to move to the urban areas in search of jobs. Be that as it may, stringent racial labor policies coupled with other apartheid social policies served the interests of the gold mining industry for almost a century. However, the very development of capitalism exacerbated inequalities between blacks and whites, especially during the period of high apartheid, 1948 to 1973. After Sharpeville, in 1961, apartheid repression was so severe that African protests declined for more than a decade. However, this reality was to change from the mid-1970s onwards.

CHALLENGES TO THE APARTHEID "CHEAP LABOR" SYSTEM

Africans never accepted the coercive racist enactments imposed by the state and industry in the workplace and in social life. Instead, they went on strikes and tried in vain to organize themselves into trade unions and political parties. The odds were against them, as capital colluded with the state to reinforce their subjugation. On the labor front, Clement Kadalie organized a mass-based African trade union in the 1920s and 1930s through the Industrial and Commercial Workers Union of Africa (ICU). On the hope of a potential bargaining avenue, the movement succeeded in drawing affiliates, but its aversion to strikes and the fact that employers refused to negotiate with it led to its demise. It was not statutorily sanctioned, and the South African Trade Union Congress refused its affiliation. Ultimately, the ICU collapsed.

On the political front, Africans' predicament was buttressed by the fact that during its formative years, the ANC sought to acquire relief for blacks through persuasion and constitutional means with both the British and the South African governments.[63] The movement was fundamentally elitist, non-violent and a Western-oriented response to the policies of a European government.[64] The aim, as then President John Dube put it, was "not to approach government with assegais (spears) but respectfully as loyal subjects with the intention of airing their grievances and removing obstacles of poverty, prejudice and discriminating legislation."[65]

With a government that was not prepared to listen, deputations were sent to London (1914) and at the signing of the Treaty of Versailles (1919), in the hope that the colonial master would side with the Africans in their grievances. The deputations had little if any political effect. The movement also relied heavily on passive resistance protest strategies, the legacy of Mahatma Gandhi's *satayagraha* (passive resistance) experience in South Africa. Within South Africa, many of those who supported the cause of the South African Native National Congress, predecessor to today's ANC, in its struggle for liberation lost hope in the prospects of the organization achieving anything politically significant.

There was enthusiasm that the post World War I period would usher in a new dimension to black people's lives as a reward to their participation in the war in support of the British. However, the economic recession of the early 1920s dashed out ANC's expectations when black employment fell by nearly 20 percent. The bitter pill was made all the more difficult by successive demands on the part of white labor in the 1922 recession and the Rand Revolt for the consolidation and protection of white privilege. Blacks were made to bear the brunt of economic hardship while some white people enjoyed the wealth. Despite this, the ANC maintained its aloof constitutional approach, even though such efforts yielded few results, but trust in the possibility of compromise persisted.[66]

ANC leaders' conviction remained positive that the British would be lenient and sympathize with their cause for freedom. This optimism largely rested on the belief that England would eventually extend her liberal tradition in the Cape Colony—where blacks and coloured people were able to vote—to the other three provinces. With time, this belief withered. It was realized that the struggle from then onwards had to rely on *internal power* for it to succeed. With the rise of the Communist Party of South Africa (SACP) in 1921 and the ANC's association with it, the struggle adopted ideological substance. The emphasis was on "awakening the African proletariat," leading to a revolution that would eventually overthrow the state.

Dale McKinley argues that the association with the SACP was due to the ANC's moderate leadership's inability to transcend its own limited vision.[67] This may be true, but the ANC at this stage had acknowledged the weaknesses of deputation politics and the need to rethink its strategy. The answer rested on Leninist approaches to a people's struggle, that is, a struggle driven by the masses at the direction of the leadership, a 'people's front.' The majority of the people, who were seen as the vanguard of the struggle, were mainly workers, many of them affiliated to leftist oriented ideologies inspired by the Communist Party.[68] After all, the two were fighting for the same cause of freedom, united they would get stronger, so the leadership believed. Having changed its name from the South African Native National Congress to the African National Congress (ANC) in 1923, the ANC appeared to have been like a dormant volcano throughout the 1920s to 1940s. The organization was plagued by internal squabbles over its leaders' close ties with the SACP. In 1930, the ANC executive even resigned in protest against President Josiah Gumede's (elected in 1928) close ties with the Communists. As though that was not enough, ANC radicals in the Cape even formed an independent ANC in 1930.

Much of the party's weaknesses during this period can be attributed to the fact that its larger constituency, mainly working class and peasants, saw the party as dominated by intellectuals who in many ways did not share their peasantry experiences. Further complications were compounded by the fact that the ICU and the SACP also had their fair share of supporters, among the mainly African working class masses taking charge of their struggle outside the intellectual ivory tower of the ANC. Many would-be supporters, especially on the rural side, may have been disillusioned by long period of oppression, the only one they knew and therefore felt the idea of change was an illusion. The emergence of the ANC Youth League in 1943 (among its leaders was Nelson Mandela, Walter Sisulu and Oliver Tambo), was a youthful response to the leadership they call a "dying order of pseudo-liberalism and conservatism, of appeasement and compromise."[69] This marks the turning point in the course of the struggle. It was the militant approach of the Youth League that strengthened the position of the ANC.[70] After the Defiance Campaign of 1952, a non-violence protest against unjust laws, the belief in non-violence as the way of expressing discontent diminished. With the ban of African political organizations in 1960, the apartheid regime increased its repression and after the Sharpeville massacre, Africans protests subsided until the early 1970s.

*   *   *   *   *

In 1974, two disconnected developments outside South Africa took place that threatened the century-old gold mining industry's access to "cheap labor." The first development was an airplane crash near Francistown in Botswana in which 72 Malawian miners were killed. The plane was owned by the WNLA and was ferrying miners between their home and the railway link to the mines. In response to this incident, Malawi's President Hastings Kamazu Banda announced that further recruiting of Malawians to the South African mines was to be stopped. He further ordered the return of Malawian miners from South Africa. In the 54 years that the Chamber of Mines had been recruiting in Malawi, it had become so reliant upon this distant labor source that the number of Malawian miners had risen to 119,141 by 1973, making up as much as 30 percent of the total number of miners. The withdrawal cost the industry R7 million in airfares alone.[71]

The decision by Dr. Banda certainly compelled the Chamber of Mines to revisit its expansionist recruitment policy and reliance on foreign labor, despite the fact that it had successfully helped the industry to maintain a "cheap labor" policy. While the Malawian government relied heavily on the remittances of migrant laborers in the mines for foreign exchange earnings, Dr. Banda was prepared to sever ties with the source of that valuable economic resource. Politically, Dr. Banda's decision had an even greater impact on South Africa's relations with other African states. For in 1967, Malawi was one of the very few countries that opposed the Organization of African Unity's hostile attitude towards South Africa. Subsequently, Malawi and South Africa exchanged diplomatic representatives, while no other Southern African country was interested.

The second development was more profound, the military coup in Lisbon, Portugal, the colonial power administering Angola and Mozambique. This development had both economic and political implications for South Africa. On the political front, it replaced the *cordon sanitaire* of the white colonial regimes sympathetic to South Africa with black Marxist-Leninist regimes. Although Rhodesia, present day Zimbabwe, remained, the intensified guerrilla war was proving effective against Ian Smith's regime. South Africa was confronted with a dual problem of containing the growth of communism in Southern Africa, as Marxist-Leninists were on the verge of gaining political power in Angola, Mozambique and Namibia. The paranoia of B.J. Vorster, South Africa's Prime Minister at the time, led to military entanglements in the Angolan quagmire, largely as an American proxy. On the economic front, for years, South Africa had relied heavily on its relationship with the Portuguese rulers in Mozambique to get its much-needed labor. By 1970, Mozambique was supplying as much as 25 percent of miners, some 100,000 men to the South African gold mines.

Economically *naïve*, the Marxist-Leninist Frelimo freedom fighters in Mozambique proclaimed that they would suspend sending their miners to South Africa. This, they argued, indirectly supported the apartheid system, which they strongly opposed. Frelimo's threats of withdrawing 100,000 men and Malawi's 120,000 to be withdrawn the same year meant that over 50 percent of the industry's labor force was to be withdrawn within the same year. However, Frelimo's Marxists were to drop their rhetoric once they gained power at independence on June 25, 1975. Mozambique did not withdraw its nationals after independence in 1975, instead sending as many as 114,385 miners in 1976. The relationship between South Africa and Mozambique was *improved* (although South Africa continued to support Renamo), as reflected in the signing of the Nkomati Accord, a non-aggression pact between Presidents Samora Machel and P.W. Botha in 1984.[72] Botha agreed to suspend his support of Renamo while Samora Machel agreed to expel the ANC from Mozambique, although as we now know, Botha did not abide by the agreement.

Because of both incidents, the Chamber became acutely aware of its vulnerability due to its inability to control labor sources and feared the potential disruption of production if the over-reliance on foreign labor was not reduced. From then onwards, foreign miners were kept at reasonable numbers that could not disrupt production if their governments decided to pull them out at short notice. Alternatively, the industry internalized its recruitment machinery by beefing up its recruitment campaign in the emerging *newly independent homelands*. Meanwhile, the industry had to drop its long-standing argument that black South Africans were not prepared to work for what it was willing to pay. While the industry had for over 100 years refused to pay more, it now had to do it under duress because during this period the price of gold went up, and the gold industry was able to afford higher wages for miners.

Miners detested the migrant labor system and its exploitation. They challenged the conventional wisdom, of spatial separation of home and workplace—which also made them vulnerable, divided and disposable.[73] The miners' lack of representation was expressed through violence in the compounds. With B.J. Vorster's unconventional approach to industry's grievances (unconventional in the sense that the mining industry always received attention and assistance from the state, but Vorster was not interested) and his reluctance to intervene in the ensuing compound violence, the seemingly invincible state-capital alliance that had survived for almost a century was to face its most formidable challenge. The political unwillingness to intervene in the compound violence led the industry to rethink using its formidable weapon: financial muscle. However, with P.W. Botha as Prime Minister in 1979, the police were called in to Carletonville to suppress miners' unrest. As Terreblanche puts it, this reality prompted the *Financial Mail* to call on business people to mobilize the full force of what it called 'business power" to enforce the changes it regarded as necessary for restoring, the corporations' short-term profitability. As he further puts it, "this was the beginning of an extraordinary politicization of the business sector."[74] Despite a long-standing state-capital consensus on African labor policy, mine management stressed the need for collective bargaining with Africans

Chamber of Mines and Labor

and as they argued, "union leaders would give early warning of grievances, provide a means for conflict resolution and forestall violence."[75]

*   *   *   *   *

Because of increasing gold prices after the fixed price system was abandoned in the early 1970s, enough profits accrued and wages could be raised to attract large numbers of African miners in the homelands who had generally shunned mine work. The industry saw this factor, together with B.J. Vorster's disinterest in its concerns, as a signal of the political change of mood regarding the industry's interests. This marked the turning point in the state-capital alliance that had been in place since the turn of the century. The industry, however, was still reluctant to change its policies—although it did increase wages, the fundamental structure that forms the overall systematic exploitation of the migrant labor system remained.

Francis Wilson's study of the gold mines revealed that "despite the enormous development of the industry during the first eighty years of its existence the real wages of black miners did not increase at all; indeed, over the period 1889 to 1969, they seem to have fallen, while real earnings of whites increased by at least two-thirds."[76] With the gold price boom that increased the industry's profits, African wages improved by 320 percent from R16 to R67 between 1972 and 1980, while white wages increased by only 12 percent.[77] However, wage increases were not accompanied by an increase in productivity output. Essentially, average wage increases slowed down the rate of capital accumulation. This reality presented more problems when the National Union of Mineworkers emerged and demanded more wage increases between 1983 and 1987, while the level of productivity remained the same as it was in the 1970s.

The rationale for improving African wages was: first, to attract black South Africans whose increasing unemployment and despair was becoming militant, especially after the inspiration of the 1976 Soweto uprising. This internalization process marked the beginning of bourgeoning black South African labor power once the government and industry lifted the ban on black unionization in the mines. Second, in the period of recurring uncertainties, the industry desperately wanted to reduce the over-reliance on foreign labor, which was becoming increasingly unreliable. At last the industry was forced to violate the color bar and do exactly what it avoided for decades—employing a cadre of dedicated and reliable well-paid career miners as opposed to sourcing labor where it was cheapest. The table below indicates the ratio of white and black wages in the gold mines and the actual amount in rands for the period 1968 to 1980.

Table 2.4. White and Black Miners' Wages, 1968–1980[78]

Indexed and deflated by the consumer price (January 1968=100)			Actual (Rands per month)		White/black wage ratio
	White	Black	White	Black	:1
1968	100.4	98.7	337	16.41	20.54
1969	99.4	99.6	347	17.06	20.34
1970	104.7	98.8	386	17.82	21.66
1971	106.5	99.3	414	18.96	21.84
1972	106.8	107.6	450	21.96	20.49
1973	123.7	133.3	576	29.93	19.24
1974	124.3	193.6	649	48.69	13.33
1975	123.1	285.9	734	81.38	9.02
1976	122.0	301.9	802	95.33	8.41
1977	119.3	307.6	872	108.09	8.07
1978	112.8	317.2	930	124.33	7.48
1979	108.9	324.7	1023	144.82	7.06
1980	112.5	345.9	1191	214.97	5.54

In 1968, white miners earned R337 per month and Africans earned one twentieth as much, R16.41. Although African wages were increased, by 1980, they were still paid much less than what whites earned twelve years before in 1968. This difference between black and white wages increased the profit margins for the industry and reveals the extent to which the industry was committed to enforcing an exploitative "cheap labor" system. The point worth emphasizing is that there is no way the industry could have afforded the salary discrepancy without government's statutory provisions that legalized discrimination. The "cheap labor" system and the accompanying extreme exploitation were responsible for high percentages of economic growth. Radical salary increases for African miners appeared to stem from then increasing militancy of the bargaining processes. The industry had to adjust African wages to narrow differentials, but this inadvertently afforded African miners a realization that the industry was acceding to their demands and therefore losing its grip. Widespread labor unrest ushered a new era beginning in the 1980s, which severely put the industry and the South African state itself under a legitimacy crisis.

THE EMERGENCE OF THE NATIONAL UNION OF MINEWORKERS

Until the early 1980s, the state-capital collusion had for almost a century of its existence refused African trade unionization in the gold mining industry. While the gold mining industry had often solicited coercive and sometimes brutal neutralization of African industrial protests from the state security apparatus, from the mid-1970s, the size of the mine labor force and its militancy that largely stemmed from growing feelings of alienation could not be easily contained. This militancy was both a displacement and a defensive strategy as Africans sought to protect themselves in the absence of formal trade union recognition and overall political representation. Furthermore, there was also the influence of the Black Consciousness Movement and the influences of the Soweto uprising in 1976, from which miners were not politically insulated. It was an outcome of the failures of labor control. Put bluntly, one of the unintended consequences of apartheid was its glaring contradictions: how were employers going to negotiate with hundreds of miners? There were no practical ways, except negotiating with them on a football field, which was not feasible.

In the absence of negotiations, if the industry were to continue its traditional coercive approach, it would have had to contend with half-a-million miners who were not insulated from the highly explosive political atmosphere of the early 1980s. The political environment of the late 1970s and early 1980s was so confrontational that the state did not want to risk another 'Soweto scenario.' The Black Consciousness Movement had successfully sowed the seeds of provocative political expression that dominated the later half of the 1970s. With the coming to power of P.W. Botha as Prime Minister in 1978 (previously Minister of Defense for 12 years), a new era characterized by the changing of the state-capital relations that dominated the century had begun, as the state reinforced its security apparatus to confront rising African militancy.

Although to the extreme right, Botha, unlike his predecessor, B.J. Vorster, was prepared to yield under political pressure and introduce reforms. The first of these reforms was lifting the ban on African trade unionism in the mining industry and the introduction of limited cosmetic political reforms. Between 1977 and 1979, under the purview of labor minister, Fanie Botha, the Wiehahn Commission (appointed by Prime Minister Vorster) inquired into industrial relations and its 1979 report advocated official recognition of African trade unionism. According to Wilmot James, through Wiehahn, "reformist officials in the Labor and Manpower ministries of the state sought to depoliticize production, and to minimize the state's presence in what increasingly was seen as the 'private' sphere of accumulation."[79] As Dan O'Meara puts it, "a gradual extension of trade union rights attempted to institutionalize and regulate industrial conflict, and, through tight controls on the unions, to isolate and depoliticize the work place struggles."[80]

The state wanted to retreat from direct involvement in the economic and labor spheres to commit its resources to the emerging militance of the black political consciousness sparked by Soweto, the prominence of the Black Consciousness Movement and its military entanglements in Angola and Namibia. This revealed Afrikaner determination to remain within the straightjacket of grand apartheid despite explicit African militant discontent. In 1946, the Fagan Commission commenced its deliberations on "native policy" and recommended limited recognition of black trade unions in 1948. The Chamber of Mines vigorously opposed this recommendation. However, 35 years latter, the Chamber would change its position. The emerging unionization directly threatened the gold mining industry's profitability, which was premised on a "cheap labor" policy.

*   *   *   *   *

In January 1980, international gold price jumped to an all-time record of US$835 an ounce. South Africa was a major beneficiary of this meteoric rise in price resulting in an economic boom. Aware of Wiehahn Commission's investigation into African labor issues, African gold miners certainly expected improvements not only in their financial position, but also in the workplace. There was reason for optimism, at least in light of wage increases of the 1970s, that the state and the gold mining industry was prepared to relax some of the conditions gold miners faced, either at the workplace or in the compounds. Indeed, as a result of the high gold price, the value of the daily trading on the Johannesburg Stock Exchange was over R3 million, which was more than an entire week's figure of less than a year previously. The economic boom was seen as an opportunity for the government to redress its racial policies, but Botha's reforms faltered in the face of far-right discontent within the National Party and his preoccupation with "total strategy" against the "total onslaught." This campaign served to strengthen African nationalism, and Botha lost the opportunity afforded by the favorable gold boom to redress racial issues.

In 1982, the economic boom came to an end as the gold price dropped below US$300 an ounce. The rand followed by losing 23 percent of its value against the U.S. dollar and inflation was as high as 15 percent, the worst since the 1920s. The fall in gold revenue had a serious impact on South Africa's balance of payments. As a result, South Africa had to request US$1 billion from the IMF, which was granted in November 1982. Because of the fall in gold price, miners received a lower than expected wage increase, and riots broke out at Gencor and GoldFields mines near Johannesburg involving some 75,000 black miners and resulting in 10 deaths. However, this does not necessarily mean that other mining houses like AngloGold were not affected by the riots, since working conditions were the same. Africans were the worst affected and in the absence of safety nets, they resorted to anti-government demonstrations and sabotage resulting in the destruction of oil storage tanks at Sasolburg.

On the basis of the Wiehahn Commission's report, government lifted the ban on African trade unionism in the mines in 1981. This development meant that all statutory provisions that prohibited African trade unionism in the mines became irrelevant. In the following year, following protests in the mines, the Chamber of Mines announced that it was prepared to bargain with miners' representatives. For the first time, the barrier that protected the Chamber of Mines for almost a century was removed. As John Lang put it, "there was a new consensus in the ranks of South Africa's mining companies as they tried to put the past behind. The companies opted instead, for an enlightened approach."[81] At least from then onwards, the implicit moral contract that governed relations between mineworkers and low-level management became explicit.[82] The implicit contract specified, amongst others, formal rules that set limits on the coercive treatment of the work force and also allowed a measure of latitude to regulate their private lives in the compounds. At last, the long-awaited era of collective bargaining rights for Africans had arrived.

The National Union of Mineworkers emerged in mid-1982 and had to reverse repressive measures on which the Chamber of Mines had assiduously worked to perfect for almost a century.[83] For its part, the Chamber of Mines even assisted the newly formed union by providing office space as it struggled to sign up mine workers. This, however, does not appear to have been a benign initiative, because the prevailing conventional wisdom within the Chamber held the view that migrancy and unionism were mutually incompatible.[84] But the odds were against the union and a statement by the then Secretary General Cyril Ramaphosa, expressing the difficulties the union confronted, is worth quoting at some length:

When the National Union of Mineworkers was formed an experienced unionist said to me 'organizing workers in South Africa is the art of the impossible.' But organizing workers in the mining industry is the art of the impossible . . . impossible because it has been the art of trying to make a fundamental change in a system by using structures and instruments that were designed to perpetuate that system . . . the art of making a revolution with modern tools that were invented to prevent a revolution. Because of the nature of the mining industry, which is conservative or ultra-conservative by any definition, the black miner has been condemned to seek radical ends within a framework, which was designed to prevent radical ends. In order to understand the full flavour of this system, one must see the industry against the larger canvas of a country, which has permitted one nation to systematically oppress a whole people as a matter of public policy. It is within this larger context that the mining industry, its ancient industrial relations practices, its mindlessness, its violence, must be situated.[85]

It did not take long to prove the Chamber wrong and it paid dearly for its miscalculation. For instance, by 1986, the NUM had 155,315 paying members with a further 167,546 signed up.[86] By 1987, in a labor force 500,000 strong, the NUM had a membership of 360,000, representing over 60 percent of the workforce on the gold and coal mines.[87] This rapid development, as Roger Southall put it, "belied previously held academic and corporate notions that migrants were not interested in unions."[88] The industry's recruitment drive and its expansion which resulted in labor force of more than half a million in the gold mines alone by 1986, proved to be a potent threat to the industry, as foreign migrant workers whom the industry deemed averse to unionization enlisted in huge numbers. This presented a threat as miners consistently demanded improvements, both in terms of wages and living conditions in the compounds, which cost money for the mining houses. The point worth emphasizing here is that increasing unionization threatened the gold mining industry. Whether the majority of unionized miners were foreign or South African was insignificant.

Migrant workers knew that they were easily disposable, but that was not enough to deter them from affiliating to the union. NUM's easier access to the compounds and some of the mining houses' willingness to assist the newly formed union facilitated the recruitment drive. Besides, when an opportunity to be represented appeared, it was unthinkable to refrain from participation, especially as the NUM appealed to broader political issues outside the scope of industrial grievances. As Wilmot James, puts it:

The NUM wanted to see improvements in the conditions of mine work, particularly with regard to health, safety and remuneration levels. They pressed for the rights of workers against unfair and arbitrary managerial treatment. They opposed the colour bar in employment and the privileged position of white miners, and criticized the migrant labor system and mine compounds for their inhumane and undesirable social consequences.[89]

Eventually, by 1986, 44.6 percent of foreign migrant workers were union members, as opposed to 55.4 percent of South Africans (including the homelands). When the NUM affiliated itself to the newly formed Congress of South African Trade Unions (Cosatu), they formed a lethal political Molotov cocktail waiting to be ignited. To broaden its appeal, the NUM supported sanctions and disinvestment as part of the broader anti-apartheid movement.[90] As an insult to the apartheid government, in 1986, while still in prison, Nelson Mandela was voted life president of the union, and together with Cosatu, in 1987 the NUM adopted the Freedom Charter of the African National Congress, and therefore, pledges for the nationalization of the mines and socialist South Africa (see Chapter Four). Still, its weakness was that it was a union largely composed of migrant workers who became trespassers in accordance with the Urban Areas Act, once they were dismissed for industrial action.

With the emergence of the union movement, for the first time, Africans could reconcile their differences in the compounds and harness their energies to fight their common enemies: government and the Chamber of Mines. Although labor grievances could be settled with the Chamber of Mines through the negotiating platform of the NUM, it was increasingly becoming clear that the grievances were inseparable from the broader anti-apartheid political movement.[91] It is from this perspective that the militancy of the NUM can be properly understood. Thus, in the absence of African political representation and suffrage, the labor front became the vehicle with which blacks could coerce the government to reform. The government was aware of the potential threat and was so intimidated that it even planted a bomb at Cosatu house that blew six or more storeys into the basement.[92] The militancy of the NUM against the Chamber of Mines culminated in the 1987 strike, by far the largest industrial action in the history of South Africa.[93]

The 1987 NUM Strike

Wage differentials between white miners and African miners have always been a contentious issue in the mining industry. As such, amongst other grievances the NUM wanted to confront head on was ensuring that the wage gap was narrowed or closed within a relatively short period of time. To this end, in 1986, the union demanded a 45 percent wage increase across the board. The Chamber offered 17 percent for the lowest categories and 12 percent for the highest. A settlement was reached without industrial action by the union, but future wage negotiations were not going to be as smooth.

For in the 1987 wage negotiations, the NUM demanded a 55 percent increase for unskilled and semi-skilled miners and a 40 percent increase for skilled miners. This demand was the essential catalyst for the strike that ensued when the Chamber of Mines refused the demanded wage increases. The NUM went on strike on August 9, 1987. This was the most decisive mine industrial action since 1946. The strike obviously exacerbated the position of the mining industry, even though the industry managed to cut 50,000 miners, 46,000 of whom were later reinstated. More than 250,000 miners were believed to have participated in the action, which affected 16 of the country's 44 gold and coal mines. Some 11 miners died, 300 were injured and 400 arrested before the NUM was forced to accept the Chamber of Mines' original offer of a 15–23 percent raise on August 30, 1987. However, the victory was costly as the mines suffered an estimated US$125–225 million in production losses. Still, the NUM claimed that it had learned valuable lessons during the strike and that the strike was a dress rehearsal for further action.

As Bobby Godsell, now Chief Executive of AngloGold later put it, "it was a big mistake to think that giving people room to organize means we give up our ability aggressively, assertively and effectively to promote vital interests."[94] Although the NUM did not achieve its objectives, its opening salvo, however, managed to stop production for three weeks. The strike was a test of the worker's strength and determination, but the industry also demonstrated the limits of union bargaining power. More importantly, because of widespread unemployment, the industry was able to find new labor to substitute for the striking miners.

Table 2.5. Gold Production and Average Labor Employed, 1973–1987[95]

Year	KGs	Labor	Year	KGs	Labor
1973	837,419	378,826	1981	601,125	478,938
1974	743,995	349,985	1982	610,750	475,769
1975	701,203	321,846	1983	622,371	487,761
1976	697,258	342,507	1984	619,044	498,421
1977	651,783	373,487	1985	604,117	513,832
1978	657,451	388,794	1986	577,218	534,255
1979	649,879	399,123	1987	540,900	530,574
1980	620,924	469,257			

As a result, for the period 1980 to 1985, sporadic work stoppages by the NUM coupled with falling gold prices meant that Chamber Members' gold production never increased in real terms (672,875 Kilograms in 1980 to 670,755 in 1985). However, labor increased from 469,257 in 1980 to 513,832 in 1985. Despite the incremental decline in gold production, labor increased to a peak of 534,255 miners in 1986. From a peak of 679,952 kgs in 1984, gold production fell to 601,775 kgs in 1987. Aware of the eventualities of political uncertainty, in the period following the 1987 strike, the Chamber of Mines began to re-position itself by restructuring and reorganizing its labor force through retrenchments in a manner that would not disrupt production in the future. This enabled the gold industry to cut escalating costs, especially its wage bill which was an outcome of the NUM's successful bargaining. Because the sanctions campaign excluded gold exports, this enabled the government to continue earning the much-needed foreign exchange.[96] However, the industry could not remain insulated and sanctions broadly turned the terms of trade against the accumulation strategy. On the basis of the political consciousness within the NUM, it can be argued that the strike was more of a political statement in the escalating political and economic crisis by exerting pressure on one of South Africa's most prominent industries.

CONCLUDING REMARKS

This chapter sought to summarize the history of South Africa's gold mining industry and its centrality both in the development of a "cheap labor" system and in the South African economy. As economic historians have pointed out, gold mining powered South Africa's industrial revolution. The chapter also demonstrated the extent to which the gold industry's quest for "cheap labor" led it to collude with the government of the day to secure a privileged access to labor that was central to its survival during its infancy. It was important that three problems were overcome to secure maximum labor exploitation; namely: sufficient capital to finance production; sufficient supply of low-cost labor power; and the overall maintenance of a low cost structure. As demonstrated, the mining industry managed to address all these problems within the first 20 years after gold was discovered. The need to offset costs culminated in the setting up of a vast labor recruitment apparatus to scour labor throughout the sub-continent.

Although these initiatives reduced production costs, African miners paid the price. They were not allowed to form trade unions and could therefore not bargain for better working conditions, until the early 1980s. The "cheap labor" system served the interests of the gold mining industry and as Crush *et al* noted "if an ore body similar to South Africa's had been discovered in Australia, Canada, or the United States, it would almost certainly have been left in the ground because of the inability to mobilize the right type of workforce."[97] Therefore, the historical key to unlocking the promise of gold was black labor, cheap, disposable and exploitable. The relationship that emerged between the mining industry and successive South African governments, especially after the Boer War, laid the foundation for black subjugation in the form of racial segregation. However, this mode of regulation started crumbling in the early 1970s. From then onwards, the South African gold mining industry has been facing a crisis of accumulation. The state was however, more absorbed in controlling the increasingly violent black protest. With this background on South Africa's gold mining industry, we can now begin with an analysis of the gold mining industry and labor in the post-apartheid period.

Chapter Three
Evaluating GEAR: Labor and Employment Trends in the Chamber Affiliated Gold Mines

INTRODUCTION

After curtailing African demands for equitable working conditions for over 100 years, the 1987 NUM strike induced a comprehensive restructuring process in the South African gold mining industry. This restructuring was necessitated by the changing locus of gold mining internationally as reflected in declining South African gold output; the increasing depth of old shafts, which were becoming too costly to operate; overall rising production costs—overburdened by a large, overly *unproductive* "cheap labor" force; weak international gold prices, which have declined from a peak of US$835 an ounce in 1980, US$381 in 1989 and US$271 by 2001. For local capital, the political transition opened an escape hatch. As such restructuring process was accelerated by increasing output from green-fields explorations abroad, which have been comparatively cheaper.

Of all these factors, the overly *unproductive* "cheap labor" force, which was once controllable, was becoming militant. The frequency of industrial action and rising demands for equitable working conditions augmented other challenges confronting the mining industry. For as Segal and Malherbe puts it, "the union action contributed to the further rise of a third in unskilled wages between 1982 and 1998."[1] As such, the restructuring exercise included a labor haemorrhage process, the "downscaling" as it is appropriately known, in the drive to reposition the gold mining industry in the South African and global economy. The table below shows the trend:

Table 3.1. Gold Production and Average Labor Employed, 1987–1993[2]

Year	KGs	Labor
1987	540,900	530,574
1988	554,267	515,739
1989	569,883	505,262
1990	565,653	473,685
1991	562,023	424,250
1992	574,319	406,792
1993	578,011	386,653

Between 1987 and 1993, the job losses in the gold mining industry should be understood from this perspective. As the table shows, despite a reduction in labor by as much as 143,921 miners in seven years (1987–1993), gold production increased from 540,900 kilograms in 1987 to 578,011 kilograms in 1993. However, production began to fall slightly in the late 1990s. As Segal and Malherbe put it, "the scale of contraction in gold mining—in output terms from 566 tons in 1990 to 420 tons in 1998—created the impression that mining in South Africa was a sunset industry heading for marginal status in the economy."[3]

With this restructuring, old ways of working suddenly changed after persisting for the better part of a century. In the changing political landscape of the period 1987–1993, statutory overhaul of legislation tailored for the gold mining industry specifically, could not be ruled out. For an industry that has been the driving force of the South African economy, it enjoyed privileges that were not extended to any other industry. It ran parallel employment regulations outside the parameters of formal employment policies, even running a parallel immigration system through the bilateral treaties. With the restructuring of the labor market, new challenges confronted the mining industry, gold in particular. These factors outlined presented challenges and opportunities for the mining industry, unless transformation was accelerated to sustain profits. This required adjustments in accordance with new employment regulations. This chapter analyzes labor trends in the South African gold mining industry and assess their relationship to GEAR.

ALL THAT GLITTERS? GOLD MINING INDUSTRY IN SOUTH AFRICA'S ECONOMY

After more than a century of full-scale mining, South Africa's gold ore reserves are still estimated at 25,000 tons. At 4,000 meters below the surface, 65 percent of this is still economically recoverable, that is, about 16,500 tons can be mined.[4] The figure below shows the amount of economically recoverable gold at different working levels. Thus, depending on the price of gold, which varies at different periods, a certain amount of gold can be mined economically at different working levels. For instance, if the gold price rises, and the unit production cost per ounce is kept low, the industry is able to extract more gold from the ground.

In 2001, for all gold producers, the roughly US$380 seems to have been the desirable price as all of them—Australia, Canada, South Africa and the United States—were producing an ounce of gold at a cost of roughly US$240.[5] However, the unit cost of production varies across countries. A lower price of gold means less gold is mined. For South Africa's low-grade ore, the amount of gold recoverable at different levels varies. It is important to note that the amount of recoverable gold at different working costs does not vary in any specific year and therefore remains roughly the same even when the price of gold fluctuates:

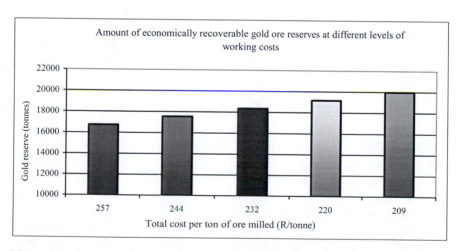

Figure 3.1. Amount of Economically Recoverable Gold Ore at Different Working Costs.

Source: Unpublished Data: Chamber of Mines' Economics Division

South Africa remains the world's largest gold producer, producing 394 tons in 2001, although that was the lowest production level since 1956. At the height of its production, South Africa's gold contributed as much as 50 percent, and even more, of total world output. South Africa's gold mines are largely underground operations, reaching depths of over 3.8 kilometres. The right type of labor for this mining was mobilized successfully with the benefit of state assistance. Even today, this legacy has made the mining industry one of the most exploitative and dehumanizing industries in the South African economy. Because this exploitation was accompanied by a substantial degree of economic output, which the government desperately needed to earn foreign hard currency, the industry enjoyed privileges, which were not accorded to any other industry.

While the overall contribution of gold to South Africa's GDP has been on a continuous decline, it continues to contribute substantially to the national economy. In light of gold's declining importance in the economy and the industry's restructuring, the South African government has been steering the economy away from its historical over-reliance on gold as the major economic stimulus. The shift has not completely downplayed the role that gold may still play in the economy, but as far as mining is concerned, the emphasis has been on the ever-increasing production of platinum group metals and on manufacturing. However, the government has at the same time been helping the gold mining industry where it can. In the year 2000, the platinum group metals surpassed gold in aggregate value and became South Africa's largest export with R27.1 billion against R25.1 billion for gold.[6] Gold is no longer playing the central monetary role it once did and international economic patterns give no indication that it would once again become a reserve in backing up national currencies.

For instance, in the past decade the total percentage of gold as a monetary reserve in the world has been on a continuous decline.[7] In 1990, the amount of gold as a world reserve stood at 29 percent and this fell to 11 percent in 2001. Evident in this trend is that the glittering power of gold has been waning, especially in the more traditional areas of its consumption. Simultaneously, new avenues for the demand of gold have emerged, thus giving reasonable hope for continuing exploration, but strictly in those areas where the cost of production remains cheap and economically viable. Although there are new applications for gold, they do not, however, require the large quantities the reserve era once did. These new applications include, amongst others, gold being used as a catalyst—that is, as a substance that accelerates the rate of chemical reaction without itself being consumed by the reaction. There is also a potential for gold to function as a heterogeneous catalyst for the synthesis of gas conversion to methanol, which has become a research project by the University of Cape Town together with the Royal Institution of Great Britain. Gold has also become a vital material in the modern electronics industry ensuring reliability of more products ranging from cell phones to credit cards.

The declining importance of gold in driving the South African economy is equally accompanied by the fall in the grade per ton of ore milled and the increasing depths. For an example, in 1970, gold mining was extracting an average grade of 13.5 grams per ton of ore milled, and during this period, whatever was mined made a profit. In the year 2002, the grade per ton of gold had declined to about four grams. In production cost terms, this means that 35 percent of the ore-body is uneconomic to mine. For every ton of ore milled, there has been a massive reduction in grade. The industry tried to compensate for the declining ore grade by increasing the amount of ore milled. All these features, together with the fall in the international gold price, have successfully combined to decelerate the pace of gold production. Overall, gold's share of total mining output, compared with all minerals output combined, is steadily decreasing. In 2002, gold alone contributed 24.6 percent of total mining output, compared with 75.4 percent of all other minerals combined. In 1985, gold mining's share stood at 56.1 percent and other minerals combined made up a total of 43.9 percent.[8]

With a 24.6 percent contribution in total mining output, the gold mining industry still contributes substantially to South Africa's GDP. However, the ever-increasing price and value of platinum group metals and the shift from gold as the main export undermines the future role of gold in the South African economy. This does not necessarily threaten its mining as the world's reliance on nuclear fuel increases.[9] The uranium needed for both the manufacture of nuclear weapons and fuel for nuclear power reactors is produced in abundance in South Africa as a by-product of gold mining.[10] While the output of gold decreases, the output of other mining activities increases.

* * * * *

Economists estimate that in the gold and uranium industry, a one percent increase in output will cause a 0.64 percent increase in total labor levels, a 0.43 percent increase in high skilled labor, a 0.485 percent increase in skilled labor, and a 0.67 percent increase in semi and unskilled labor. However, it is estimated that increased union power will cause the substitution of skilled, semi-skilled and unskilled employment with highly skilled employment. An increase of one percent of workers that are members of unions will cause a 0.00926 percent decline in total employment, a 0.00144 percent decline in skilled employment, a 0.00816 percent decline in semi-skilled and unskilled employment, as well as 0.0182 percent increase in highly skilled employment.[11]

The industry is however, not interested in increasing its labor turnover and, as a result, there has not been substantial recruitment of novice miners. The rationale is that the industry saw labor as a cost to control following the 1987 industrial action and the post-apartheid labor statutory regime. The mining companies were under serious cost pressures, and the cost of production in real rand terms had escalated from R40,000 per kilogram of gold to about R70, 000. Coupled with the fall in the price of gold, there was a massive profit squeeze that rendered large-scale traditional labor retention unprofitable. In the early 1990s the industry had to focus on restructuring to balance the widening gap between cost and productivity. Essentially, restructuring meant reducing production costs in order to enhance the profitability of operating shafts. This reality necessitated a shift from unskilled to skilled labor, the most compelling reason for the change in interests of capitalists.

The future of gold mining was no longer dependent on the abundance of cheap unskilled and exploitable labor, but on a free, mobile and competitive labor market. The post-apartheid economic system that emphasizes competitiveness could not coexist with an apartheid residue that rendered labor unproductive. For the South African economy in general, the restructuring was inevitable as apartheid raised the cost of production and made exports uncompetitive, partly because protection of high cost apartheid products against imports favoured production for the protected domestic market. The changing balance of costs and benefits led to a growing pressure by capitalists against aspects of apartheid and contributed to the erosion of economic and social apartheid that took place between the late 1960s and the 1980s.

To achieve this change, it was necessary to offer incentives and introduce new working and management techniques.[12] Regarding working techniques, in an agreement reached between the Chamber of Mines and the National Union of Mineworkers amidst the collapsing gold price, the two agreed that the implementation of full wage increases was made conditional on productivity agreements at mine level. Such mine level productivity agreements were struck at most mines, and include some of the following elements: additional shifts or full calendar operations; the introduction of productivity committees or monitoring forums; broad-banding and upgrading lower categories of employees; changed incentives through a bonus system, in addition to the centrally agreed salary which is linked to production targets.

On the management side, the mining houses have reduced the diversity of their investments. For instance, Billiton and Gencor divested from their paper, oil and consumer interests though an unbundling process. In addition, Anglovaal has split into three groups focusing on mining, consumer goods and engineering. In the process, the traditional mining house has been destroyed and replaced by holding companies, among them, Billiton and Anglo-American. In 1998, the Chamber of Mines also appointed its first black chief executive in more than 100 years, Mr. Mzolisi Diliza. However, his appointment does not seem to offer the NUM hope. According to one interviewee, "Diliza has done nothing to improve the working conditions of thousands of his fellow brothers—mineworkers." In the words of another interviewee from the NUM, since Diliza's appointment: "the industry has not changed its diversity or its employment regulations, it has not made any difference."[13] Conversely, the Chamber of Mines holds a different view and as one executive interviewee puts it, "he has changed the image of the industry . . . he is not a front office *Nigger*, but a fantastic individual of high integrity."[14]

In the restructuring process that ensued, most mining houses also started globalizing their operations as apartheid and the sanctions campaign prevented them from diversify their base. South African mining companies have new mining operations in Australia, Ghana, Mali, Tanzania, and others. Earlier in 1999, AngloGold purchased 50 percent of Ashanti Gold Fields' Geita mine located in the Lake Victoria Goldfields. AngloGold also has 46.2 percent of a joint venture with Perez Companc S.A. and the Santa Cruz Province on the Cerro Vanguardia gold mine located in Santa Cruz, Mexico. It solely owns and operates the Navachab gold mine located in central Namibia and also owns 67 percent of a joint venture with Golden Cycle Corporation on the Cripple Creek and Victor Gold Mines located southwest of Colorado Springs in Colorado. The group has a 70 percent interest with Meridian Jerritt Canyon Gold Mine located near the town of Elko in Nevada.

Together with the Canadian IAMGold Corporation, AngloGold has a 38 percent interests in the Sadiola Hill Gold Mine in Brazil.[15] Accordingly, these new projects combined with South African growth, were expected to have increased the gold reserve base by an additional 20 percent to reserves within South Africa by the end of 2002. Furthermore, AngloGold now operates in Colombia, Alaska, Laos, the Philippines, Mongolia, China and Russia. It is important to note, as Figure 3.4 above indicates, that the amount of reserves depends on the unit cost for producing an ounce.[16]

In addition to AngloGold, GoldFields owns gold mines in Ghana and Australia. In December 2003, GoldFields purchased 92 percent of the voting shares of Sociedad Minera La Cima owned by the Cerro Corona gold and copper project in Peru.[17] GoldFields has also entered into a strategic partnership with the Chinese company Fujian Zijin Mining Industry to explore and develop gold mines in China. Prior to this announcement, GoldFields was already part of an exploration joint venture with Sino Mining in Shandong province of China.[18]

The shareholder base has also changed with the majority of shares increasingly held by foreigners. Criticisms of the mining's globalization activities have been that it is increasingly integrating itself with international capital and not seeing itself as South African capital that has to develop the South African mining industry. Interestingly, it is also acknowledged that this does not have much to do with the GEAR document but the opening up of the economy. "GEAR as free market is not the GEAR on paper." [19] The focus is now on productivity from all inputs, capital, labor and technology.

The process of globalization has given the NUM an opportunity to demand the same working standards as those that apply in countries such as Australia, Canada and the U.S., where South African gold mining companies operate. For instance, as one NUM senior official puts it, "of fundamental importance to us has been the demand for global standards consistent with the industry's globalizing trends . . . We have been able to challenge discriminatory policies."[20] Still, other structural features of the migrant labor system remain. For instance, in an interview with the *Sunday Times*, Gwede Manthashe, President of the NUM, argued that the mining industry is not humane because it has consistently dodged the phasing out of single sex hostels[21] in which 71 percent of miners still live.[22]

The Contribution of Gold to South Africa's GDP

Over the past 120 years, the South African gold mining industry has been a vital foundation for economic growth and development of the economy. The gold mines provided a substantial proportion of government revenue and often over half of total export earnings.[23] The huge capital investments required for efficient extraction of gold made the industry a key driver of fixed capital investment. Increasing depths meant more investment and enabled the industry to increase its share of contribution to GDP.

Despite the evident decline of gold mining's importance relative to other minerals, the gold sector still contributes significantly to South Africa's GDP. In the year 2001, mining alone accounted for 41 percent (R690 billion) of the total market capitalization of the Johannesburg Securities Exchange.[24] As the figure below shows, the total mining contribution to GDP peaked in 1980 when it reached 25 percent. Of this, gold alone contributed over 17 percent to the country's GDP. This is explained by the fluctuating gold price, which reached a high of US$800 an ounce by 1978, and the threat by Malawi and Mozambique to withdraw foreign black labor, which led to a rapid rise in African wages. Since then, rising labor costs, a non-negligible amount, intensified the incentives to mechanize, which increased the demand for skilled and semi-skilled labor.

Although this was not taken seriously in the early 1980s, it was to be pursued vigorously towards the end of that decade. There has been a decline since then, and in 1991 it was estimated that mining's contribution to the country's GDP had declined significantly to 10.1 percent (1960s levels). In the same period, gold mining's share of this was 2.11 percent directly to the GDP and approximately 15 percent, if the indirect multiplier effects associated with the industry's influence on the economy are included. According to the Chamber of Mines, these multiplier effects include amongst others:

- *Backward linkages*—arising from the purchase of goods and services by the mining industry, which stimulate industrial production and the provision of services;
- *Forward linkages*—from the use of mineral products in other domestic industries, such as energy production (about 30 percent of South Africa's liquid fuels and 90 percent of electricity are produced from coal), steel production, jewellery fabrication and production of refined and branded good delivery gold;
- *Social multipliers*—the result from the role of mining in the development of human resources and infrastructure, such as schools, colleges, clinics, roads and housing.

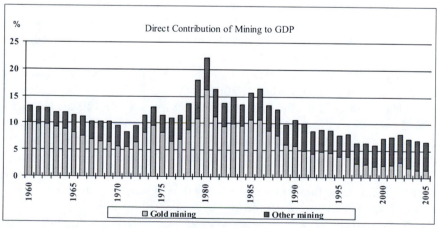

Figure 3.2. Direct Contribution of Mining to GDP

Source: Chamber of Mines' Economics Division

However, the following year, in 1992, the figure declined to 9.6 percent, and by 1993, it stood at 8.7 percent.

According to the Chamber of Mines, for the first time since 1999 the direct contribution of mining to South Africa's GDP had increased from 6.1 percent to 6.5 percent in the year 2000. The decrease in gold production led to a decline of -2.6 percent in the economic growth rate of the gold sector. In addition, the mining industry—driven by increased sales value of platinum group metals, coal and iron ore—resulted in a 15.8 percent increase in the economic growth rate of the sector. Observable from the figure is that "other mining's" contribution to the country's GDP has remained fairly constant throughout, while gold mining's contribution fluctuated between 1960 and 1980 and began a downward trend, which was at its lowest point in 1999 and stabilized in 2000–2001. The high contribution rate for 1980 can be attributed to the abandonment of fixed gold price in 1972, after which the price rose from US$36 an ounce to reach well over US$800 by 1980.[25]

In 2002, the mining industry paid about R16.1 billion in taxes to the state.[26] From 1996 onwards, the contribution of "other mining" overtook that of gold. In 2001, "other mining" contributed 5.28 percent to the country's GDP while the equivalent for gold was 2.26 percent. This is explained by platinum's increased exports as compared to gold. The downside of it all is that the platinum industry employs far fewer workers, when compared with the gold industry, which is responsible for 56 percent of South Africa's overall mine labor force. While the figure indicates that gold still contribute substantially to the economy, this appears deceptive as much of the profits can be attributed to the value of gold output in relation to the value of the rand, which depreciated significantly in the period 1996–2001.[27] For instance, during the latter half of 2001, the decline in the rand exchange rate resulted in the rand gold price escalating to R3,210 an ounce in December whereas it had been roughly R 2,338 an ounce in the period prior to September 11, 2001.[28]

The main gold producing area in the Witwatersrand Basin has been mined for more than 100 years, yet it still remains the greatest unmined source of gold in the world.[29] Even with such wealth in gold reserve, the number of new mines in South Africa has decreased, thus raising fears about the long-term future of the industry. The point worth repeating is that, in making these projections, what is often forgotten is that the South African gold mining industry has successfully launched itself into the global market by buying new mines and exploration rights outside of South Africa. The figure below shows South Africa's share of new mine supply in tones of gold as contrasted with other major gold producers.

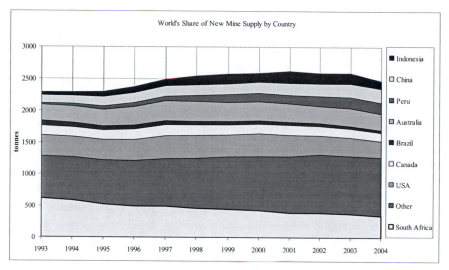

Figure 3.3. World's Share of New Mine Supply, 1993–2004.

Source: Unpublished Data: Chamber of Mines' Economics Division

According to the above figure, South Africa's share of new mine supply has been on a steady decline between 1993 and 2004. A comparative trend with other major gold producers, namely Australia, Brazil, Canada and U.S., does not look encouraging. While these countries' share of new mine supply has remained fairly constant throughout the period, it is only South Africa's that has been declining, and the trend continues. Ultimately, what can be deduced from this comparison is that South Africa will soon be overtaken as a major gold producer. Although the figure indicates the share of new mine supply, it does not indicate the ownership or parent companies of those mines—many of which, in Canada, the U.S. and Australia, are increasingly owned by South African mining companies.

Of interest is that the category of "other" countries in the above figure is also characterized by the investments of major South African gold mining corporations as they move out of the country to areas where gold exploration is comparatively cheap, and labor costs are lower. These include countries that are not directly mentioned in the above figure in which South African mining companies operate, such as Peru, Namibia, Mali, Argentina, Ghana, Tanzania and Mongolia. For instance, in August 2003, Ghana's Ashanti Goldfields was at the center of US$1.8 billion bidding by two major South African companies, AngloGold and Randgold Resources.[30] Eventually, what appears certain is that, while South Africa's gold production may decrease in the long term—that may not necessarily mean that

South African companies would be producing less, as they own a fair share of new mine supply abroad.

FROM VOLUME TO VALUE: LABOR IN THE CHAMBER GOLD MINES

While it is true that there have been significant job losses in the economy throughout the last decade, the assumption has often been made, albeit erroneously, that these job losses were solely as a result of GEAR. There is, however, an indirect impact of GEAR on job losses since 1996. Explanations for the claim that job losses are as a result of GEAR vary, and they all depend on a variety of factors including, amongst others, each analyst's own idiosyncratic and ideological commitments. For instance, when asked about the fundamental weaknesses of GEAR in relation to labor specifically in the gold mining industry, one interviewee aptly put it, "I have a passionate hatred of GEAR,—a neo-liberal economic policy, and a self-imposed structural adjustment programme."[31]

Despite the fact that South Africa's organized labor has been agitating against job losses, even going on strikes that further strained its alliance with the ANC government, there has not been comprehensive research from the union movement that assesses the impact of GEAR on labor in a specific industry. Notwithstanding this overt lack of empirical evidence, the rhetoric on the correlation between GEAR and job losses has intensified in the media, political circles, and in the public domain. The economy had to be restructured by the political process or the free market logic would take matters to itself, restructure the economy and set the conditions on which it would be run.[32]

Although the National Union of Mineworkers is adamant that GEAR is responsible for job losses in the gold mining industry, a meticulous dissection reveals minimal correlation between the two. Substantive argument for this assertion is premised on the observation that there appeared to be two kinds of GEAR. The first is a macroeconomic stabilization policy the ANC government introduced in mid-1996 in the form of a document entitled, *Growth, Employment and Redistribution: A Macroeconomic Strategy.* The second is one that has spontaneously developed in people's psyche, as the rhetoric on the former came to dominate the media and public discussions. This does not have much to do with the technical macroeconomic stabilization policy, its substance and rationale, but more to do with the ideological package that encapsulates it: the neo-liberal agenda. In an era where protests against globalization and the overwhelming influence of International Financial Institutions have become common, a policy that is modeled on the prerequisites of these institutions is bound to attract ferocious attacks and criticisms.

Thus, in seeking to advance any particular position on GEAR, either as a macroeconomic stabilization policy or as neo-liberal economic orthodoxy, there is a need for a better understanding of the logic behind what it sought to achieve and the degree to which its targets, goals and objectives have been achieved. This is important to demystify and debunk some of the myths that have cloaked GEAR and its relationship to job losses. Although there have been undesirable job losses in the South African economy, it would be an arduous task to prove that they were solely caused by GEAR, as it is understood as macroeconomic policy. This research has not established any direct correlation between GEAR and the trend of job losses in the gold mining industry. However, the accompanying neo-liberal ideology may have had unintended consequences for labor in other industries. Neo-liberal policies are good for business, but bad for labor as they seek to maximize profit with little or no regard for the improvement of working conditions.

For an industry whose profits have largely been determined by gold prices fixed in foreign currencies in the London Stock Exchange and not in the Johannesburg Securities Exchange, it is hard to prove that the job losses that have taken place were as a result of domestic policy in the form of the GEAR macroeconomic policy. For, in the gold mining industry, the job losses have been a predominant phenomenon for at least a decade prior to GEAR's implementation. The shift from a cheap to a more expensive, but more skilled and reliable, labor force can largely be attributed to the fluctuating gold price. In simple terms, reductions in the labor force had very little to do with GEAR, but with the structural realities of capitalist restructuring in response to the challenges that characterized the South African gold mining industry in the face of competition at global level. Apart from this, the following factors need to be taken into account: first, there was a decline in the grade of gold per ton of ore milled; second there has been an unstable price of gold; third the era of fluctuating exchange rate; and fourth the introduction of the new labor statutory regime. All these combined, together with the restructuring inevitabilities brought by the changing political landscape and the new exploration avenues at the global level, presented the mining industry with unique constraints and opportunities.

In the logic of this analysis, the industry therefore had to restructure itself to deal with the constraints that hindered full maximization of opportunities. The rationale behind the mining industry's restructuring of the last decade and the job losses that took place should be understood in that context. For instance, as far as gold production is concerned, it peaked in the 1970s, and since then the amount of gold produced has been on a continuous

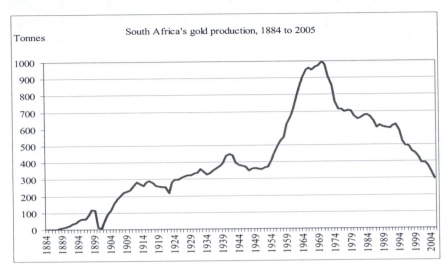

Figure 3.4. South Africa's Gold Production, 1884–2005.

Source: Chamber of Mines Economic Division.

decline. This is largely attributed to the end of gold as a reserve in backing international currencies and with it, the international demand for gold. This decline in the demand for gold internationally reduced the production of gold. The figure above shows the trend:

At the peak of its production, the South African gold mining industry produced a thousand tons of gold in 1971–2. Since then, however, production has been falling to the year 2005 level of about 300 tons. Thus, by the year 2005, South Africa produced 296 343 kilograms of gold, which is roughly equivalent to the amount of gold it last produced in 1924 (297 817 kilograms). The rate of production decline is alarming. Essentially, in 2005, South Africa's gold mining industry produced half the amount of gold it produced in 1994. If production decline continues at this pace South Africa will soon be producing less than 200 000 kilograms of gold in the next few years. Overall, the decline since 1974 had something to do with America's economic advantages over the rest of the world, which were rapidly dissipating, while other countries were catching up economically—Japan and Germany in particular.

With recovery from the devastation of the Second World War, Western European economies (America's allies—especially France and Germany), became very concerned about the impact of the erosion in the dollar's value as the world's reserve currency. Ultimately, these problems led to the U.S. abandonment of the Bretton Woods fixed exchange rate system and to the emergence of a more volatile era of floating exchange rates. The question of how much gold and foreign exchange the U.S. government held compared to Germany or Japan was beside the point, when the U.S. was the only government capable of creating dollar assets that are accepted and saleable worldwide. In some sense, a financial system largely operating in dollars did not need gold reserves.[33]

The business rationale in any industry dictates that labor costs should be covered by the amount of profits made. From this rationale, the South African gold mining industry required new approaches to the organization of work, and some innovations if the industry were to remain commercially viable. Inevitably, the profound changes that the gold mining industry has experienced have been caused by both local and international conditions. Cost increases in the gold mining industry have been significant, while both the tonnage and the grade of the ore have declined. The trend that is clearly visible is that less and less gold has been produced since the early 1970s up to the current period, although the decline seems to be proceeding more slowly than the rise of production between 1954 and 1971.

To remain in business, it was therefore essential that the industry radically restructure itself to maximize profits in the face of declining ore grade and deep level mining. According to the Chamber of Mines, the restructuring preceded the political transition, as the industry was not making significant increases in profits. From 1987 onwards—for at least five years to 1992—profits in the gold mining industry stagnated (see shaded blocks in the table below). Even gold's contribution to GDP during this period shows a significant decline (see figure 3.2 above). However, all these were to change as gold profits rose from R17 billion as a result of the 1987 strike to R41 billion in 2002. By 2004, profits declined to R29 billion, the value equivalent to 2001 level.

As the table shows, for six years, 1987–1992, profitability of the gold mining industry stagnated and only started to recover by 1993. Furthermore, the average grade was also fluctuating in addition to the declining percentage of South Africa's share of total world gold output from the peak of 79 percent in 1970 to 43 percent in 1987 and, as low as 14 percent in 2004, which is three times lower than the 1987 average. These realities have convinced mining executives that their industry restructuring must intensify.

Even though the profits fluctuated, they stabilized between 1997 and 1999. Since then, there has generally been an increase, largely due to the fall of the rand against the U.S. dollar in 2001–2002. To make the industry profitable, a vigorous comprehensive restructuring process had

Table 3.2. South Africa's Gold Output and Sales, 1987–2004[34]

	SA Gold Production (tons)	Average Grade	Realized Value R billion	World Gold Production In tons	SA as a % of Total World
1987	568.7	5.28	17,500.1	1,383.4	43.82
1988	581.6	5.13	19,675.5	1,550.8	40.03
1989	569.8	4.99	19,387.8	1,682.0	36.12
1990	565.6	5.05	19,239.3	1,757.1	34.42
1991	562.0	5.20	19,224.4	1,788.7	33.63
1992	574.3	5.37	19,468.3	1,871.8	32.81
1993	619.5	5.56	23,239.3	2,290.9	27.04
1994	583.9	5.40	24,953.1	2,284.9	25.55
1995	522.4	4.87	23,465.2	2,291.3	22.80
1996	494.6	4.91	26,467.5	2,375.3	20.82
1997	492.5	4.95	24,904.7	2,492.6	19.76
1998	464.4	5.09	24,294.6	2,542.0	18.27
1999	449.5	4.62	24,990.4	2,573.8	17.46
2000	428.0	4.50	25,272.1	2,591.1	16.52
2001	393.5	4.13	29,011.6	2,620.8	15.00
2002	395.2	4.27	41,386.1	2,589.9	15.28
2003	375.8	4.56	32,908.8	2 592.6	14.50
2004	342.7	4.72	28,937.7	2 464.4	13.91

to be undertaken to extricate the industry from its profit crisis. Unfortunately, the casualties of the process have been labor. The crisis itself has been a result of apartheid policies that benefited the industry through access to a cheap, but largely low productivity, labor force. Inadvertently, the gold mining industry is being haunted by the incarnation of century-old spectres of those it exploited and dehumanized through inhuman labor practices that benefited it handsomely.

Labor and Productivity in the Chamber Gold Mines

The productivity hypothesis argues that the size-wage effect reflects an underlying size-productivity relationship.[35] Large companies usually invest in physical capital, which results in higher levels of complementary investment in skilled labor. As a result of increasing costs, a decline in tonnage and the grade of the ore mined, and a drop in the gold price, employment levels in the gold mining industry have decreased significantly over the past ten years. Seidman's (1995) analysis also attributed the fall in employment levels to the same explanation. As she puts it, "this has entailed a shift away from the large, relatively unskilled African work-forces that have been an historical feature of the industry to smaller more stable work-forces whose higher wages would be offset by higher productivity."[36] Certainly, productivity could not be postulated with the rate of profit sufficient to undertake production. As such large supplies of largely unskilled labor could not be sustained.

This remains true today, as the few miners that have remained have greater long-term opportunities for career growth. Moreover, forced to restructure and modernize to maintain profitability, some mines also reached the end of their working lives. From a total of approximately 530,000 miners employed in the gold mining sector in 1987,[37] there has been a decline to a 2004 employment level of around 148,712—a decline by over 70 percent in 18 years.[38]

For the first time in the history of the Chamber, there was excess labor, and the well-oiled labor recruitment machinery that once sourced labor as far as China, had to be retired. Certainly, this change in labor demand and supply has alienated labor sources with geographic prox-imity to the industry; a relic of apartheid intended to service the labor demand.[39] The abolition of Pass Laws in 1985 also meant that many people could move to the cities with neither restrictions nor proper regu-lation for urban migration, inevitably exacerbating informal settlements in urban areas. At one point, it was a crime to be black, unemployed and in the urban areas. It was the lifting of the Pass Laws, which made the 1987 NUM industrial action more decisive, as the state could not, as in the past, arrest thousands of miners for trespassing. Indeed, this reality has led to remarkable black urbanization, which is now exacerbated by the inability to find a job.[40]

The Chamber of Mines has attributed labor decline to natural attri-tion, as the gold industry moved from a mass employer of limited, contract, unskilled labor, to an employer of more permanent, mostly semi-skilled or skilled labor. Thus, the crisis of gold meant that the job bar (which restricted black miners from doing "skilled work"), which for over a cen-tury, maimed and killed thousands of blacks at the rock face, had to be raised to expand the base of skilled labor. An additional element was, of cause, the lifting of sanctions and the subsequent opening up of the econ-omy, all of which took place before GEAR was introduced. For instance, in

1994, the RDP acknowledged the increasing trend of retrenchment in the gold mining industry in particular:

> Up to now, the heaviest burdens associated with downscaling have been borne by miners, one third of whom have been retrenched. The RDP must put into place mechanisms to ensure orderly downscaling of our mines so as to minimize the suffering of workers and their families. Measures should include the re-skilling and training of workers for other forms of employment.[41]

According to the Chamber, the move from being a mass employer of unskilled labor force to semi-skilled and skilled labor reflects the industry's commitment to the development of human capital and the provision of career paths with adequate training.[42] In essence, the move was intended to maximize output with less labor through an increase in labor productivity. To a large extent, there have been remarkable successes in these initiatives. While this is true, the NUM argues that, "the mining industry sabotaged the government policy of job creation."[43]

All the above factors combined explain why the gold mining industry, despite playing such a prominent role in South Africa's economy, is presently experiencing significant new challenges to its economic survival.[44] Issues of productivity and profitability are central to the industry's future. However, with declining grades, increased depths and a slide in the gold price, costs have begun to rise and production has been steadily falling. In the face of new challenges, mines have undergone major business re-structuring and have reduced costs significantly.

*   *   *   *   *

In the last decade, there has been rapid intensification in technology with concomitant increases in the demand for skilled labor. Mechanization was accelerated in tandem with new labor recruitment techniques. Often when the rand rallies against the dollar and the gold price weakens, making underground mining unprofitable, the industry reverts to reprocessing old mine dumps or tailings (processed material), which is comparatively more cost effective than underground mining. These mining dumps cover approximately 40,000 hectares in the Witwatersrand basin alone.[45] Most of them were processed with the use of Nobel's blasting galantine invented in 1874, followed by the MacArthur-Forrest cyanide process, patented in 1878.[46] Advances in Biotechnology and chemical engineering have cumulatively made reduction plants, where the mineral is extracted from the mineral-bearing rock more efficient. Furthermore, Segal and Mal-herbe points out that:

> New technologies such as satellite imaging and information technology
> have revolutionised exploration. Electromagnetic spectrum analysis
> of the target landmass gathered from satellite is now the first stage of
> many exploration efforts, enabling geologists to home in on promising
> areas, which are then supplemented by geomagnetic information gath-
> ered from aircraft and, ultimately, exploration drilling. Satellites now
> fully update spectral data every 16 days for the entire portion of the
> globe between the latitudes of 81 degrees north and 81 degrees south.
> Satellite sensors acquire spectral data on seven bands, two of which
> have direct application to mining.[47]

At the Rand Refinery, improved computerised Electrolytic Refin-ing method now refines gold to 99.99 percent fineness. In addition, even bacteria has become useful in the extraction of gold from certain types of gold bearing rock through a process known as bioleaching, which was pioneered by Gencor's BOIX process in South Africa (South African firms, Mintek and Bateman are leading consultants in this field). Biole-aching is now used at mines around the world to raise fold yields and to increase project feasibility. The process can profitably recover gold with a grade as low as 0.7 grams per ton, meaning that the current four grams per ton extraction does not threaten profits. Advances like these increase supply.

The new "microwave technology makes commercially viable those mineral resources which have previously been rejected as uneconomic because of the difficulties of extraction."[48] Furthermore, the state-spon-sored Mintek's Floatstar flotation system, which has been installed in plati-num, gold and base metals operations, is said to improve recoveries by 0.5 percent to 1.3 percent. With new technological innovations, reprocessing the tailings does yield results, as most of them were processed using primi-tive technology by today's standards. According to the Chamber of Mines, by reprocessing the tailings in Johannesburg the industry is able to extract one gram of gold per ton cheaper than the four grams per ton of ore from the ground, which is not always worth lifting up from four kilometres below the surface.

These mining residues, which characterize the Johannesburg land-scape, have impacted negatively on the social and economic development of the area.[49] In the early days of gold mining, economic rather than environmental factors dictated the sites of mine waste disposal. It was not conceivable that Johannesburg would grow to the size it is today. Furthermore, apart from their economic value, the dumps were erected with no environmental concern. As one interviewee aptly puts it, " . . . the idea is really to relocate them to suitable areas."[50] The Chamber of Mines' *Mining News* announced that the Chamber had begun a R6 million clean up of over 38 sites where mines have dumped radioactive material. The gold mines had come to accept that they were collectively one of the major sources of the radioactive material that contaminated the sites in Gauteng and the Free State areas.[51] New gold mining technology seems to be paying off. [52] As one Chamber of Mines interviewee puts it, "we have changed technology. Most of our mining technology was developed in the 1950s, but in the last five years (1998–2002) we have developed new techniques. Whereas the old drill and blast method would have required 6,000 miners, now the new techniques only need at least 600."[53]

In the gold mines today, it is machines that do most of the drilling, just as it is in tunnel constructions, not humans as it used to be in the past. South African company, Boart Longyear, is the largest supplier of pneumatic drills in the world. The company provides services in the form of contract drilling or exploration drilling to the South African gold mining industry. Extracting gold at four kilometres below the earth's surface is certainly different from an opencast gold mine and can only be undertaken successfully by applying modern technology. In this regard, South Africa's gold mining industry is amongst the world leaders in mining explosives, drilling equipment, abrasives and metallurgical processes. Mining technology is also one of the few fast-moving technology spheres where a significant number of South African companies are at the frontier of innovation.[54] For instance, AECI[55], and SASOL[56] are leading suppliers of mining explosives, Boart International is a world leader in abrasives and two South African firms KR and Bateman are among the most important mining consultancies in the world. Other South African firms like LTA and Cementation Mining play a major role in specialist contract mining.

In addition, this modern technology includes new refrigeration system for cooling down the shaft and the mining floor. At four kilometres down the surface, it is roughly 60 degrees Celsius. However, the new cooling system reduces that by half to at least 30 degree's Celsius. The application of this technology means that some of the shafts that may be roughly three kilometres deep that were closed because of the heat can be re-opened. Other unproductive or marginal shafts are sold to consortiums of Black

Economic Empowerment as smaller companies can operate them better. In the process, new technology is enabling the gold mining industry to expedite Black Economic Empowerment at less cost since some of the unproductive shafts and mines are easily becoming available, thus meeting the empowerment target cheaply. The target is to have 40 percent of the shares in the Johannesburg Stock Exchange (JSE) owned by black business. Because of improved technology, there are new gold projects in South Africa. As Segal and Malherbe points out:

> The most important new gold project in South Africa is South Deep, a joint venture of Western Areas and Canada's Placer Dome, and involving investment exceeding R3 billion and fill production of 700,000 ounces per year. Avgold's Target Mine near Bothaville is another important development. By using new technology, Target Mine will be able to mine below 2,200 meters at a cash cost well below US$200 an ounce. AngloGold are currently involved in exploration of the Western Ultra Deeps Level Property (WUDLS), which is the down-dip extension to the Western Deep Levels, Elandsrand and Deelkraal mining leases.[57]

As the figure below indicates, the application of new technology saved the gold mining industry:

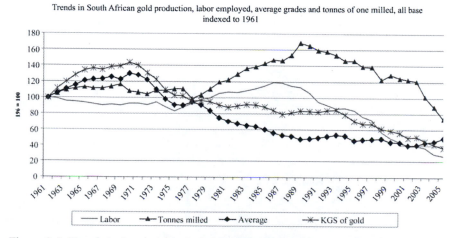

Figure 3.5. Trends in South Africa's Gold Mining Industry Base Indexed to 1961.
Source: Unpublished Date: Chamber of Mines' Economics Division

According to the indexes, the declining ore grade necessitated an increase in the amount of ore milled to produce an ounce of gold. Thus, from 1989, while the amount of ore milled has been declining incrementally, it has however remained profitable as the cost was reduced by shedding labor. As indicated below, labor accounted for 56 percent of total cash operating costs for gold mines in 2004. By 2002, for instance, the industry needed half the amount of labor to produce gold output equivalent to its level in the 1980s. Measuring productivity requires interpreting the invisible figures behind the trends. For instance, in 1970 when the average grade of gold per ton of ore milled was at its highest (13.51), 982,019 kilograms of gold were produced from 726,960,000 tons of ore milled with a labor force of 416,846. In contrast, by the year 2001 (31 years later) the average grade of gold had declined to 4.13 gram per ton of ore milled but the amount of gold produced was 342,551, from 829,620 000 tons of ore milled, roughly half of what was produced in 1970, but this time with a labor force of only 159,803. By 2005, the labor trend went below all other trends, a reflection of the degree to which labor has borne the brunt of industry's restructuring. Overall, all trends have been declining continuously since the late 1980s. The consequence of the low grade but massive quantity of gold ore could only pay off if other costs are continually kept low.

The massive reduction in labor was balanced by increasing the amount of ore milled, and this offset enabled the gold mining industry to

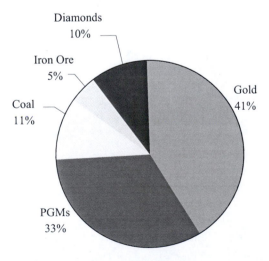

Figure 3.6. Employment in SA Mines by Commodity, 2004.

compensate for the decline in the average grade and earn reasonable profits. In the process—for the first time since 1978—the gold mining industry was able to produce more gold with less labor, despite the fall in grade. Evident in figure 3.5 is that by 1987, the mining industry had a huge labor force that was largely unproductive and after restructuring, the industry made less labor more productive that is, "producing more with less,"[58] (see also figure 3.1 above). Whereas gold accounted for 51 percent of total mine employment by 2001, by July 2004, the figure had declined to 41 percent. Comparably, while PGMs accounted for 14 percent of total mine employment in 2001, by July 2004, its share of total mine employment increased to 33 percent, an increase by more than 100 percent.

On the basis of this analysis, it is hard to accuse GEAR as solely responsible for job losses in the gold mining industry. By the time GEAR was implemented, as indicated in the figure, the gold mining industry had already shed more than half of the labor force it had in 1987. If anything, the industry has overwhelmingly achieved the productivity rate that GEAR sought to encourage in the South African work place. A comparison with the manufacturing industry reveals the same pattern: an increase in productivity and value with less labor input. According to South Africa's *Year Book 2003/2004*, in 2003, manufacturing grew by 5.4 percent which was the fastest growth since 1995. In terms of manufacturing output, the sector is expected to be 40 percent bigger in 2007 than it was in 1995. The table below reflects comparative figures with mining and other sectors:

Manufacturing has replaced commodities as the centerpiece of the South African economy, far exceeding mining in importance. This can be attributed to the declining gold production, and with it, a decline in its contribution to the country's GDP, from 16.3 in 1980 to less than two percent by 2004. As the table above shows, mining stagnated in the fourth quarter of 2003, although its output subsequently increased in the first quarter of 2004 to three percent. This can be attributed to the high gold price. For instance, gold price rose from US$392 per fine ounce in the fourth quarter of 2003 to US$409 per fine ounce in the first quarter of 2004. It is important also to acknowledge that the category of mining includes other minerals besides gold.

In the manufacturing industry, there has been a boom. A prime example of this is the automotive industry, which, since 1996, has taken off to remarkable heights, growing tenfold by 2002, in real terms of vehicles and components. According to the Bureau for Economic Research of the University of Stellenbosch, at the end of August 2002, annual growth in manufacturing exports was 8.7 percent.[60] Investment in the automotive industry grew by 6.3 percent and is expected to continue to grow around six percent

Table 3.3. Contributions to Real Gross Domestic Product, 2002–2004[59]

Percentage change at seasonally adjusted rates

Quarter	2002					2003					2004				
	1st	2nd	3rd	4th	Year	1st	2nd	3rd	4th	Year	1st	2nd	3rd	4th	Year
Primary Sectors	7	7.5	5.5	3	3	-2.5	-6.5	-6.5	-4	-1	3	5	9.5	0.5	3.5
Agriculture	13.5	14	9.5	5.5	6.5	-5.5	-19.5	-22	-9.5	-6	2.5	7.5	11.5	4	1
Mining	2	3	2.5	1.5	.5	.5	5	6	0	2.5	3.5	3.5	9	-1	4
Secondary sector	4.5	8.5	6	1.5	4.5	-3	-3	-.5	-1.5	0	3	5	6.5	3	3
Manufacturing	5	10	7.5	0	5.5	-4.5	-4.5	-1.5	-3.5	-1	2.5	5.5	6.5	2.5	2.5
Tertiary Sectors	3	3.5	3	3	3.5	3	3	3	3	3	3.5	3.5	5	5	4
Non-Agricultural	3.5	5	4	2.5	3.5	1	1.5	2	1.5	2	3.5	4	5.4	4	4
Total	4	5	5	2.5	3.5	1	.5	1	1.5	2	3	4	5.4	4	3.5

a year from 2003 to 2006. The growth in manufacturing can be attributed to the export oriented products that have to compete with other, equally, if not better producers. These two industries, mining and manufacturing, remain the major contributors of South Africa's exports. According to the South African Reserve Bank, (see table above) the real value added by the manufacturing sector increased in the first quarter of 2004 after having declined significantly for four successive quarters. The resurgence in real manufacturing output was evident in the increased production volumes of several sub-sectors.[61]

The legitimate question to ask is whether this is because of GEAR or not. This research leads one to conclude that it has more to do with the commercial imperatives of competitiveness. However, GEAR as both policy and ideology helped accelerate the restructuring process. The point worth noting about the RDP is that while it is not possible to judge the success of what was not implemented, it is also difficult to assess the successes or failures of what was done. It is not clear how the RDP would have reversed the negative growth trajectory that characterized the economy. Although it was a development strategy, the RDP could not be implemented on an economy in a regression trajectory. The remarkable economic growth that has occurred has enabled the South African economy to create jobs, although far less than the desirable levels.

In his study on labor demand in post-apartheid South Africa, Haroon Bhorat found that on the contrary, between 1995 and 1999 970,000 jobs were created across all sectors of the economy.[62] Drawing from results of Census 2001, in the same period, 1995–2002, the economy lost more than one million jobs.[63] It is only in the post 2000 period that the economic picture emerges that shows that GEAR may not necessarily be a completely bad policy after all. On the contrary, its performance is overshadowed by discontent over its ideological commitment. With the poor, even negative, growth rates that characterized the stagnant economy of the early 1990s, the economy would have shed jobs and the absence of any meaningful economic growth would have made the situation far worse than it was by 2004–2005. Despite this achievement, organized labor remains adamant in its rejection of GEAR, what then is the basis for that rejection?

NUM AND SUB-CONTRACTING: A REARGUARD STRUGGLE?

The NUM, which remains the country's biggest single labor union, has been hit hard by job losses of the past decade particularly in the gold mining industry. Whereas the Union had over 300,000 affiliates in the gold mining industry alone prior to its 1987 industrial action, the number decreased equally with the pace of retrenchments. The changing nature of the mining industry in relation to its hiring practices does not leave much optimism for increased union power in the long term. While new miners are employed, it is the platinum group of metals that is increasing labor turnover. For instance, in 1997, the platinum sector employed 90,876 workers. Since then, at least 36,800 jobs have been created and platinum mining was estimated to provide about 127,672 jobs at the end of 2003.[64]

After the end of the wage negotiations between NUM and the Chamber in August 2003, a miner was earning about R2,200 per month. The union managed to secure a 10 percent wage increase. This was a short-term achievement whose long-term consequences threaten the viability of gold mining itself, as labor still accounted for 58.3 percent of total operating costs by 2004.

In the usual wage jiggle, the more the NUM push for better working conditions, the more determined capital becomes in weakening its power with retrenchments. This could not have come at a worse time than in early October 2003, roughly a month after the successful negotiations. The rand strengthened to less than seven to the U.S. dollar. With this development, the mining industry warned that it might lay off as many as 70,000 mineworkers and halt up to R100 billion worth of capital investments. At last,

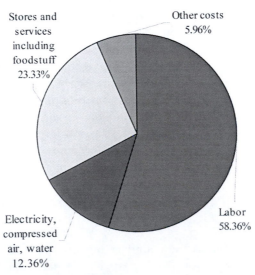

Figure 3.7. Cross-Sectional View of Total Cash Operating Costs for Gold Mines, 2004

the labor haemorrhaging attracted the attention of the government. President Mbeki wrote in the ANC online publication, *ANC Today*:

> We had hoped that, at least, the corporate citizens, who are proposing or acting to bring despair to thousands of our working people and their families through retrenchments, allegedly because of the strength of the rand, would have had the decency to discuss this serious matter with our government before they made their announcements.[65]

While at the same time the gold price strengthened, the mining industry appeared to be attempting to reverse the 10 percent wage increase. Apart from wage increases, administrative costs of running the mining industry have increased by 30 percent on average since 1987. These have been pushed higher by an eight percent increase in electricity costs and a 53 percent rise in general tariffs charged by *Spoornet*, government owned railway company.[66]

In 2004, electricity and water combined constituted 12 percent of total cash operating costs for gold mines. The figure above indicates the breakdown in percentages.[67] The percentages for "other" and "other stores" include repairs and maintenance. As indicated in the figure, the reasons for massive layoffs become clear. Water costs are kept low because the deep level gold mining re-treats its water for cooling and dust allaying purposes. The mining industry is the major source of raw materials needed for electricity, coal and uranium. Ninety-two percent of South Africa's electricity is produced from coal of which South Africa is also the world's seventh largest exporter. In 2001, 218,682,050 tons were produced, 70 percent of which was exported to the European Union. During the sanctions campaign, the oil embargo proved costly and South Africa's chemical giant SASOL successfully extracted oil from coal. South Africa has two nuclear power reactors of 1,840 MW and is constructing a fail-safe and highly efficient nuclear technology in the form of a pebble bed modular reactor (PBMR) in an attempt to beef-up its electrical power generating capacity.

As most areas of the country average more than 2,500 hours of sunshine per year, annual photovoltaic (PV) panel assembly capacity totals four Mega Watts, and the number of companies manufacturing solar water-heaters is increasing. The point of all this is that electricity prices may remain low for some time, especially as government tries to use cheap electricity costs to attract foreign investors. Furthermore, because electricity is an instrument of policy in terms of government's housing-electrification campaign, it can be deduced that it will not be privatised for some time to come.

In the midst of all this, capital remains viable by compensating for the labor losses through strengthening its use of sub-contracted labor; that is, casual or outsourced labor, which has improved gold mining industry output with remarkable success. For instance, Target Mine in the northern Free State produces about 350,000 ounces of gold per year, yet it employs only 500 workers plus 1,000 contract employees. In comparison, a conventional South African gold mine of its capacity normally employs up to 2,500 miners.[68] In the early days of the gold mining industry, before the mines could put their labor recruitment machinery in place, independent contractors supplied labor at a specific rate. The point raised in Chapter Two that is worth re-emphasizing is that the problem with the arrangement was that contractors negotiated better deals for Africans who were also able to choose the mines they preferred. Obviously, this created problems for *undesirable* mines with bad safety records. To overcome this hurdle, it was necessary for the Chamber to crack the unyielding monopoly private contractors exercised over the supply of labor. By 1920, the Chamber of Mines had largely succeeded in displacing independent contractors. However, specialized tasks such as shaft sinking, cementation and certain types of development remained largely in the hands of contractors.[69]

Why rehearse the old story? While the industry fought vigorously to put independent contractors out of business in the early days of mining, in the face of post-apartheid restructuring, challenges of competitiveness and an unbiased labor market which demands standard conditions of employment, the industry has demonstrated its preference for sub-contractors. It is an alternative to hiring novices as it enables the gold mining industry to continue its quest for "cheap labor" by "other" means. Internationally, sub-contractors' short terms of engagement facilitate the drive to maximize profits. More importantly, sub-contracted miners are largely not affiliated to the NUM (which means that the mining industry can easily negotiate favourable conditions of employment including wages), which sees the mining industry's facilitation of the formation of makeshift contractors as a deliberate attempt to avert regulations stipulated under Labor Relations Act of 1997, and the Basic Conditions of Employment Act of 1998.[70]

*   *   *   *   *

For the mining industry in general, sub-contractors made up three percent of workers in South African gold mines in 1987. By 1998 the figure had risen to 16 percent. Capital cites the drive for higher productivity, labor flexibility and cost cutting to explain their preference for sub-contracted labor. The trend depicts a deliberate attempt by mining companies to circumvent years of bargaining and hard-won benefits of unionized labor force largely affiliated to the NUM. It would be interesting to know what the impact of capital's assault on labor has been on the economies of the sub-region, especially in the case of Lesotho, Mozambique and Swaziland, which have traditionally relied heavily on remittances of their mine workers in South Africa to supplement their economies. Earlier, when the industry was starting with retrenchments (see figure 3.8 below), Laubschane and Muller warned that:

> A complicating factor in the problem of labor migration is that many of South Africa's neighbouring countries rely on income earned from the export of labor to keep their economies going. Any significant reduction in migration of this kind could be seriously to the disadvantage of the rest of the region.[71]

While there are positive commercial attractions to sub-contracting, there is an adverse side of it, which is often concealed by increases in output and profits. Thus, while business makes profit, it is often at the expense of workers. Amongst others, these disadvantages are:

- Through sub-contracting, enterprises reduce costs by paying non-continuous workers only when they are on the job;
- The instability and insecurity of their employment means that sub-contract workers tend to have fewer employment benefits, worse working conditions and lower wages than normal workers;
- Sub-contracting can be a way for firms to deny workers the high wages and better working conditions won by unions. Workers employed by contractors are notoriously difficult to organize. This may be the result of insecurity and instability, but many employers actively discourage union membership;
- Employers may increase their use of sub-contracting to weaken union strength and numbers.[72]

The NUM has argued that sub-contracting divides workers into permanent workers—who are unionized—and casual workers—who are not unionized. The labor movement in general recognizes that outsourcing may be profitable for firms, but argues that it is socially suboptimal because it results in a decrease in employment and wages, reductions in conditions of employment and the erosion of union power.[73] It also undermines previous agreements struck between the union and industry. A senior NUM official insisted that a sub-contractor should have basic coverage, amongst others, for health and pensions as it applies in the formal labor force. As he puts it, "it is not safe . . . they cut corners and invest in least resources."[74] As another NUM interviewee puts it:

> The problem is that the Labor Relations Act's definition of employee does not cover sub-contracts . . . In fact, no legislation compels sub-contractors to register and this makes it difficult to deal with them as they simply change their company's name.[75]

In the gold sector a considerable number of the more than 50,000 workers retrenched in 1996 and in the last half of 1997, were sub-contracted. As miners told me, "this is mining gold cheap . . . Mine companies exploit our people and faction fights are already taking place."[76] In our discussions, miners did not mention any relationship between job losses in the gold mines and GEAR. Instead, they attributed severe job losses to new exploration opportunities for South African mining industries outside South Africa. As they put it, "the whole mining industry is affected by globalization, there are no new projects and no new shafts sunk. Instead, they are opting for open cast mining in other African countries which are cheaper than South Africa."[77] As in other industries such as manufacturing, the consequence of sub-contracting has been a reduction in permanent formal employment.[78] Destructive as it may seem, in the gold mining industry sub-contracting has enabled the industry to survive plunging gold prices of the late 1990s.[79] Sub-contracted miners have been employed as follows:

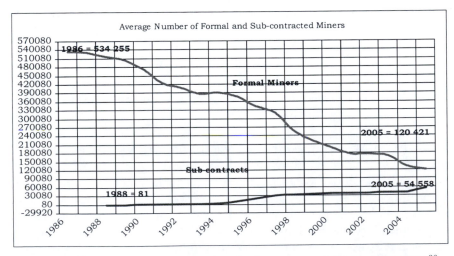

Figure 3.8. Average Number of Formal and Sub-contracted Miners, 1986–2005[80]
Source: NUM, Chamber of Mines and Department of Mineral and Energy Affairs

What is observable is that between 1986 and 2004, the number of formal miners decreased from 534,255 in 1986 to 120,421 by 2005. Observable in the "formal miners" trend is that between 1986 and 2005, 413,834 miners lost their jobs through retrenchments in the gold mining industry. Overall, the number of sub-contracts, a mere 81 by 1987, blossomed to 54,558 by 2005. However, while there have been job loses, they have largely targeted the foreign component of labor. For historical reasons that have more to do with large numbers of Basotho in the South Africa's gold mines and their dominance within the NUM, they have borne the brunt of retrenchments.

Thus, while there are job loses in the gold mining industry, this is not only a problem for South Africa, but is also one for Lesotho and Swaziland to a lesser extent. The number of Mozambicans has increased in the past few years while the number of Basotho decreased, revealing the industry's preferences for less militant Mozambican miners, who are largely not affiliated with the NUM. In 1987, there were 105,506 Basotho miners engaged by the Chamber of Mines. By 1994, that number had dropped to 80,200.[81] In 1988, for instance, Harmony gold mine in the Free State employed nearly 32,000 workers (nearly all Basotho). By early 1993, it had cut its workforce to about 14,586. In other words, 17,500 workers were retrenched in the space of five years (1988–1993).

CONCLUDING REMARKS

In South Africa, the beneficiaries (corporate South Africa, whites and black elites) of the system have ensured they retain their relative position by pressing the apartheid government towards a negotiated settlement. In the process, they have successfully managed to salvage their aspirations for capital accumulation in the long term. As this analysis demonstrates, this was achieved in the gold mines through shedding excess labor and driving the production costs down. On the basis of the above analysis, there was no direct relationship between GEAR and the continuing job losses that have characterized the gold mining industry up to 2004.

Although GEAR may not have been the best policy, it has largely succeeded in stabilizing the economy. The analysis has demonstrated the extent to which mining capital benefited by pushing for a favourable capital accumulation strategy, GEAR. Under the new mode of regulation, the industry was able to globalize its operations and invest abroad and compete at the international level. This could not be achieved under sanctions and international isolation during apartheid. The analysis shows how the industry prepared itself for competition at the international level, and how the new regime of accumulation, neo-liberalism has saved it through globalizing its activities.

GEAR, however, should be understood purely as an economic policy that was not designed to work for a country that has a past history of deliberately engineered poverty like South Africa. Bad as it may be, the policy suits the wishes of corporate South Africa at the expense of the impoverished majority's hope for "a better life for all." It is clear that progressive business people and entrepreneurs spearheaded South Africa's transition because apartheid and the sanctions campaign constrained their entrepreneurial spirit. The analysis went on to present the position of the mining industry throughout the transition period in contrast to its performance during the sanctions era and how the political transition has allowed it to globalize its activities.

In the process of presenting the gold mining industry's successes, the analysis also demonstrate that retrenchments of miners had nothing to do with GEAR. This was demonstrated by arguing that downscaling started in 1987 and was fast-tracked by the era of fluctuating exchange rates since 1995 with the signing of an agreement with the World Trade Organization in March 1995. This preceded GEAR, which was released in June 1996. Furthermore, through statistics on gold as far back in the pre-GEAR era as possible, the analysis also demonstrated the extent to which GEAR and the retrenchments in the gold mining industry are unrelated. Privatization of those areas that would have a direct impact on the gold mining industry's operation has yet to take place. For instance, the cost of electricity and water remains around 12 percent of total costs, while labor still accounts for over 50 percent of the industry's production costs.

The problem with GEAR is that although macroeconomic stability has been achieved, it has not been linked with labor retention within the economy in general. In essence, there has been an increase of structural unemployment. The targets that GEAR set for itself have meant that revisiting these targets for any revision would weaken the confidence of foreign investors regarding government's commitment to a strict neo-liberal macroeconomic policy. While this is true, this analysis has demonstrated that the gold mining industry's contribution towards the increase of structural unemployment was not solely caused by GEAR.

Chapter Four

From RDP to GEAR: The Political Economy of South Africa's Transition

INTRODUCTION

> The nationalization of mines, banks and monopoly industries is the policy of the ANC and a change or modification of our views in this regard is inconceivable.
>
> Nelson Mandela, 1990.[1]

> In our economic policies, there is not a single reference to things like nationalization, and this is not accidental. There is not a single slogan that will connect us with any Marxist ideology.
>
> Nelson Mandela, 1994.[2]

The new ANC government enacted various laws in attempts to redress the imbalances created by apartheid's relentless pursuit of "cheap labor." More importantly, a Presidential Labor Commission was set up in 1995, charged with the responsibility of establishing a framework in which labor market policies could evolve. The need for restructuring arose out of the acknowledgement that apartheid was designed to make black people inferior politically, socially and economically to whites. However, despite the changes introduced, to this day, the South African labor market is still *de facto* divided along racial lines with whites tending to occupy positions in the skilled labor market and blacks occupying low-paid jobs in the unskilled labor market.[3] According to the International Labor Organization (ILO) study by Standing *et al*, in 1996, 48.3 percent of the workforce was African; 18.4 percent was colored; 7.5 percent was Indian; and 15.8 percent was white.[4] According to Statistics South Africa census in 1996, of these racial categories, the actual number of those employed and unemployed in 1996 was as follows:

The Experience of Economic Redistribution

Table 4.1. Economically Active Population by Race and Gender, 1996[5]

	Employed	Unemployed	Total
African	5,682,476	4,205,992	9,888,468
Colored	1,129,515	299,231	1,428,746
Asian	363,486	50,379	413,865
White	1,856,456	89,066	1,945,518
Other	81,917	26,980	108,897
Male	5,481,903	2,039,917	7,521,820
Female	3,631,944	2,631,730	6,263,674

The challenge has been how to restructure the economy and labor market policies to make them consistent with both the democratic ideals and new constitutional obligations. While this goal is of primary importance, it has since been contradicted by the adoption of neo-liberal macroeconomic policy and subsequent job losses that directly undercut that initiative. This is often attributed to the fact that South Africa's transition began at a time when the ideological climate of the global economy was dominated by the pundits who, as Paul Williams reminds us, claimed "there was no alternative" to the neo-liberal path to economic growth.[6]

Ultimately, the adoption of neo-liberal macroeconomic policies meant that the long-awaited freedom brought with it new problems that will torment South Africans for some time to come. For in light of high expectations for employment, good economic prospects and "a better life for all" arising from the successful struggle against the malignant apartheid state, a very large percentage of the population—amongst them many of the most desperately poor people in the world—are being sacrificed on the altar of the neo-liberal logic of global capitalism.[7] Notwithstanding its ideology and rhetoric while in exile and opposition, once in power, the ANC government implemented orthodox macroeconomic policy that focused on deficit reduction and a strict monetary policy that coalesced with trade liberalization.[8]

By 1994, three-quarters of the population of 40 million were black Africans. They had voted for the first time and it was estimated that a quarter of them (or about seven million) lived in squatter camps or crude temporary housing; over 40 percent of them (or about 12 million) had no access to clean water; and over half of them (or about 15 million) were illiterate. Of all rural African households only about a tenth had access to basic sanitation and only five percent had access to electricity.[9] The contemporary discourse on South Africa's political economy of transition largely centers on the long-term implications of neo-liberalism on issues of social justice. For there is overwhelming pessimism among academics, trade unions and the general public that the vast majority of the people in South Africa will find their lives improved by the neo-liberal economic policies.

Indeed, something the reverse appears to be the far more likely outcome. Throughout the transition, there have been demonstrations against job losses, privatization, the removal of state subsidies and poor service delivery. This chapter seeks to examine the political economy of South Africa's transition, focusing specifically at the shift in macroeconomic policies from the Reconstruction and Development Programme (RDP) to the Growth, Employment and Redistribution Strategy (GEAR) and how that shift affected labor and the government's promise for a "better life for all."

THE POLITICAL ECONOMY OF SOUTH AFRICA'S TRANSITION

With political liberalization in South Africa, there were genuine fears of a violent and disorderly transition of a Congo-type scenario. More importantly, corporate South Africa and whites in general feared the prospects of an ANC government, especially when it came to the economy and its management. These fears were justified by the fact that the ANC had a long history of fraternal ties to the socialist regimes of Cuba, the former USSR and the former Soviet bloc states. Having been largely a broad-church comprising several groups, the ANC's ideology throughout the anti-apartheid struggle, if not pure Marxist, was at least clearly on the centre-left. Its intellectual coherence was drawn largely from the SACP. As a result, the ANC tended to be socialist in its outlook and policies. The leftist oriented party's economic position was spelled out earlier in the Freedom Charter adopted in Kliptown, June 26, 1955, which reads:

> The mineral wealth beneath the soil, the banks and monopoly industry shall be transferred to the ownership of the people as a whole; all other industry and trade shall be controlled to assist the well being of the people.[10]

Until 1994, the Freedom Charter remained the ANC's explicit articulation of economic policy and vision. During the years of massive repression under apartheid, armed struggle and the need to acquire international recognition had transcended every other objective, and the need to hatch an economic strategy was therefore overshadowed by these strategic considerations. This meant that when the movement was unbanned in 1990, transforming itself into a credible political party required that it articulate its economic blue print for a new South Africa. At an international level, the first opportunity for the ANC to voice its economic orientation came just two months after its ban was lifted. It was at the Harare Economic Conference in April of 1990 that, contrary to the views espoused in the Freedom Charter, the ANC ruled out any radical or far-reaching economic restructuring in post-apart-heid South Africa.[11] Almost three decades without legal political activity explicitly revealed the weakness of the ANC's position. An economic policy urgently needed to be formulated and this presented the opportunities and challenges for the political transition, both domestically and in accordance with the prevailing international political economy.

By 1991, ANC was already contemplating a synthesis of free market elements and state intervention in the economy, but what was not definite was how the party would translate this broad approach into specific policy initia-tives.[12] At the University of Pittsburgh in December 1991, Mandela stressed:

> We are convinced that the private sector must and will play the central
> and decisive role in the struggle to achieve many of these objectives.
> Contrary to what you might have heard or read, let me assure you that
> the ANC is not an enemy of private enterprise or the market system.[13]

By this time, the ANC understood that development could no longer be regarded as the responsibility of government alone. It required a part-nership of government with other social actors including the private sector, labor and non-governmental organizations.[14] Mandela further emphasized that the ANC was open to suggestions, noting that ". . . . our ideal is a mixed economy in which government interference would be no greater than that in Italy, Germany or France." During this period, the ANC was moving further away from the nostrums of the Freedom Charter.

Today, the core of the ANC is dominated by those whose aggressive pursuit of orthodox economic policies has been uncompromising, largely for self-enriching purposes. It is this group that is benefiting handsomely from GEAR democracy or neo-liberalism in general, through Black Eco-nomic Empowerment. In just over a decade after democracy, their grasp-ing acquisitiveness has become the hallmark of affluence in the midst of abject poverty. The irony of it is that, just like in other political transitions elsewhere, the benefits tend to be reaped by few with very little redistribu-tion—if any—to the less-well-off.

In a rather quick conversion, the ANC (under Mandela's leadership) became an advocate of the prevailing neo-liberal orthodoxy. After a rather brief period of negotiations and intermittent violence, a power-sharing post-apartheid democratic framework was worked out. In this framework, the ANC assumed power after the 1994 elections and within a relatively short period, "not only were free enterprise and property rights enshrined in the Constitution itself, but also full-blown neo-liberalism became the dominant (if not universal) phenomenon within the ANC policy-making elite" resulting in what Patrick Bond aptly refers to as *elite transition*.[15]

With Southern African economies already reeling in the face of globalization and the imposition of Structural Adjustment Programs by the World Bank and the International Monetary Fund, it is more complicated to explain the ANC's deliberate decision to discard its durable commitment on state-centered development and embrace neo-liberalism. However, the fact that the process was almost entirely driven internally seems to have given the ANC enough leverage to avoid the economic pitfalls those in exile witnessed throughout Southern Africa. Whether it was possible to resist neo-liberalism is beside the point as South Africa's policies were self-imposed. If a country with a comparatively smaller economy such as Ethiopia could resist the IMF, South Africa would probably have had more leverage.[16] However, it is important to emphasize that the ANC would have had to contend with the overwhelming power of domestic capital that was lobbying for neo-liberal macroeconomic policies as they suit their business imperatives.

* * * * *

There is no doubt that South Africa's transition to democracy occurred in difficult economic conditions in which intensified international competition has made entry into external markets extremely difficult. At the same time, the developing countries have been subjected to severe coercion under the General Agreements on Trade and Tariffs (GATT) and World Trade Organization trade arrangements to open up their domestic markets. Within the current international political economy, developing countries—in Africa in particular—have received only a limited share of foreign direct investment flows, which are concentrated largely among the emerging economies in Asia and Latin America.

The awareness of these realities makes it more complex to explain the ANC's economic choices, especially within such a relatively short period of time. Japan, South Korea and Taiwan integrated into the world economy under very different conditions that offered enough protection, even encouragement, by the U.S. However, serious irreversible losses like complete economic collapse in the case of Zimbabwe or the Thailand currency crisis that sparked the East Asian economic meltdown may indeed occur if the wrong kind of openness is attempted or the timing and sequence are incorrect.[17]

The ANC's change of economic policy can be understood through internal socio-economic challenges and external factors that made economic choice other than neo-liberalism difficult if not impossible. For a variety of reasons, most analysts have argued that South Africa was not well placed to resist the neo-liberal orthodoxy. The first problem was a lack of any tradition of substantive economic policy debate within the ANC, which left the movement in 1990 with virtually no informed ideas of its own about economic issues. Second, aspects of the constitutional settlement, most notably the decision to grant the South African Reserve Bank (SARB) policy independence, effectively removed important policy-levers from government, largely because this was considered important in renewing access to private international capital markets.[18]

The move towards neo-liberalism has not been properly understood, as the ANC had traditionally opposed capitalist economic directions. As one SACP interviewee puts it, "international financial institutions did not have conditionalities on South Africa."[19] In 1996, when neo-liberal macroeconomic policy was introduced in the form of the GEAR, South Africa was not beset by any fiscal imbalances that called for stabilization measures. Still, changes in the locus of international influence that arose out of the collapse of the Soviet Union and the Eastern bloc made any meaningful implementation of leftist-oriented economic development policy impossible. More importantly it also ensured that the most important international actors in South Africa's transition were to be the U.S. and its allies, Britain, Germany and Japan. The price these powers demanded for *disciplining* the apartheid governments and extending promises of material aid to the ANC was a commitment by the latter to follow the Washington Consensus.[20]

What is most fascinating about South Africa's transition is its uniqueness. It was a process largely managed by South Africans themselves and not brokered by the United Nations, as in Namibia, or by the former colonial power, as in Zimbabwe. The negotiated settlement also meant that the basic maintenance of the previous economic system remains, including respect for private property. There are clear winners and losers out of the Convention for a Democratic South Africa's (CODESA) deliberations. The political aspects may have been settled appropriately, but the economic imperatives are increasingly exacerbating the plight of the poor, especially people's legitimate expectations. What is important is that while the rest of Southern Africa had the imposition of development strategies by the International Financial Institutions, in South Africa this has been largely internally driven and self-imposed.

* * * * *

Internationally, while some governments have formulated sound economic policies for growth and redistribution, forces beyond their control often thwarted their efforts. There is evidence that powerful external forces operating on the ANC and new democratic government influenced economic policy towards neo-liberalism. Thus, in the language of John Gray, in seeking to force every economy into a straight-jacket sewn from the singular practices of American capitalism, South Africa was minimally compelled to adopt economic policies that do not fit its history and needs (in the sense that South Africans were allowed to craft their own neo-liberal macroeconomic policy as opposed to countries like Zimbabwe where the policies where simply imposed).[21] In an interview, Alexander Erwin, then South African Trade and Industry Minister, stated that, "a country such as South Africa, which started its economic reform in the 1990s, was prevented from using interventionist methods by World Trade Organization rules." Accordingly, as he puts it, "we therefore tend to implement policy packages that are similar to those of other advanced developing countries."[22] Patrick Bond argued that International Financial Institutions, together with Western governments, have been an influence over ANC economic thinking since the early 1990s, albeit theirs has been more a successful exercise in moral suasion or indirect lobbying. For, as he puts it, the Bretton Woods organizations have not had much direct leverage (via loan conditionality) over the direction of ANC economic policy since 1994.[23]

The power and influence of the Bretton Woods institutions should not be underestimated. After 1990, the World Bank whose working style Arturo Escobar, equates to the "God trick of seeing everything from nowhere,"[24] "opened its channels to the ANC and the trade union movement, and enlisted researchers associated with the democratic movement in its projects where they were fed a steady diet of neo-liberal economics."[25] According to Hein Marais, its representative later boasted, "this is the only country where we speak to the opposition."[26] In addition to these robust external forces, the ANC also had to contend with its own members who vigorously pursued capitalism for carefully planned long-term economic and material personal gains. In the dissection of South Africa's political economy of transition, the powerful influence of senior ANC figures towards a neo-liberal oriented economic policy has been underestimated. Furthermore, soon after the ANC was unbanned, white South African businessmen enticed black businessmen, intellectuals and politicians by offering them attractive directorships and share holdings in established companies; ironically, it is these groups that were latter chastised by President Mandela for criticizing the economic policy reversals.[27]

South Africa's powerful conglomerates lost little time after the ANC was unbanned in 1990 in bringing their views to the ANC leadership; the faster abolition of the then existing exchange controls (which the Reserve Bank and government agreed to abolish only gradually) had been a major focus of their lobbying activities.[28] Hein Marais argues that plethora of much more capital-friendly corporate planning, unleashed after 1990, inundated the ANC's economic thinking. In addition to the influence of the Bretton Woods institutions, these corporate planning exercises explain why in 1993 the ANC effectively rejected the policy findings of its own economic think tank; the Macro-Economic Research Group (MERG), which it had set up to formulate a post-1994 economic policy. MERG called for a programme of fiscal expansion directed towards social and physical infrastructure, a balanced monetary policy, and a more active role for the state in the economy.[29]

The first of these corporate scenario-planning exercises was Nedcor/Old Mutual's prospects for a "Successful Transition," launched in late 1990 and completed in 1993. The insurance conglomerate Sanlam's "Platform for Investment" scenario and the social-democratic "Mont Fleur Scenarios" followed. In addition, other documents such as the South African Chamber of Business (SACOB) *Economic Options for South Africa* were also wheeled into the main fray.[30] Bond also contends that the white establishment used black faces to gain access to the new government and often paid blacks in the form of shares in their companies.[31] Eventually, it is a handful of black people that are being enriched, through Black Economic Empowerment (BEE).

The State of the Economy in the Early 1990s

Over time throughout the 1980s, sanctions against apartheid had worked their way through the economy. Economic growth had become sluggish at between one and two percent per annum and even negative in some financial years. More importantly, from the 1970s onwards, apartheid's homeland system consumed billions of rands through subsidies from Pretoria to make them viable. The results of this profligacy in sustaining something that was not economically viable but ideologically justifiable, consistent with the idea of apartheid, were to be felt towards the end of the 1980s when sanctions began to take their toll on the economy. The stagnant economic growth rates served to constrain employment creation and therefore income expansion—a major issue that spurred the social unrest throughout the 1980s. The apartheid government clearly had no practical economic answer, but a political one in the form of a State of Emergency declared in the mid-1980s. All these factors combined meant that the ANC was to inherit an economy that had been stagnant for some time (see Table

5.2 in Chapter Five below). This reality has served to exacerbate discontent throughout the transition period, whether in service delivery or in poverty alleviation in general. For, there was little growth for any meaningful wealth distribution, which, after all, primarily accrued to the white minority.

Ravi Naidoo argues that the apartheid leaders had thoroughly plundered the state coffers, awarding themselves and white civil servants massive pensions and 'golden handshakes' between 1990 and 1994. The budget deficit was seven percent of GDP and before the ANC took over; the country barely had three weeks foreign exchange reserves, with a payment crisis looming.[32] Furthermore, the legacy of apartheid itself was and is still so severe that it required comprehensive interventions. In light of all these, to be successful, South Africa desperately needed at least six percent economic growth rate sufficient for creating 300,000 jobs per year to cut into the 30 percent unemployment rate.

Furthermore, the economy was and still is characterized by a highly unequal distribution of wealth and income, high levels of poverty, and a very high unemployment rate, as well as being situated in one of the worst performing economic regions of the world.[33] It remains, however, the strongest economy in the weak African periphery. In 1995 South Africa's Gross National Product was almost five times more than that of the rest of the sub-region combined, making it the economic hub for sub-Saharan Africa. However, the end of apartheid meant that South Africa was no longer a "cheap labor" economy, something that lured investors in the past. While some may argue that South Africa was no longer a "cheap labor" economy before 1994, that conclusion seems to suggest that black people had already managed to close the wage gap. That is not true. It was only after 1994 with the introduction of new labor laws setting up minimum wage that the gap was statutorily closed. However, unscrupulous employers still exploit the loopholes that currently exist, especially in the more conservative industries like agriculture.

Rampant crime and the scourge of HIV/AIDS deprive South Africa of the comparative advantages that allow countries like China or Malaysia to fashion hybrid strategies, which incorporate (but are not determined by) neo-liberal adjustments. Saddled with a structurally weak economy and handicapped by balance of payments constraints and a sizeable (but not extravagant) debt burden, Marais argues that the state's room for manoeuvre was been severely cramped.[34] Despite these shortcomings, the ANC government had to live up to the economic and social expectations of its constituency. More importantly, while in exile and in opposition, the ANC had held its own diverse constituencies in check by emphasizing a litany of grievances, which it promised, without any order of preference, to address once it gained access to political power.[35] In order to meet these undertakings, the major challenge was to re-ignite the economy through macroeconomic changes. This was based on the logic that a healthy economy would alleviate most of the socio-economic woes by absorbing the unemployed.

FROM THE RPD TO GEAR

Macroeconomic Populism—RDP

> The rates of economic growth we seek cannot be achieved without important inflows of foreign capital. We are determined to create the necessary climate, which the foreign investor will find attractive.
>
> Nelson Mandela, 1991.[36]

In April 1994, when ANC leaders entered the Union Buildings, the seat of government in Pretoria, they understood that apartheid had left a legacy of such distortions in the operation of the South African economy that extensive state intervention was required for reconstruction.[37] A meaningful reversal of these distortions necessitated reigniting the economy and a major overhaul of the entire socio-economic apparatus. Emphasis was thus put on achieving vibrant economic growth; the assumption was based on the premise that it would lay the basis for reducing unemployment and an equitable redistribution of income and wealth would follow. It was against this background that in September 1994 the RDP was re-worked into a white paper that spelled out government policy. Although the RDP was a socialist oriented development strategy, it is interesting that it was crafted at a time when the ANC was clearly subscribing to the neo-liberal economic orthodoxy.

The RDP is credited for understanding comprehensively, the economic realities and major problems of South Africa in the early 1990s. According to John Weeks, these challenges were: first, the need to increase the rate of economic growth; second, the need to increase the rate of investment in order to stimulate economic growth and modernize production; and third, to achieve these in a manner that would achieve increased wage employment, better wages for those in the employment, and greater equality in the distribution of income and wealth.[38] Articulating these challenges made the RDP an integrated, "coherent socio-economic policy framework that sought to mobilize all South Africans and the country's resources toward the final eradication of apartheid by building a democratic, non-racial and non-sexist future."[39]

The RDP became a mantra for government policy, appearing to stand for the total transformation of South Africa and a yardstick against which government's success could be assessed.[40] It was premised on the understanding that neither economic growth by itself or redistribution on its own would resolve the serious crisis in which South Africa found itself.[41] Therefore, government policy would have to involve the promotion of a more equitable pattern of growth, an equitable distribution of assets and the maintenance of macroeconomic stability. This made it a people-centered development strategy, but it did not make clear exactly where the envisaged growth would come from. Be that as it may, the RDP was conceived on the understanding that:

- South Africa's history has been a bitter one dominated by colonialism, racism, apartheid, sexism and repressive labor policies. The result is that poverty and degradation exist side by side with modern cities and a developed mining, industrial and commercial infrastructure. Racially distorted income distribution, which ranks as one of the most unequal in the world, lavish wealth and abject poverty characterize South African society;
- The economy was built on systematically enforced racial division of labor in every sphere of society. Rural areas had been divided into underdeveloped Bantustans and well-developed, white-owned commercial farming areas. Towns and cities have been divided into townships without basic infrastructure for blacks and well-resourced suburbs for whites;
- Segregation in education, health, welfare, transport and employment left deep scars of inequality and economic inefficiency. In commerce and industry, large conglomerates dominated by whites control large parts of the economy. "Cheap labor" policies and employment segregation concentrated skills in white hands and poorly equipped workers to meet the rapid changes taking place in the world economy;
- The result is that in every sphere of South African society—economic, social, political, moral, cultural and environmental—South Africans were confronted by serious problems. The apartheid arrangement left no sector untouched by the ravages of apartheid. Whole regions of the country suffer as a direct result of the apartheid policies and their collapse.[42]

It was understood that apartheid was directly responsible not only for the structural violence of poverty, but also the related deprivations, and the RDP was designed to address these deficiencies. As Southall puts it, the RDP's emphasis was "on coaxing and disciplining the dominant private sector into helping to overcome huge historical racial and social inequalities (which it helped to create), without which there could be no sustainable future for capitalism in South Africa."[43] The strategy was spelled out in an ANC discussion document on economic policy in 1990. The document argued that:

> The engine of growth in the economy of a democratic, non-racial and non-sexist South Africa should be the growing satisfaction of the basic needs of the impoverished and deprived majority of our people. . . . We thus call for a program of Growth through Redistribution in which redistribution acts as a spur to growth and in which the fruits of growth are redistributed to satisfy basic needs.[44]

The RDP reinforced the ANC's growth through redistribution strategy that was dominant in the 1980s. This strategy suggests that vigorous income redistribution can pay for itself by serving as a source of economic growth. It provided firm targets for redistribution, which aimed at doubling the national income share of the poorest 40 percent of households by the year 2005. It was understood that in South Africa's demand-constrained economy, black people were too poor to generate sufficient demand to increase employment and overcome the seemingly substantial overcapacity in various sectors of the economy.

As John Weeks points out, this presented a rather radical proposal. Assuming that South Africa's economy were to grow by at least 4.2 percent per annum during the period 1996–2000 and a sustained six percent growth rate during 2001–2005, this would imply an average growth rate of 5.1 percent in ten years. The RDP certainly could not otherwise achieve its targets, as it emphasized growth though redistribution—but where was the growth to come from? Indeed, the government was in a financial crisis. For instance, when the Minister of Finance presented the national budget to parliament in March 1995, the total revenue was estimated at R124 billion, while the total government expenditure was estimated at R153 billion, which had to be financed through a variety of debt instruments. The government simply did not have the economic means to implement the RDP. For, as then Deputy President Mbeki informed students at the University of Potchefstroom:

> The budget we inherited from the previous government requires that 91 percent be spent on recurrent expenditures, including wages, welfare and the servicing of foreign debt. This means only nine percent is available for housing and new infrastructure. We cannot produce miracles with nine percent of the budget.[45]

As for servicing foreign debt, the 1995/96 budget set aside about R28.385 billion. This was about 18 percent of the total state expenditure for the year, which was second to the expenditure in education. When this reality is put in perspective, the RDP appears to have been economically unviable, except for justifying redistribution.

* * * * *

Economists have pointed out that growth through redistribution presented a rosy picture of demand-oriented redistribution that benefits everyone at the expense of no one.[46] This macroeconomic populism of the RDP was characterized by the belief—then shared by many—that income redistribution can be achieved through changes in the level or structure of aggregate demand, at little or no cost. Estian Calitz defines macroeconomic populism as economic management, which emphasizes economic growth and income distribution, and under-emphasize the risks of inflation, deficit financing, external constraints and the reaction of economic agents to aggressive non-market policies.[47]

The RDP was modeled on this understanding. It set targets for growth which included the creation of 2.5 million jobs over a ten-year period; the building of one million houses by the year 2000, the connection to the national electricity grid of 2.5 million homes by 2000; the provision of running water and sewage to one million households and other goods. Its widespread acceptance by the public averted the worst fears of social unrest in the early 1990s by providing a reasonable balance of hope and optimism, thus stabilizing reverberating ferments of the delicate political landscape. Overall, it is important to emphasize that through the RDP, the ANC acknowledged the need for pro-poor macroeconomics and therefore oriented the public policy machinery towards "a better life for all" and poverty reduction.

After only two years, the RDP was discarded in favor of a much more neo-liberal macro-economic framework in the form of the Growth Employment and Redistribution Strategy (GEAR). The ANC had changed its orientation after successful persuasion that, "growth through redistribution was risky macroeconomic populism" in that the stimulus to demand, through what would necessarily be deficit spending, would likely be inflationary and detrimental to the balance of payments."[48] The implementation of macroeconomic populism in other countries has not been encouraging either. For instance, the Austral, Cruzado and Inti Plans introduced in 1985–1986 in Argentina, Brazil and Peru led to an improvement in growth, inflation and poverty performance over the first two years, but to a worsening situation over the medium term.[49] It remains doubtful whether the RDP's performance would have satisfied the left's wishes for social democratic development. Because government claims it is using the GEAR strategy to achieve RDP envisioned objectives, it is difficult to asses the success of the RDP before GEAR took over, as it had only been official government policy for two years.

African Renaissance [of] Economic Orthodoxy?—GEAR

> In order to make a serious dent on unemployment we need to grow the economy at a faster rate and this requires that we address issues related to increasing investments as well as resolving the skills constraint. Further economic growth must also lead to social development.
>
> Nelson Mandela, 1991.[50]

Deserting the RDP was a betrayal of the ANC's own creed and revealed an imperative policy change towards economic pragmatism and a less vigorous pursuit of broad socio economic development objectives that conventional economic wisdom held were obstructing real or meaningful investment. In the nationalization rhetoric of the early 1990s, investors would not invest if they felt that Damocles sword of nationalization pledge hung over their heads.[51] The switch to neo-liberal policies was not a *faux pas* but indeed an outcome of the government's increasing free market as opposed to interventionist leanings and the basic impracticalities of economic self-reliance in a globalizing economy.[52] This was born from the need to re-establish pre-conditions for growth and the belief that economic growth in itself, along with robust safety nets through welfare provision, would take care of gripping poverty. However, internal determinants were more important that external determinants towards a neo-liberal orientation. While South Africa had been liberated politically, the demise of future prospects of vigorously pursuing socialism led to the semi-capitalist class within the ANC linking itself with "undefeated capital."[53]

It is generally accepted that under the RDP (1994–1996), the economy was not achieving the desired growth rates. This reality constrained the RDP from realizing its targets. In essence, this meant that it could not attain an equitable balance between economic objectives and political imperatives. Foreign direct investment was minimal, as investors and International Financial Institutions demanded more clarity on macroeconomic policy.[54] This clarity was whether the ANC would cling to its socialist development policy or economic pragmatism would prevail. The message was clear, the ANC either had to craft its own neo-liberal economic policy or worse, it would be crafted elsewhere and imposed, just as it has been throughout the developing world. Of the two, the former was the best alternative, although it has attracted enormous criticisms. Being the "magical elixir," it seems the market had to be liberated to boost the waning confidence of foreign direct investors who took a wait-and-see approach.

With the African capitalist renaissance rhetoric of the time, the stage was set for unleashing the market forces and when they were unleashed, it was with such rigor that the commitment to principles enshrined in the RDP became moot. Neo-liberal economic policies are often negotiated in secret and South Africa was not an exception. A small team of economists was secretly assembled in December 1999 by the then Deputy Minister of Finance, Alexander Erwin, to begin work on a new macroeconomic policy. With the assistance of the South African Reserve Bank (SARB), the World Bank, the Development Bank of Southern Africa (DBSA) and the University of Stellenbosch, GEAR was secretly produced—almost entirely by white consultants.[55]

It is doubtful whether the outcome would have been different had Africans constituted a significant component of the panel. Joseph Stiglitz points out that the problem with economists, especially for the World Bank in crafting policies is that the core curricula in which modern economists are trained, involves models in which there is never any unemployment.[56] This sentiment was echoed earlier by Andre Gunder Frank. He argued that ". . . . our theoretical categories and guides to development policy have been distilled exclusively from the historical experience of the European and North American advanced capitalist nations.[57] More importantly, Frank asserts that "our ignorance of the underdeveloped countries' history leads us to assume that their past and indeed their present resemble earlier stages of the history of the now developed countries." Notwithstanding these realities, the policy formulation process had to be expedited "because it was meant to reassure business, not as a way to transform government policy."[58] So although the government was serious with the policy, that seriousness was undermined by the fact that macroeconomic stability overshadowed economic redistribution.

Eventually, in June 1996 GEAR was unveiled. The clear message from government was that GEAR is the vehicle for furthering goals set out in the RDP document. As Alexander Erwin, then Minister of Trade and Industry put it in May of 1997, "the need to create employment and a better life for our people is the central objective of the economic policy of this government. The RDP remains the basic policy of this government, while GEAR is the associated macroeconomic strategy used."[59] With all the hallmarks of the Washington Consensus, including, amongst others fiscal discipline, public expenditure priorities, trade liberalization, and privatization, GEAR's major objectives were to achieve sustainable economic growth, predicted at a 5.2 percent rate per annum between 1996 and 2000. This magnificent proposal was to be accompanied by the creation of employment at a rate of 270,000 new jobs per annum by the year 2000.

After GEAR's release, the Asian economic crisis, which was triggered by the floating of the Thai baht on July 1997, had serious repercussions for financial markets worldwide, and South Africa was not spared.[60] The crisis prompted acrimonious debates on fundamental issues of macroeconomic policy formulation, the rightward shift and the abandonment of the social democratic RDP in favor of GEAR.[61] Both Cosatu and SACP leadership expressed reservations about the nature of consultation, and the general vagueness of GEAR's contents. As Cosatu's discussion paper later put it, "when it comes to policy, the alliance engaged only the product."[62] A contrast was made with the very broad-ranging and consultative process that underpinned the drafting of the RDP base document.[63]

Inevitably, unlike the RDP, GEAR did not enjoy the political support of Cosatu and the SACP. The underlying premise of GEAR strategy was that growth would be best promoted by freeing the private sector from the fetters of the distorted racist logic and constraints of the country's apartheid past. The GEAR document acknowledged the necessity for initiatives that will generate the demand stimulus to achieve the projected growth rate of 5.2 percent for the years 1996–2000. It proposed to achieve this by arguing that growth was mainly an outcome of steady increases in fixed investment and manufactured exports.

The strategy of GEAR aimed at a significant improvement in economic growth and development for all and a meaningful decline in unemployment. The logic of GEAR is that to provide jobs and redistribute wealth, growth must be achieved first. In GEAR's language:

> As South Africa moves towards the next century, we seek a competitive fast growing economy which creates jobs for all jobseekers; a distribution of opportunities and income in favor of the poor; a society in which sound health, education and other services are available to all; and an environment in which homes are secure and places of work are productive.[64]

A careful reading of the GEAR document, however, suggests that its recommended growth scenario actually implied an increase in inequality.

For instance, it was well known that the privatization of state owned enterprises would be accompanied by massive job losses. Initally this reality was overlooked for strategic objectives of achieving macroeconomic stability. Overall, GEAR was intended to improve South Africa's international competitiveness by further reducing tariffs and encouraging foreign investment. In his speech to the National Assembly on June 14, 1996, Thabo Mbeki (then Deputy President) made it clear that GEAR was the central compass which will guide all growth and development programs of the government aimed at achieving the objectives of the RDP, but in a rather circuitous and devious route.

In the then-President Nelson Mandela's acerbic annotation, GEAR was 'not negotiable.' Despite continuing objection from its alliance partners, the SACP and Cosatu, the ANC went ahead with privatization in part under the guise of using the proceeds to fund some of the programs envisioned in the RDP.[65] This awkward embrace of neo-liberalism has strained the relationship between the ANC and its alliance partners. So far, a shared history of the struggle against apartheid and inter-dependence makes them hang together. Observers have warned that if managed recklessly, in time this animosity in the alliance may spell a far greater disaster (see Chapter Five below for a discussion on alliance politics). Some leftist-oriented analysts argue that even though the RDP may have been failing, it could have been reworked without discarding it altogether. Certainly, armchair critics see things different as opposed to politicians who have more to consider than petty fascination with ideological commitment.

GEAR, with its privatization, retrenchments, cuts in government spending, versus the demands of the black working-class for redistribution and empowerment, became the central fault line between the ANC and its alliance partners. These agendas are mutually incompatible and cannot be reconciled. This is the basic factor undermining the alliance, splitting it into two camps: ANC, which supports GEAR, and SACP/Cosatu, which do not. GEAR set targets, and the performance results have been the benchmarks for those who denounce it. In the table below, the middle column shows GEAR's targets for each of the policy objectives and the right column shows the percentage of actual targets that were achieved:

Clearly, GEAR failed to achieve all of its targets, and, if anything, it has made life for the poor and the destitute more miserable. For instance, while private wage growth was 1.4 percent per annum prior to GEAR, it was projected to grow at a meager 0.8 percent per year. However, as the table indicates, this has not been the case and there was a

Table 4.2. GEAR's Projections, 1996–2000[66]

GEAR Objectives: Prior, Targeted and Actual, 1996–2000			
Policy objectives	Prior to GEAR	GEAR's target	Actual
Export growth	6.9%	8.4%	6.6%
Real private investment	5.6%	11.7%	2.4%
Real public investment	2.7%	7.6%	3.8%
Real GDP growth	2.8%	4.2%	2.5%
CPI inflation	9.5%	8.2%	6.7%
Current account deficit (% of GDP)	1.4%	2.4%	1.0%
Private wage growth	1.4%	0.8%	2.5%
Formal job growth	1.0%	2.9%	-0.3%
New formal jobs ('000)	104	270	30

salary growth rate of 2.5 percent in the private sector in the period 1996 to 2000, more than twice GEAR's projection, thus widening the divide between the rich and the poor. The government has used this reality to argue that in some way the private sector is undermining national priorities through excessive salary increases far above inflation. Amongst the reasons why GEAR failed: there were mistaken assumptions regarding the export response; there were unintended consequences of the anti-inflation budget bias which restrained public investment; and there were mistaken policies regarding monetary defense of the rand, giving rise to debilitating interest rate shocks. More important was the inability to attract foreign direct investment on which GEAR's success was predicated.

There was also an inability to control private sector wage growth leading to formal job shrinkage. According to Cosatu, what contributed to GEAR's failure was a very restrictive macroeconomic policy, including cutting the state budget. As one interviewee told me, "very few countries in the world cut their budget and GEAR came at a time when there was an economic down turn. Something could have been done at the time for more targeted growth action. Regrettably, that did not happen."[67] The other problem was that GEAR had a profound impact on the contraction of the economy, much more than was expected. Essentially, government locked itself into a rather rigid macroeconomic framework.

WAITING FOR GODOT? THE MYTH OF FOREIGN DIRECT INVESTMENT—FDI

> We believe that South Africa depended to a large extent on foreign cap-
> ital and foreign trade. We felt that planned destruction of power plants,
> and interference with rail and telephone communications, would tend
> to scare away capital from the country . . . and would in the long run
> be a heavy drain on the economic life of the country, thus compelling
> the voters to re-think their position.
>
> Nelson Mandela, 1963.[68]

Whereas the ANC had been a vigorous campaigner for disinvestment in South Africa at the height of the sanctions campaign of the 1980s, by the early 1990s, it was canvassing for foreign investors to return to South Africa. This seems to have been a little late, as international investors already heeded its call, disinvested and invested elsewhere. In the post-1990 period, domestic instability and the accompanying political uncertainties prior to the 1994 elections discouraged potential investors. After South Africa's debt crisis of the mid-1980s, the country's position in the international capital markets became precarious. While it took a great deal of persuasion for the disinvestment campaign to succeed, it is proving equally difficult to lure investors back to South Africa. After all, capital moves to where the margins of profits are higher—and like water, it flows to where there is least resistance.

In 1996, the IMF argued that the end of apartheid and sanctions created the opportunity for external capital flows to return and play the role they played in the quarter century before the mid-1980s, when foreign savings averaged more than 5.5 percent of the GDP.[69] Ironically, the IMF failed to recognize that the high rates of profits achieved then were largely based on extreme exploitation and low wages of apartheid's "cheap labor" policies. With trade liberalization, South Africa now has higher wage costs than most of Asia and Latin America and its market size has become insignificant for international corporations. In addition, while the apartheid "cheap labor" system has largely been phased out, working conditions and requirements in the new labor market regime discourage both employers and potential investors. As a result, there appears to be little incentive to locate new investment in the country.

In the past decades, the International Financial Institutions have insisted on trade liberalization and the opening up of the economy as prerequisites to attracting foreign direct investment in support of development initiatives.

Apart from the International Financial Institutions, lately the Monterrey Consensus, the New Partnership for Africa's Development, the 2002 OECD Ministerial, Johannesburg World Summit on Sustainable Development and the Millennium Development Goals all underscored the importance of international investment in achieving sustainable development. Inspired by this belief in the magic of foreign direct investment, through GEAR, it was assumed—**wrongly**—that foreign direct investment would act as a developmental *deus ex machina*, and register a nine-fold increase to enable its employment targets to be met.[70] Also envisaged was that with state facilitation the domestic private sector would expand and drive the economy.

This understanding was based on the absurd premise that GEAR would open up the economy and as the International Financial Institutions' panacea prescribes, foreign direct investment would follow. While GEAR may have appeared the appropriate alternative, achieving its targets has been undermined by the trickling inflow of much anticipated foreign direct investment. For instance, while an economic growth rate of six percent was projected, in reality, the economy has grown on average by 2.8 percent over the last decade.[71] The Bureau for Economic Research at the University of Stellenbosch forecast that growth could accelerate if manufacturing, which accounts for 25 percent of GDP (a contribution equivalent to the mining industry in 1980), continues to improve. There is room for optimism as manufactured exports have increased from 6.7 percent of GDP in 1990 to 39.7 percent in 2000.[72] In 2004, Trevor Manuel, the Finance Minister, also reiterated that a combination of positive elements—lower inflation and interest rates, vastly improved tax collection, better government spending and more domestic investment [not foreign direct investment] will lead to 3.7 percent growth.[73]

However, if the economy were to grow by six percent as projected, South Africa would substantially increase its GDP. To achieve this, perceptions of risk, for instance, crime rate and its impact on doing business in South Africa, the rigid labor market regime, which most investors feel inhibit investment, have to be altered to increase domestic fixed investment from 15 percent of GDP to at least 25 percent.[74] The figure below shows the trends:

This is central to South Africa's economic successes as overall fixed investment has remained fairly constant at 15 percent since 1990. Even by comparison, other successful developing countries such as Korea have maintained more than 20 percent of fixed capital formation since the 1970s. If the level of fixed investment were to increase to roughly 30 percent—as it was in the 1980s, it would help accelerate South Africa's economic

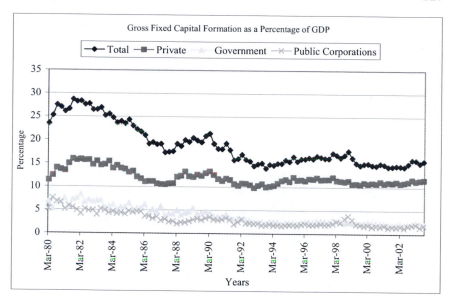

Figure 4.1. South Africa's Gross Fixed Capital Formation as a Percentage of GDP
Source: South African Reserve Bank

growth rates. However, the fact that GEAR's success was largely predicated on successful attraction of foreign direct investment meant that domestic investments were overlooked. Exacerbating poor levels of domestic investments has been the generally low savings rate. As Figure 4.1 indicates, private investments have largely kept the economy floating, while government and public corporations investments have been declining from five percent in 1985 to less than three percent overall. To accelerate South Africa's economic growth rate, the challenge remains how to improve the ratio of foreign direct investment to GDP from its 2003 level of one percent. Foreign direct investment is usually measured by the percentage of people employed by foreign companies within their country. It includes significant investments by foreign companies, such as construction of production facilities or ownership stakes taken by foreign businesses. Foreign direct investment not only creates new jobs, it can also lead to an infusion of innovative technologies, management strategies and workforce practices—so the litany goes.

With such a legacy of apartheid in which most people in their prime years are functionally illiterate, this presents obstacles to realizing meaningful growth rates. As one interviewee told me, "the education system does not produce enough human capital for sustaining desired growth rate."[75] Bhorat *et al*, points out that in the early years of National Party rule, expenditure on

African education fell in per capita terms, declining from 13 percent of white levels in 1953 to only 10 percent in 1961. According to the 2001 census, 22 percent of Africans were completely illiterate, whilst five percent have some form of tertiary education as compared to 30 percent of whites. As late as 1989, the state continued to spend 4.4 times more on white child than on a black child—this having fallen to 16.6 times in the 1970s.[76] Alistar Sparks also points out that:

> White public education was equal to the best in the developed world, while black education was poorer than many in the Third World: buildings were derelict, 30 percent had no electricity, 25 percent no water, 50 percent no sanitation and one-third of the teachers were unqualified and many more were underqualified.[77]

As a result, a dysfunctional education system meant that African high-school graduates entered the labor market at a severe disadvantage.[78] This reality has led to the argument that most of those who are unemployed are simply unemployable.

The reason for the trickling of foreign direct investment inflow has been attributed to the *relatively* high perception of the risk of doing business in South Africa. However, in 2003, South Africa ranked 70 out of 140 nations in terms of investment risk.[79] In October 2003, results of the U.S. based research group, Russell 20–20, scored South Africa higher in banking, capital markets, corporate governance, rule of law, political stability and macroeconomic fundamentals compared to developed markets.[80]

Apart from the trickling foreign direct investment, the failures of GEAR to achieve targets in respect of economic growth and employment are strongly related to the rigid labor market conditions that followed the implementation of such legislation as the Basic Conditions of Employment Act (1997) and the Employment Equity Act (1998) (discussion below). In response to this, progress was made during 2001 with legislative amendments aimed at improving the efficiency of the labor market. Labor market reform is necessary to reduce structural impediments to employment. To this end, workers' rights may have to be reversed in the interest of higher growth rates. Hard choices will have to be made from a calculus of competing interests.

The tabling in Parliament of the Labor Relations Amendment and Basic Conditions of Employment Amendment Bills was approved in August of 2001. In addition to proposed legislative changes to the Labor Relations Act and the Basic Conditions of Employment Act, the Minister of Labor also turned his attention to the traditionally vulnerable sectors, recommending the establishment of minimum working conditions and wages for domestic and farm workers.[81] The excessive costs in the hiring and dismissals of people are notorious for their devastating effect on employment. The labor market rigidities appear to be typical insider-outsider phenomenon and apart from their inhibiting effect on employment, they inadvertently discourage both domestic and foreign direct investment. For South Africa's economy, an investment strategy should, first and foremost, be to get domestic entrepreneurs proud of their own economy.[82]

While this remains crucial, domestic investment has been reduced by the departure of Anglo-American, Old Mutual, South African Breweries, Dimension Data and others to primary listing in the London and New York Stock Exchanges. This was done to access cheaper capital and to facilitate their foreign expansion.[83] The neo-liberal ideology at Treasury permitted the move, capital had to flow freely. As one interviewee put it, "the treasury felt that the weight of economic ideology was so heavy that they had to let them go . . . Although this was not an argument that everybody in government supported, it was a big mistake."[84] In retrospect, in the logic of this analysis, the move seems to have been a conscious one by the ANC as it served as a pressure valve to reduce the power of these corporations in the political sphere. Between 1994 and 1998, Africa received 42 percent of the outward investment by South African companies, which makes South Africa amongst the top ten African investors. In the same period, the European Union received 18 percent.[85]

Within Africa, major South African investments include Mozal the aluminum smelter outside Maputo which cost US$1.3 billion; Sasol, the petrochemical giant completed the US$1.1 billion, 865 kilometer pipeline from Temane gas fields to Secunda in Mpumalanga; MTN (mobile phone network provider), one of its major investments has been in Nigeria, where it paid US$280 million in license fees in an investment estimated at US$900 million; Vodacom, committed to investing US$260 million in Mozambique, having already poured US$150 million each into Tanzania and the Democratic Republic of the Congo; AngloPlatinum, is set to plough US$90 million into Unki, Zimbabwe, bringing spending in the region to US$150 million; AngloGold, currently has direct investments of US$93.3 million in Mali, accompanied by US$309 million indirect investment; Eskom, has committed to a US$1 billion Inga project in the Democratic Republic of the Congo; and SABMiller has US$50 million breweries in Maputo and Beira Mozambique. In addition to these, Stanbic Africa is now valued at R1.6 billion, with assets of between R20 and R25 billion. The enormous offshore investment is more than what South Africa has received each year in foreign direct investment up to 2000.[86]

In its first year as a London listed company, 1999–2000, Anglo-American posted a 24 percent increase in its profits.[87] This was largely as a result of the appreciation of the dollar, the currency in which commodities are traded, versus the rand, the currency in which the bulk of its operating costs are paid. This however, revived negative imperial recollection as London was re-established as the dominant command and control center of the South African economy. Thus, aspects of both South Africa's colonial and apartheid history are being inscribed or reinforced by the current restructuring. Although the move was intended to assist these companies' globalization aspirations and reduce what was and still is largely a monopolistic economy, it, however, drained confidence among local corporate and potential foreign investors.

While there was a drive for outward investment, internationally, the flow of foreign direct investment to the developing world has been very trivial. The 14.9 percent of total international share of foreign direct investment since 1997 is roughly half the amount of foreign direct investment South Africa requires per annum for reducing unemployment. By 2002, South Africa was still far behind other African countries in attracting foreign direct investment from the U.S. For instance, in the same financial year, South Africa received US$112 million in foreign direct investment, while Nigeria received US$922 million.[88] Because of sanctions, comparative figures for South Africa are only available from 1994 onwards. However, despite the new democracy and the opening up of the economy, in Africa's three top earners of foreign direct investment, South Africa does not come first:

However, South Africa's free trade agreement with the U.S., is expected to boost the trickling foreign direct investment. Further obstructing realization of this goal is the low rate of productivity in South Africa. For instance,

Table 4.3. FDI Net Flow Units: Million US$, 1994–2000[89]

FDI: Net Flow Units: Millions US$							
	1994	1995	1996	1997	1998	1999	2000
Angola	170	472	181	412	1.114	2.471	1.698
Nigeria	1.959	1.079	1.593	1.539	1.051	1.004	1.082
South Africa	374	1.248	816	3.811	500	1.503	961

Table 4.4. The Flow of Foreign Direct Investment: US$, 1997–2002[91]

The Flow of World's Total Foreign Direct Investment, 1997–2002						
	1997	1998	1999	2000	2001	2002
China	44.2	43.8	38.8	38.4	44.2	52.7
Indonesia	4.7	-0.4	-2.7	-4.6	-3.3	-2.3
Malaysia	5.1	2.2	3.9	3.8	0.6	..
Singapore	10.7	6.4	11.8	5.4	8.6	..
Russia	4.9	2.8	3.3	2.7	2.5	2.4
South Africa	3.8	0.6	1.5	1.0	7.3	0.7

in manufacturing for every dollar of labor that is purchased, the output is only two dollars, whereas for South Africa's competitors like Brazil and South Korea, the output is five dollars, over twice as much.[90] Thus, their relative productivity is about twice as much as South Africa's. South Africa needs to make a quantum leap in order to attract sufficient direct investment required for real development and to cut through unemployment. This would require total reform of the labor market and the education system.

As the table shows, in the six years between 1997 and 2002, China attracted half of foreign direct investment destined for the developing world, while South Africa was only able to attract a total of 14.9 in the same six year period. According to the United States International Trade Commission, in 2002, U.S. Sub-Saharan Africa merchandize trade totaled US$24.1 billion, down from US$27.8 billion in 2001. Unlike foreign direct investment, which is unpredictable, increased domestic investment safeguards the economy in the face of adverse effects. According to Rodrick at least four institutions are required for this initiative: a) property rights and contract enforcement institutions; b) institutions governing economies of scale concerning companies; c) institutions for monetary and fiscal management; and d) institutions for social protection and insurance.[92]

It is growth that generates the means in the form of taxes to pay for the delivered development. GEAR's limited success in achieving growth rates of at least three percent of the targeted six percent obviously revealed its acceptance by capital, regrettably, with desultory benefits to labor. Ultimately, over time the continuing unemployment crisis may reduce government's tax base. It was out of this understanding that a Growth and Development Summit took place in June 2003. The summit, consisting of government, labor and business pledged to work together towards the provision of investment necessary for economic growth. This marked the beginning of collective action by government, labor and the private sector towards a proper development strategy, which GEAR is not. It was understood that the current growth rates of between two and three percent coupled with investment levels of 15 percent of GDP are not adequate to reduce unemployment. A key area of discussion at the summit was that cutting into the growing unemployment rate requires a six percent growth rate and increased domestic investment, which is necessary for the latter. In the words of President Mbeki, the "Growth and Development Summit" had the following principal objectives.

> First, to build an enduring and lasting partnership between government and the social partners, namely business, labor and the community. Such a partnership is crucial to ensure that a shared vision and commitment to tackle the legacy of unemployment, poverty, and challenge of social development and economic growth is developed. Second, there is a need to tackle urgent challenges that face the country. There is also a need for joint interventions that have the potential to make the biggest impact in the shortest possible time. These interventions relate to accelerating investments, job creation, greater equity, and the fairer distribution of economic opportunities. Of cause, all partners had their own ideas about how that investment and the subsequent job creation will be generated, promoted and sustained.[93]

A breakdown of their different views is as follows:

The summit expressed a realization that government alone cannot create enough jobs, address the challenge of increasing investments, or resolve the skills constraint. It requires a partnership with other stakeholders in the economy based on a shared vision. As an outcome of the Growth and Development Summit, the constituencies recognized that the aggregate levels of fixed direct investment are central for growth and that current levels are insufficient to achieve the desired growth and employment rates. An agreement was reached in which the constituencies agreed to encourage investment, including business (local, foreign, public and private), retirement funds, the life assurance industry, government, labor and community organizations, to work towards investing at least five percent of their income in appropriate financial institutions.[95] How these initiatives will take place remains to be worked out.

Through GEAR, the government has assiduously worked to achieve internationally acceptable standards of orthodox economic management.

Table 4.5. What the Social Partners Wanted[94]

Business	Labor	Government
Investment • The creation of an investment friendly environment, for example, labor market reform and reviewing of micro-economic factors.	Cosatu: Restructure the formal sector by gearing the economy towards job creation growth, for example, labor-based methods in construction and training for project managers. Fedusa: The construction of new social and economic infrastructure centered on a labor-based rather than an equipment-based approach.	• A focus on public infrastructure investment that, for example, includes the construction of social and economic infrastructure and the formation of a joint task team to address urban and rural development investment. To strengthen the design of public-private partnerships.
Job creation • A public works program to provide small income and skills development for the unemployed. • The implementation of a Regulatory Impact Assessment to ensure the level and costs of regulation for small business are appropriate.	Cosatu: public works and community service programs should create 500,000 jobs a year. • All major players in the public and private sectors should include in their annual report an assessment of their progress in creating jobs both directly and indirectly in line with the Johannesburg Stock Exchange sustainability index. • A workforce of one million people at R1, 000 per month would cost R12 billion per year.	• Expanded public works program through labor intensive methods. • Enterprise support and empowerment by strengthening small business incentives, improving access to financial services, training and mentorship. • Labor based social, municipal service delivery and community development programs.

There were implicit assumptions that once that recognition has been secured, foreign direct investment necessary to achieve GEAR's targets would inevitably follow. In essence, GEAR sought to solicit foreign direct investment to South Africa by presenting an image of a credible government committed to austere practices of the neo-liberal economic regime. This in itself has very broad appeals, but lessons from the flow of foreign direct investment internationally reveal that investors do not invest to extricate an economy from its morass. Instead, as the example of China shows in the table above, investment follows rather than leads economic growth, there is an element of reciprocity. As one interviewee puts it, "investors are attracted by real opportunities on the ground."[96] Growth, which was predicated on growing foreign direct investment, has so far remained sluggish and deep social inequalities are instead increasing.[97] Susan George reminds us that, "it is not accidental that, depending on the year, two-thirds or three-quarters of all the money labeled 'foreign direct investment' is not devoted to new job-creating investment but to mergers and acquisition, which almost invariably result in job losses."[98]

The absence of foreign investment has now sparked an old African debate on self-reliance through increased domestic investment as opposed to dependency on foreign direct investment. The hard lesson from GEAR, as Hein Marais points out, is that macroeconomic stability is a necessary condition, but not a sufficient one for growth and development; wealth generation does not necessarily reduce poverty. The richest country on earth, the U.S., exhibits disturbing levels of inequality, while one of the poorest, Cuba, justifiably earn kudos for lessening inequality.[99]

GEAR AND THE LABOR MARKET

With the introduction of GEAR, government envisaged the development of a humane labor market together with skills development programs to encourage job creation.[100] Conversely, a closer analysis of South Africa's transition reveals that it was actually GEAR's envisaged development of this flexible labor market that has caused enormous job losses. In terms of GEAR's projections, there were meant to be 101,000 new jobs in 1997 and 84,000 in 1998. In practice, there was a net loss of more than 130,000 jobs by the end of 1998.[101] Recent official statistics for the year 2002 reveal that unemployment increased from 16 percent in 1995 to 40 percent in 2002. During this period, 1995–2002, the economy lost more than one million jobs.[102] This is contrary to GEAR's projection of employment creation of 1.3 million jobs for the same period.

The casualties have, however, been African youth and those in the rural areas. People under the age of 30 faced a 47 percent unemployment rate in 2001—70 percent of all unemployed.[103] In total, there were 40.5 million people in 1996 and there were 44.8 million in 2001. This is very critical at a time when reducing unemployment remains the key to an improved economy. The proponents of GEAR justified their relative positions through reference to its predecessor, the RDP. They described it as a framework that made possible the sustainable implementation of the RDP, through ensuring macroeconomic stability. Opponents of GEAR argue that the framework was not appropriate to the implementation of the RDP; it served, in fact, to seriously undermine the state's ability to address the inherited apartheid legacy, or "social deficit."[104] The reason for this is that GEAR was introduced to gain investor confidence. As one Cosatu interviewee puts it, "the focus has been on efficiency and competencies, here there has been remarkable success, but it has not been linked to labor retention. Competencies and efficiencies require high skills which we do not have owing to high illiteracy."[105]

The lack of consultation with the alliance partners, Cosatu and the SACP meant that the consequences of GEAR were not properly thought through, especially regarding the labor market. Indeed, as Parsons, put it, "macroeconomic policy was too readily assumed to be a panacea for all structural problems in the South African economy."[106] The lack of consultation meant that important institutions for the national bargaining forum such as the National Economic Development and Labor Council (NEDLAC), which deliberates on socio-economic and development policies, and consists of representatives from employers, workers, government and community organizations, played a very insignificant role. More importantly, the key public finance and monetary policy chamber in NEDLAC was boycotted by Cosatu and the SACP after GEAR was announced unilaterally. As Parsons puts it, "the NEDLAC chamber became a lightning conductor for opposition to GEAR."[107]

It is important to note that the power to bring GEAR to all its outcomes did not rest on it being a macroeconomic policy, but to the consensus within the alliance partners, which would have resulted in a different policy altogether. Unfortunately, policy-makers deliberately avoided seeking consensus. Even in democracies, some issues are not open for debate. New evidence reveal that in the midst of opposition to GEAR, Trevor Manuel (the Finance Minister) "was nonetheless able and willing to have regular bilateral policy sessions with business associations like the South African Chamber of Business and the Chamber of Mines," the main beneficiaries of GEAR.[108] GEAR could not balance fiscal conservatism with the need for social justice.

THE NEW LABOR LAWS

Because apartheid was based on the need for "cheap labor," of which the gold mining industry was the main beneficiary, the new democratic order changed the labor market regime in accordance with the Bill of Rights. The centrality of labor exploitation and its dehumanizing aspects, particularly in unskilled work, meant that reviewing labor laws became central to the post-apartheid reconstruction. Andre Roux notes that "an economy growing at three percent would have no prospect of resolving South Africa's endemic unemployment crisis, unless there was a miraculous improvement in labor absorption."[109] The need for such labor absorption was contradicted by legislative instruments that were to be implemented, which sought primarily to protect workers and fundamentally change the conditions of employment. The laws introduced include the following; Labor Relations Act (1995), the Basic Conditions of Employment Act (1997), the Employment Equity Act (1998). The laws focus more on the welfare of workers in formal employment, ignoring the plight of the real poor, those in the informal economy, that is, the space within which those who are marginalized from the first economy operate—and the unemployed.[110] The table below presents the main features of these pieces of legislation:

While there was genuine need for worker protection, the timing for introducing labor laws seems to have been taken for granted, as the country faced a 33 percent unemployment rate by the time both GEAR and the labor laws were introduced (1995–1998). Instead of encouraging employers to hire, the new labor laws imposed stringent requirements on employers. The legislation received support from organized labor, but is perceived by business and investors as being in conflict with the spirit of GEAR because of the increased labor market regulation it embodies. The legislation demanded an element of responsibility, requiring employers to implement new work practices at a time when industries were more concerned about cutting production costs and the need to be competitive at the global level. In essence, the laws undermined competitiveness at the international level, and, therefore, investment.[112] What eventually happened was the replacement of unregulated low-wage employment with a state-regulated labor market system. In fact, labor productivity grew by four percent, but it was achieved only at the cost of a significant reduction in formal-sector employment.

The labor legislation formed the cornerstone of South Africa's labor market transformation. The main benefit of the Labor Relations Act has been the strengthening of workers organizational and trade union rights, protec-

Table 4.6. New Labor Laws, 1994–1999[111]

Name of Act	Key Aims	Institutional Implications	Key Provisions
Labor Relations Act, 1995	Promote orderly collective bargaining, workplace democracy and effective resolution of labor disputes.	• New dispute resolution institutions including the Labor Court and the Commission for Conciliation, Mediation and Arbitration (CCMA).	• Voluntary centralized industry-level collective bargaining through the setting up of bargaining, and statutory councils; • Extension of bargaining Council agreements to non-parties and provision for exemptions; • The establishment of workplace forums • Regulation of unfair Dismissals.
Basic Conditions of Employment Act, 1997	• Extend and improved 'floor' of rights to all workers; • Improve enforcement mechanisms.	• Replacement of Wage Board by an Employment Conditions Commission (ECC) Labor inspectorate to be improved and given responsibility for monitoring and enforcement.	• Introduction of a 45-hour week (goal of 40 hour week); • Increase in overtime payment, 21 days' annual leave, 4 months' maternity leave, and family responsibility leave; • Changes to notice provisions, and new regulations on termination of employment.

(continued)

Table 4.6. New Labor Laws, 1994–1999[111] (continued)

Name of Act	Key Aims	Institutional Implications	Key Provisions
Employment Equity Act, 1998	• Eliminate unfair discrimination; • Ensure the implementation of affirmative action.	• Commission for Employment Equity (CEE), responsible for advising the Minister on codes of good practice.	• Prohibition of unfair Dismissal; • Designated employers draw up employment equity plans that will be submitted to the Department of Labor; • Every designated employer must take measures to reduce *wage differentials* subject to such guidance as may be given by the Minister of Labor (upon advice of CEE).

tion of workers in legal strikes and extension of unions to cover all workers, including historically excluded public service, farm, domestic and mine workers. The Basic Conditions of Employment Act's aim was to provide a floor of basic employment standards for all workers, such as the phasing-in of paid maternity leave for four months. The Employment Equity Act sought to advance the constitutional right to equality and called for the implementation of measures to redress past imbalances and prohibit as well as prevent unfair discrimination in the employment context as stipulated in Section 9(1) and (2) of the Constitution which read: "Everyone is equal before the law and has the right to equal protection and benefit of the law. Equality concludes the full and equal enjoyment of all rights and freedoms."

Such legislation posed a threat to the mining industry's privileged access to "cheap labor," as for the first time the unions demanded their application to the mines. For the NUM, the laws had some benefits and as one interviewee puts it, "we have been accorded new opportunities to bargain for medical aid and social services that benefit miners."[113] In response, the mining industry became more determined to not employ new entrants under stringent laws that require an element of responsibility towards employees. Indeed, as one interviewee with the Chamber of Mines put it, "wage increases (required by the Employment Equity Act, 1998) have had the consequences of job loses."[114] It can be argued that these shortcomings were and still are well known to the ANC. For instance, in his State of the Nation address on February 4, 2000, President Mbeki acknowledged that "certain aspects of the legislative instruments aimed at giving effect to the government's labor market policy have had unintended consequences."[115] They have, in the words of former Director General of the National Treasury, "reduced the labor absorption capacity of the formal economy."[116]

The concerns with the labor laws led in 2002 to a major development in an agreement reached between labor and business to amend the Labor Relations Act and the Basic Conditions of Employment Act. The amendments relax those sections of legislation that make it difficult to hire employees, amongst others, the right to dismiss workers even where there are reasonable grounds to do so. In this regard, business made concessions on terms and conditions of retrenchment and labor accepted employer's right to retrench after consultation.

* * * * *

Generally, in restructuring, there is often an element of trade-off between employment and the cost of labor, especially when it comes to wages. So, as the cost of labor increases, competitiveness requires that employers mechanize, thus putting substantial capital investment, which reduces the cost of production (by reducing the amount of labor) in the long term. This is the reality of the current South African labor market. Companies that once employed thousands have reduced labor turnover to become globally competitive as the economy opened up. Whereas the apartheid machinery was designed to make labor plentiful, and since its structures actually remained in place, there is an oversupply of labor as the job-creating capacity of the economy shrinks under market deregulation. Ultimately, it is the poor who absorb the impact of a malfunctioning labor market, thus strengthening their disenchantment with the system. As a result of the restructuring process, the government is increasingly confronted by negative sentiments from domestic social forces, which undermines the potential for a national development project.[117]

There have been many criticisms of GEAR as macroeconomic policy, but these criticisms are not substantiated by any rigorous analysis of its impact on a specific industry. Since GEAR came into being, the South African media has been inundated by analyses that sought to dissect its impact and performance against its own targets. While GEAR was a macroeconomic fiscal stabilization policy, the impression was created at the time of its adoption that it was also a development strategy, that is, a strategy that would deliver people from their miserable lot to the ideal "better life for all."

As a macroeconomic stabilization policy, GEAR has made remarkable strides. For instance, the budget deficit has come down from 9.5 percent in 1993 to fractionally over one percent in 2002/3. In addition, foreign reserves have risen from one month's import cover to two-and-a-half months' import cover. According to the ANC election manifesto for the 2004 general elections, "South Africa achieved a level of macro economic stability not seen in 40 years."[118] There has been an inflation rate of six percent, declining interest rates, and a stable political environment. All these look good on paper but have not been enough to propel the economy beyond three percent per year or encourage a rush of confidence among investors.[119] Although most progressive economists pointed the weakness of GEAR, in terms of job creation, their analyses were largely ignored.

Jobless Growth? An Analysis

Although South Africa is technically considered a middle-income country, it has one of the world's largest disparities between its rich and the poor, and that gap continues to be drawn largely along racial lines. This is the legacy of apartheid, but the post-apartheid economic restructuring has inadvertently served to exacerbate the divide. GEAR presents an opportunity for most employers to reduce production costs to become globally competitive. Regrettably, the casualties of this restructuring have been unskilled and semi-skilled laborers who generally have little education and no job experience.

The true victims of apartheid continue to be excluded from the formal labor market. This in itself is a legacy of economic dualism, that is, a situation "where much of the population was excluded from the formal sector."[120] In 2003, President Mbeki referred to this as the "two economies." However, the logic of GEAR was that growth in the first economy will benefit those in the second economy. But if the second economy is widely regarded as variously isolated, subsistence-based, feudal, or pre-capitalist and therefore more underdeveloped, how can it benefit if it is too marginalized to be able to share in the first economy benefits? Gunder Frank believed the thesis of economic dualism is false and cautioned against these distinctions. If acted upon, he argued that these distinctions "serve only to intensify and perpetuate the very conditions of underdevelopment they are supposedly designed to remedy."[121] Apartheid aggravated this dualism by denying the majority rights in the formal sector. In addition to this dualism, the structure of the formal sector limits job creation. Furthermore, nine years after democracy, "three million households were without houses, 7.5 million without access to running water and 21 million were without sanitation. Five million South Africans were HIV positive and the crime rate was among the highest in the world."[122]

It has been estimated that "three to four percent of the workforce will die each year from AIDS after 2003/4, and that this will cost companies that wish to invest in the country between 3.5 and 6.3 percent of their salaries and wage bill in benefits, absenteeism, retraining and other costs."[123] A survey of South Africa by the *Financial Times* of London estimated that the high HIV/AIDS infection rate would knock 17 percent off the GDP in the next decade.[124] Still, South Africa is not achieving the necessary growth rate to reduce unemployment. While the government pursues neo-liberal free market policies and remain impervious to popular rejection of neo-liberal economics, in the long run it may not be able to afford to allow the poor and the destitute (who make up the majority of its political constituency) to live without hope. The fulcrum between democracy and social entitlement has shifted significantly. As such, new ferments with deep lasting impact—service delivery protests—have already started to reverberate (see Chapter Five). It is therefore important, as Berman points out:

> The autonomy and legitimacy of the state, the fundamental separation of economic and political spheres, require constant efforts to renew and maintain them in the face of the actual involvement of states in accumulation and class struggle, ranging from the high levels of coercion during the period of primitive accumulation to the continually expanding and ever-more complex forms of state management in contemporary capitalist societies.[125]

Prior to GEAR, in 1995, 1.9 million people were unemployed. In 2002, their number blossomed to 4.9 million (officially) and 8.1 million (unofficially). The major obstacle towards realizing GEAR's employment targets has been the meagre record of economic growth rate. Making the fight against unemployment hard is that the more success South Africa has in its efforts to diversify the economy away from raw material resources, the fewer people it is able to employ. For instance, according to the Department of Trade and Industry, manufacturing production grew by 3.5 percent in 2002 and it was estimated to grow by 4.4 percent in 2003 and 5.5 percent in 2004.[126] For the year 2002 the growth in output was largely driven by exports with a favorably weaker rand against the U.S. dollar. However, due to improvements in productivity and the poor performance of sectors serving mainly the slack domestic economy, despite this growth, employment has been falling at more than two percent per year; thus, jobless growth.[127] While acknowledging improved economic growth rates, it has been a rather skewed middle-class consumer boom, while millions become victims of neo-liberal economics—impoverished and destitute. Despite the fact that government has identified insufficient rate of investment as the main culprit for sluggish economic growth rates, fiscal conservatism has taken precedent over much-needed investments in redistribution and poverty reduction.

Most economists have insisted that the solution for the jobless growth that the economy has experienced lies in pay cuts. For instance, according to Johannes Fedderke, a one percent reduction in the real cost of labor in the manufacturing sector would lead to a 0.7 expansion in job opportunities. If the manufacturing industry had taken the average inflation adjusted wage in 1998 and decreased it from R4,358.48 to R4,314.90 a month—a loss per worker of R43.58 in monthly earnings, the result would have been 9,462 jobs created in the manufacturing sector with each worker earning a slightly lower wage of R4,314.90.[128] Following this analysis, South Africa's current economic growth trajectory can best be described as "job destroying." However, given

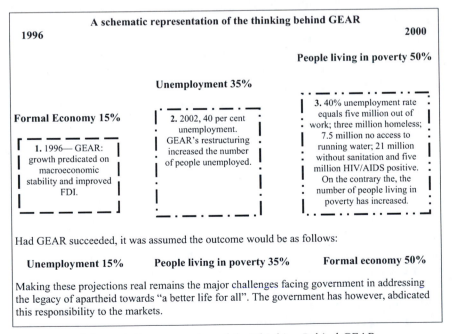

Figure 4.2. A Schematic Representation of the Thinking Behind GEAR

the orthodoxy of macroeconomic management, a World Bank-funded report attributed massive job losses to the "hastle factor associated with excessive labor market regulation and crime, rather than situating them as the results of globalization and conglomerate restructuring."[129]

As the diagram represents, South Africa needed a development strategy and GEAR is not that. GEAR is incapable of addressing the unemployment crisis in the economy.[130] Macroeconomic stabilization has become the primary government priority leaving the structural realities that constitute poverty untouched. GEAR compromises the ability of the state to be developmental as its rigid targets prevent any meaningful interventions, for instance, on issues of social justice. There is a need to redefine the growth path. Unemployment and poverty are inseparable and there are obvious implications of the growing unemployment, the most terrifying being the increasing threat of social unrest. The economy is growing, but it is a jobless growth.

CONCLUDING REMARKS

Although the RDP could not achieve meaningful economic growth rates, the adoption of GEAR reiterated the long-standing problem of African leaders since independence—balancing their desire for autonomy with their yearning need for help. This problem was identified earlier with the independence of Ghana when the then President, Kwame Nkrumah, coined the concept of neo-colonialism.[131] It was part of a burgeoning consciousness developing among postcolonial elites in Africa that gaining independence and the national sovereignty of African states was purely token and in no substantial way altered the relationship between the colonial powers and the colonized state. Thus, neo-colonialism means that the state is in theory independent and has all the outward trappings of international sovereignty, but in reality it is subject to control by external forces.

Real power is economic, and this reality is reflected in South Africa's social realities. While the struggle against apartheid took long, partially, it eventually succeeded. There is an unwillingness to believe that just at the moment when the struggle seemed won, suddenly appropriate policies towards a "better life for all" cannot be implemented, an inadvertent yet humiliating dereliction of duty. The struggle was precisely fought so that economic benefits accrue to all as apartheid intentionally skewed the balance in favor of whites. This was bad enough, and instead of the current economic policies addressing the legacy of apartheid, they are simply continuing where apartheid left off in pillaging the poor. Inevitably, organized labor argues that the ANC had reneged on its promise and deserted the poor.

The opening epigraph to this chapter reveals the economic position that Nelson Mandela believed to be the policy of the ANC. However, the political economy of South Africa's transition is centered on the extent to which capital successfully bought new devout proselytes to the neo-liberal fold in the struggle for a new accumulation strategy. When examining the political economy of South Africa's transition, especially changes from the RDP to GEAR, one gets the impression that once the ANC realized how limited its options were in terms of pursuing a socialist oriented development strategy, it swiftly embraced capitalism and became a bearer of the neo-liberal flag. It was an internal choice, after acknowledging that pursuing alternative policies would be costly or impossible. The hegemony of neo-liberalism limited the scope for choice. Difficult as it was fighting apartheid, it is equally difficult to implement sound policies that alleviate poverty. Unless there are serious reviews of the economic framework, the unemployment crisis will degenerate and the divide between the rich and the poor will continue to widen with adverse repercussions in the near future.

Inequality, crime and poverty in South Africa are driven by the lack of wage income. By failing to create jobs, GEAR has not been an antidote, as labor markets have shut the most vulnerable citizens out of jobs.[132] The absence of effective safety nets means that even those who are employed are haunted by the prospects of sliding into poverty. With the levels of discontent increasing, the poor, the unemployed and the destitute want to see immediate changes. However, for now, the ANC remains the only credible organization, one they have supported throughout the struggle, which can improve their lives, only if some policies are changed.

Echoing Gilbert Rist, the promise of a better life appears to recede like a horizon just as the unemployed, poor and destitute South Africans think they are approaching it.[133] Unfortunately, the current economic policies prioritize economic reforms at their expense. Sadly, structural realities of contemporary international political economy leave little room for alternative development paths and the levers for change are beyond the state. Although with evident uneasiness, even internationally, eternal communists (see Chapter Five) are beginning to accept the realities of capitalism, and the goal of grand socialism is steadily becoming an artifact in the museum of antiquity. Whether South Africa could have pressed on with socialist policies against the wishes of the International Financial Institutions is a moot point and would be speculative as GEAR was self-imposed.

GEAR, Gold and Labor: The Politics of Redistribution

INTRODUCTION

South Africa's transition successfully put in place a democratic system that upholds Western values: a capitalist market system, multi-party political system, human rights and tolerance. While this transition is still in process, the adoption of GEAR and the subsequent embrace of a strict form of neo-liberalism have exacerbated the weakening position of organized labor, Cosatu in general. GEAR, in the language of Presidents Nelson Mandela, Thabo Mbeki and Minister Trevor Manual, was non-negotiable, which meant that organized labor could not bargain its contents for the benefit of job preservation it had believed the ANC would support.

Since the advent of capitalism in South Africa, the workplace has, for blacks, been a source of anguished experience and thwarted aspirations. While labor had legitimate expectations, today the bourgeoning black middle class and capital continue to reap the benefits of the struggle. Even though this reality has strained the ANC alliance, improving economic performance demoralizes critics as it affords the ANC a great measure of support, especially from the constituency that seems to matter most, which is capital.

This chapter presents a retrospective analysis of the transition and dissects the position of capital, politics and labor in the post-GEAR period. It assesses the extent to which restructuring and the new mode of accumulation have benefited the gold mining industry through a comparison with other major gold producers; Australia, Canada and the U.S. The rationale for this comparison is to demonstrate the extent to which the new modes of regulation and accumulation enabled South Africa's gold industry to adjust its operations and compete with other major gold producers in the absence of "cheap labor."

It was only through the new mode of regulation that South Africa's gold industry could acquire a new lease of life, globalize its activities and compete at the international level. This could not be achieved under sanctions and international isolation during apartheid. The analysis focuses on the main thematic areas; first, the position of the gold mining industry and its relationship with the new ANC government after the transition; second, the position of labor after GEAR and third, the status of the tripartite alliance between the ANC, Cosatu and SACP in the post-GEAR period; and fourth, a synthesis of the relative positions of the state, the economy and organized labor in the first decade of democracy.

GOLD MINING IN THE NEW MILLENNIUM: AN INDUSTRY IN CRISIS?

In contrast to other industries such as manufacturing, gold mining presents unique challenges in that its profits are determined by prices fixed in foreign currencies. The introduction of a fluctuating rand exchange rate in March 1995 and GEAR's economic restructuring mean that when the rand rallies against major international currencies, especially the American dollar, on which gold prices are fixed, the gold mining industry, which has been so dependent on a stable, or fixed, gold price and an overly protected currency under apartheid, becomes unstable. Often, the fluctuations are favourable. For instance, despite a 2.9 percent decline in the average gold price from US$278 to US$271 an ounce in 2001, the 24 percent decline in the rand/dollar exchange rate resulted in the rand gold price rising by 21 percent from R1,847 to R2,338 an ounce. Accordingly, the higher rand gold price resulted in the total value of South Africa's gold sales rising by 14 percent from R25 billion in 1999 to R29 billion in 2001.

Furthermore, according to the Chamber of Mines, during the later part of 2001, the decline in the rand exchange rate resulted in the rand gold price escalating to R3.210 an ounce in December. Cost containment in production and the decline in the exchange rate resulted in South Africa's total cost of producing an ounce of gold falling from US$254 in 2000 to US$214 in 2001.[1] This helped South Africa to remain the lowest cost large-scale gold producer in the world. The higher rand gold price provided gold mines with the flexibility to mine lower grades. The total operating profit rose 38.2 percent from R1.05 billion in 2000 to R1.7 billion in 2001. Higher operating profit levels provided reasonable optimism for future exploration. At the end of 2001, the Johannesburg Stock Exchange's All Gold index was 1,775 points—103.2 percent higher than at the end of 2000.

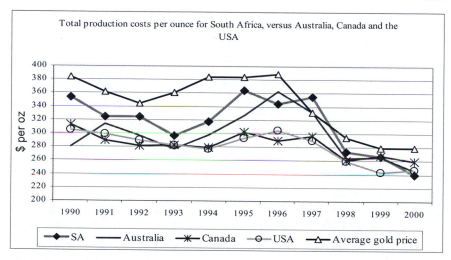

Figure 5.1. Total Production Costs per Ounce for South Africa versus Australia, Canada and the U.S., 1990–2000.

Source: Unpublished Data: Chamber of Mines' Economics Division

The currency fluctuations helped the industry earn remarkable profits. According to the Chamber of Mines' *Annual Report* for 2003, the gold mining industry was the star performer in the mineral sector in South Africa with total sales increasing by 42.7 percent to a record R41.4 billion.[2] For the first time since 1993, gold production increased by 0.4 percent to 395.2 tons as the price of gold exceeded US$400 an ounce. Gold production on Chamber member mines increased by 15 percent to 347.5 tons as a result of a 2.6 percent increase in the average grade of ore mined (4.2 grams per ton).

However, fluctuations may not always be favourable and the gold price may decline lower than the unit cost of producing an ounce. For instance, as the figure above indicates, this happened in 1997 when the fluctuation in the rand/dollar exchange made the cost of gold production in South Africa more than the unit price of gold itself. This put the future of South African gold production into question. However, production cost was immediately brought below the price of gold in 1998. Australia escaped the crisis by a small margin in the same period. The price of gold was US$385 per ounce in 1996; it dropped drastically to US$280 by 1999, and this was lower than the unit cost of production for all gold producers by 1997 prices. Eventually, all gold producers: Australia, Canada and the U.S. were forced to reduce their cost of production to at least US$240. Being an emerging economy meant that South Africa was—and still remains—vulnerable to market volatility than its competitors.

As the figure above shows, during the 1990s, South Africa's gold mining industry was on average far more costly to operate than Australia, Canada and the U.S. Ostensibly this may be attributed to the large-scale operations of the industry. To reverse the trend, urgent measures needed to be taken. The restructuring process intensified and spawned spectacular achievements, particularly through escalating the retrenchment process and reprocessing of tailings. Production costs became lower than the average gold price and even below the average cost for Australia, Canada and the U.S. With a fair degree of success, the restructuring process (new gold processing techniques and the sub-contracted component of labor, which is not unionized and therefore cheaper) salvaged South Africa's gold mining industry from its crisis.

This is clearly visible when South Africa's cost of production is compared with the average for Australia, Canada and the U.S. as one trend between 1989 and 2004. South Africa continued to mine gold cheaply at US$214 per ounce against an average of US$240 for Australia, Canada and the U.S. For South Africa, producing an ounce at US$214 by the year 2000 was a significant improvement on the US$360 in 1995, which had made profit margins insignificant. For instance South Africa's gold mining

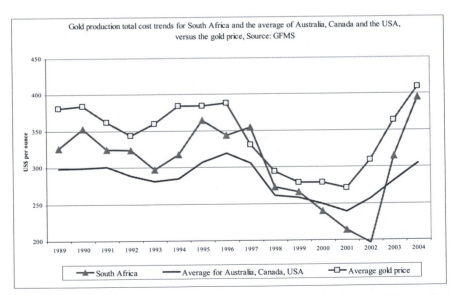

Figure 5.2. Gold Production Total Cost Trends for SA and the Average of Australia, Canada and the U.S. versus the Gold Price.

Source: Unpublished Data: Chamber of Mines' Economics Division

industry made a profit of US$25 per ounce when the gold price was US$385 as compared to the average profit of US$85 for Australia, Canada and the U.S. during the same period. However, Canada and the U.S. were producing an ounce at US$300 (that for South Africa was US$360) against the gold price of US$380 in the same period.

There are numerous explanations to the sudden rise in South Africa's production costs from mid-2002 onwards (figure 5.2 above). In December 2001, the rand reached a low point of R13.72 to the U.S. dollar. However, it appreciated by as much as 50.3 percent against the U.S. dollar to reach a high of R6.82 in October 2003, an appreciation by more than 50 percent. This made the rand to be one of the best performing emerging market currencies by 2004. The strong rand eroded profit margins leading to profit losses and shaft closures. As a result, South Africa's gold production declined by 4.7 percent to 375.8 tons in 2003. Total gold sales declined by R3.13 billion in 2003, 20 percent decline on 2002 profits. Notwithstanding high U.S. dollar commodity prices, the strong rand led to the rand values of mineral sales declining significantly since 2003. For instance, the average gold price in dollar terms for 2003 was up 15 percent to US$356.60 an ounce, but fell in rand terms by 15 percent to R88.533 a kilogram. During the same period, average cash rose some 43 percent to US$256 an ounce and total production cost rose 56 percent to US$390 an ounce by 2004. Overall, the strong rand meant that South Africa moved rapidly from being the cheapest large-scale gold producer to be the most expensive. This development put an estimated 120,000 miners at risk on marginal mines—the consequences of which could be devastating. Amongst others, factors contributing to the rand strength include the following:

- The continued weakness of the U.S. dollar;
- Continued prudent economic policies;
- Expectations of significant future foreign direct investment (FDI) flows;
- Improved international credit ratings; and
- Strong foreign currency prices of South Africa's export commodities.[3]

As indicated on Figure 3.1 in Chapter Three, at US$200 South Africa's amount of recoverable reserve ore increases to 20,000 tonnes as opposed to 17,000 tonnes at US$257 production cost an ounce. Lower production costs mean more gold can be mined. Thus, in 1995 and 1997 when South Africa was producing gold at roughly US$365 per ounce, the future of gold mining looked bleak due to the amount of recoverable gold at that price. On the profit side, if the cost of production is lower and the rand/dollar exchange rate is higher, for instance 10 rands for US$1, South Africa's gold mining industry makes remarkable profits.

When these fluctuations occur, most mines whose profits are pushed to the margins either retrench relentlessly to reduce production costs or reach the end of their production life and subsequently close down. The large scale of gold mining means that a significant number of mines are pushed to their margins. It is largely these marginal mines that consortiums of Black Economic Empowerment (BEE) buy and rehabilitate, sometimes with remarkable success depending on the value of the rand against the U.S. dollar and cost of production. In most of the closed mines, operations resume when the exchange rate and profit margins are favourable.

The fluctuations have been more volatile in South Africa since 1998 than in most emerging markets. What can be deduced from these fluctuations is that due to unstable and unpredictable market price and demand, today gold mining is no longer dependent on the abundance of "cheap labor," but on the unit price of the commodity and the margin between the cost of production and the unit price for an ounce. However, the unpredictability of currency trends means that small-scale gold producers are often caught off-guard.

With fluctuating exchange rates, some of the gold mines, and other industries that pay for raw materials in rands but count profits in dollars, have been the worst hit. One gold company, Durban Roodeport Deep (DRD), announced that it might have to cut 4,500 jobs in two mines. Buoyed by the rand's fall in early 2002, the company had responded by expanding its operations abroad. At the time, the price of gold was R2,841 an ounce and the company's cost of producing that ounce, amongst the highest for South Africa's gold mines, at R2,642.[4]

According to the Chamber of Mines' *Mining News*, DRD first warned in April 2003 that its margins had narrowed owing to the strengthening of the rand against the U.S. dollar. As the rand continued to strengthen throughout the third quarter of 2003, DRD was the top loss making gold mine in operation.[5] In response, it aimed to reduce gold output by 20 percent and reduce its workforce of 13,000 by a third in a battle to save the mine.[6] According to an interview with a National Union of Mineworkers official, it is those mines that have not restructured fast enough that are becoming marginal.[7] Paradoxically, the interviewee was referring to those mines that have not changed their operating procedures and still employ thousands of miners.

There are other variables apart from the strengthening rand, which help to explain DRD's crisis of September 2003. Normally, a strong rand has severe profit implications for mining houses as they receive dollars for their product, but report earnings in rands.[8] Surprisingly, even as the rand rallied to 6.3 to the U.S. dollar towards the end of November 2003, its strongest position in seven years, it was not accompanied by the familiar panic that characterized the gold mining industry in the late 1990s. This is because the price of gold reached a high of US$400 per ounce during the same period for the first time in seven years, even reaching a 15-year high of US$435 per ounce in April 2004. Thus, as the rand strengthened, the gold price also strengthened as a result of poor global economic performance.

Apart from the rise in gold price, the gold mining industry has been hedging its production sales. What this means is that the industry uses future sales of gold as an insurance policy against fluctuations in the price of gold. This strategy has been in place since the late 1990s when the industry's future looked bleak. According to GoldFields, hedging is important for protecting cash flows at times of significant expenditure, for specific debt servicing requirements and to safeguard the viability of higher cost operations. For instance, AngloGold has already sold the gold it will produce over a period of time at an agreed price. The strategy saved the future of the industry's operations, which, according to AngloGold's Chief Executive, Bobby Godsell, " . . . were running well and needed less insurance in 2003."[9]

THE ECONOMIC BENEFIT OF RESTRUCTURING IN THE GOLD MINES

The changing political landscape and GEAR's opening up of the economy compelled industries to restructure in order to compete at the international level. For the gold mining industry, this restructuring process has allowed the curtailment of escalation in real costs. Remarkably, although the gold mining industry became unstable with the opening up of the economy, the hedging strategy allowed the industry to sell its gold prior to extraction and processing, thus giving it a new lease of life. Overall, it is fair to argue that the South African gold mining industry has successfully weathered the storm of transition. AngloGold's *Annual Report* for 2002 noted:

Table 5.1. Delivering on Promise: AngloGold 2002[10]

What was promised for 2002	What was accomplished in 2002
Commitment to long-term target of eliminating all accidents at work	Long-term trend in lost time injuries decreased to 8.86 per million man hours, the lowest ever for Anglo-Gold.
Growing the company into the gold equity of choice and an investment that offers its shareholders competitive returns	During 2002, AngloGold was one of the top-performing resource stocks in the world. Its performance represented a total return to shareholders—a combination of share price performance and dividend of 98 per cent in dollar terms.
Drive the company down the cost curve	Total cash costs continued to decline—from US$178 per ounce by 10 per cent to US$161 per ounce—despite the impact of the strengthening rand on the South African operations.
Seek organic growth	Three new South African projects at Moab Khotsong, Tau Tona and Mponeng were on schedule. Sunrise dam expansion is complete, with the CC&V project nearing completion.
Continue near mine or Brownfields exploration	The AngloGold growth story continues, with 11.4 million ounces of new resources added at a cost of US$1.60 per ounce and 3.2 million ounces of new resources at a cost of US$4.40 per ounce.
Develop new Greenfields exploration projects	Exploration is continuing in countries in which AngloGold has operations, namely Argentina, Brazil, Tanzania, Mali, South Africa and the United States, as well as in prospective areas in Alaska, Canada and Peru. Some US$19 million was spent during the year.
Apply a disciplined acquisition strategy	AngloGold increased its stake from 46.25 per cent to 92.5 per cent in Cerro Vanguardia in Argentina during the year and continues to identify value-adding merger and acquisition opportunities.

Other South African gold mining houses such as GoldFields, Rand-Gold, Harmony and ArmGold were also able to realize significant trading profits. In its Annual Report for 2003, GoldFields reported that although its corporate strategy did not change, it has refined it and worked to consolidate the considerable momentum that has been developed in the past few years. Its vision remains to be the leading, value-adding, globally diversified, precious metals producer through "responsible, sustainable and innovative development of quality assets."[11] Its major objective remains the improvement of returns through the optimization of existing assets and diversification.

On average production costs, the gold mining industry appears to have been in crisis between 1987 and 1992 when virtually no profits were made (See also Figure 4.7. in Chapter Four). In addition, although profits improved between 1993 and 1996, the period 1997–1998 again did not register profits. As the figure below shows, this changed from 1999 onwards to 2002 when the industry registered remarkable profits.

As the figure below indicates, these losses worsened in the third quarter of 1997, but from then onwards, the industry did not suffer any

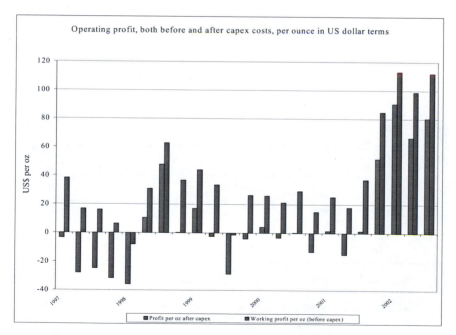

Figure 5.3. Operating Profits per Ounce in U.S. Dollars: Chamber Gold Mines
Source: Unpublished Data: Chamber of Mines' Economics Division

serious profit losses, except for the last quarter of 1999. Since 2000, the gold mining industry has been registering profits. This can be attributed to the weakening rand and a firmer gold price. Thus, the gold price has remained strong, which means that even as the rand rallies against the U.S. dollar, the industry does not find itself in a similar predicament of the late 1990s. Overall, the future looked good.

The restructuring process has meant changes in leadership; the industry consolidated and globalized its operations; management and work practices evolved towards increased productivity and efficiency and practices regarding human capital changed. These include job security and career paths that come with skilled labor. All these factors have made the gold mining industry more robust than it was in the past. For instance, the industry's domestic investment portfolio increased, with at least R20 billion committed to capital projects in South Africa between 2000 and 2004.[12] In addition, as an outcome of the Growth and Development Summit held in June 2003, the Chamber of Mines committed the mining sector's investment of R100 billion in capital projects approved for the period 2003–2007.[13] More importantly, the Chamber of Mines argues that cost containment and productivity measures are paying off, as the figure below indicates:

It is clear that the long-term prospects for mining in general look good. While gold production declined between 1999 and 2002, it is projected

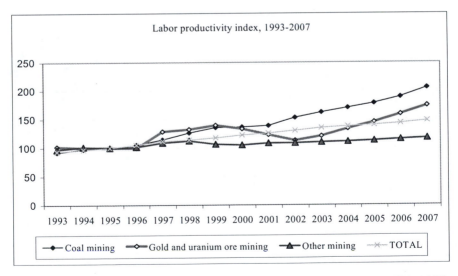

Figure 5.4. Overall Chamber of Mines Labor Productivity Projections, 1993–2007

Source: Unpublished Data: Chamber of Mines' Economics Division

to pick up significantly between 2003 and 2007. Apart from gold, overall projections for other minerals are encouraging. An increase in the demand for gold in the future cannot be ruled out. The European Central Bank's extension of the gold agreement from 2004 to 2009, which limits sales to 500 tons per year, provided the necessary stimuli for production.

The increase in gold production is projected along with a decreasing formal labor force and an increase in sub-contracted labor. These projected increases are based on a cumulative array of factors that have been positive for the gold market and for the gold price since 2002. Amongst others, the higher gold price from roughly US$270 in 2001 to over US$600 in early 2006; the weaker U.S. dollar; lower global interest rates and higher lease rates as well as increasing concerns regarding South Africa's corporate governance and the performance of major equity markets.[14]

Apart from these positive achievements, as South Africa consolidates its democracy, challenges that confront the industry in its future prospects remain. Amongst others, these include input cost pressures, which are fuelling inflation in costs (about R12.5 billion was paid to employees in the form of salaries and wages in 2004); how to continue to improve the productivity of inputs; and a rapidly changing legislative and regulatory environment which creates its own set of challenges.

Gold and Politics: Chamber of Mines and the ANC Government

The South African government has been steering the economy away from its traditional over-reliance on gold and mining generally, to other enterprises. There are at least two reasons for this shift; the first is economic, owing to the declining contribution of gold to South Africa's GDP and its fluctuations since 1994. The second may have to do with the love-hate relationship that exists between the industry and the ANC government. Owing to the industry's legacy of interference in the political landscape, it is a relationship of mutual suspicion.

While the industry played a prominent role in getting rid of apartheid, it was a strategic partner of the apartheid government and a major beneficiary of the dehumanising labor policies that were crafted. Industry's assistance in getting rid of apartheid may not have been a benign or genuine desire to see the alleviation of the plight Africans faced. Conversely, it is fair to argue that getting rid of apartheid was coerced by the classical capitalist imperatives—a need for favourable accumulation strategy that could only be realized through escaping the bottlenecks of South Africa's economic *laager* and internationalize operations. The mode of regulation reached a crisis point and could no longer support the mode of accumulation. Therefore, a new mode of regulation had to be secured first. Although gold has always been internationalized, the gold mining industry's operations were restricted to South Africa. Furthermore, the industry was the most protected in terms of its access to "cheap labor," which reduced production costs.

The Anglo American Corporation led the initiative of getting rid of apartheid once it realized the extent to which economic sanctions limited its business opportunities and finding itself confined in a saturated market, in which it had already established monopolies in every economic sphere that mattered. Since it was the mining industry's need for "cheap labor" that eventually brought misery to millions of South African for over a century, the ANC's strategy seems to have been to relocate economic focus to more potentially controllable enterprises of the economy. They certainly did not want to be held to ransom by an industry they had learned to detest for decades. Partly, the exploitations of the industry may have informed natural resource nationalization pledges of the Freedom Charter.

The industry appears to have taken a serious gamble. For, despite negotiating with the ANC to dispel its fears of the liberation movement and extending what must have appeared a cordial friendship with the enemy, the ANC, with Nelson Mandela articulating its policy, was initially determined that the nationalization of mines and minerals was still its policy. In the end, capital succeeded in convincing the ANC elites to rethink their policy, leading to the adoption of GEAR. Revolutionary nationalization pledges were renounced, economic pragmatism prevailed and a mode of accumulation whose fundamentals are even to the far right of traditionally conservative governments elsewhere was adopted. The trajectory of South Africa's accumulation strategy remained regulationist with enriched environment for companies to carry on with their business operations.

Sampie Terreblanche argues that corporate South Africa succeeded in convincing the ANC in two ways: first, by alleging that the capitalist or free market will promote "unspecified" (my emphasis) interests of the total population, irrespective of whether or not the economic system in South Africa can credibly be described as such. What was good for Anglo-American was good for the people. However, as this analysis shows, GEAR or neo-liberalism is good for business, but generally bad for the people. Second, through the contention that high economic growth rate in South Africa, despite deeply institutionalized inequalities, will automatically "trickle down" to the poor.[15] The argument that South Africa had a liberal capitalist system was wrong. As Terreblanche puts it, "if ever there was a myth that was carefully and assiduously cultivated while bearing little resemblance to reality, then this was/is it."[16] Indeed, the South African system is what Stephen Gelb has aptly referred to as "racial Fordism."[17] The mining industry's trade-off on the one hand appears to be BEE, which is diluting South Africa's racial capitalism at the top.

While GEAR has been good for the mining industry, the new labor laws, had adverse effects as they pushed the cost of production higher, but they inadvertently fast-tracked the restructuring process especially the retrenchment of miners to save costs. With new statutory provisions governing the labor market, the subordination of working conditions to production and profitability ceased. The Chamber welcomed the repeal of the new labor laws and there was no immediate cost threat to the industry's efficient operation. All along, things appeared to be falling in favour of the mining industry and its relationship with the ANC government improved, especially with the appointment of a first black chief executive of the Chamber, Mzolisi Diliza and recently, a first black president of the Chamber of Mines in more than 100 years, Lazarus Zim. The industry seems to be dealing with the ANC government by [ab]using ANC political activists and influential individuals sympathetic to the ANC's cause it could buy to its fold. As one Chamber of Mines executive told me, ". . . . if we had not had Diliza or an acceptable black chief executive, I think we would have been three or four years back down the line. I think that his credentials have so far changed the image of this industry."[18]

However, this relative comfort has changed as the government tries to maximize its returns from the industry's profits through taxation. In a move reminiscent of Paul Kruger's concession policy, the ANC government introduced statutory provisions to maximize revenue taxes paid by the mining industry. As industry's profits escalate, government became determined to maximize its returns. As the figure below indicates, as gold mining industry's profits soared, so did government taxes—but government wanted more:

Among the new statutory provisions, the first introduced was the Minerals and Petroleum Resources Development Act, (No. 28 of 2002). The Act makes special provision for the preservation of existing royalties payable by mines to communities or natural persons. This sought to redress historical injustice as communities were often forcibly removed from resource-rich areas with neither royalties nor provision of adequate alternative housing. Worse, in most instances they were dumped in arid uninhabitable areas. Second was the National Treasury's Royalty Bill, which gives effect to the Act's proposed royalty regime. It imposes a quarterly charge on holders of mineral rights for the extraction and transfer of South African mineral resources. It recognizes that the nation is entitled to a consideration for the extraction of its non-renewable mineral resources. The Royalty Bill obliges mines to pay a stipulated royalty. This amounts to a threat of double royalties. Government aimed to charge a royalty of eight percent

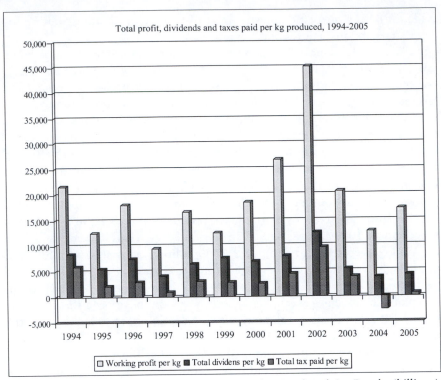

Figure 5.5. Profit, Dividends and Taxes per kg Produced in Rands (billions), 1994–2005.

Source: Unpublished Data: Chamber of Mines Economics Division

on diamonds, four percent on platinum and three percent on gold.[19] The Chamber of Mines has not been particularly pleased with government pursuit of a revenue-based taxation system and has a strong conviction that taxes should not be raised. The Chamber's view is that the Bill is neither good for the economy nor the mining industry and royalties should only be imposed on profit.[20] Introducing a revenue-based royalty will add a fixed cost to every mining operation, with a disproportionate toll on less profitable mines. The unintended consequences of this system are the increased cost of mining and possible job losses. According to the Chamber of Mines chief executive, Mzolisi Diliza:

> Our average royalty rate for gold is 1.7 percent against the Bill's three percent, platinum group metals 1.4 percent against four percent, diamonds 4.4 percent against eight percent and copper 1.2 percent against two percent. We have suggested a maximum royalty rate of

two percent for gold, platinum 2.4 percent, diamonds 6.9 percent and copper 1.3 percent.[21]

The planned royalty of three percent on gold mining raised concerns that the tax could hasten the demise of the industry, which has declined by 40 percent since 1990.[22] The Chamber argues that the three percent tax plan might force the least profitable marginal mines to close and further reduce the industry's 200,000-strong workforce (consisting of 120,421 formal and 54,558 sub-contracted miners by the end of 2005). It is important to note that most non-marginal mines generate on extraction so-called resource rents, which are a function of the scarcity value of minerals. These rents can be taxed/shared between government and the operators without impacting negatively on the economic viability of the project. The charging regime contained in the Royalty Bill maintains optimal equilibrium between government's need for adequate compensation and the imperative of maintaining international competitiveness of the mining sector. The royalty rates fall well within internationally competitive margins that can be sustained for the foreseeable future.[23]

While increased revenue would have helped redistribute wealth and more importantly, alleviated South Africa's gripping social problems, the mining industry still wields considerable power. In the end, Finance Minister Trevor Manuel backed-off by delaying the finalisation of the Mining Royalties Bill for five years to 2009 so that "unresolved issues" could be addressed and that the proposed regime be based on international best practice.[24] According to the National Treasury's chief director for tax policy, government would have raised R3.6 billion in 2003 from gold mining alone had the Royalty Bill been in force.[25] On the contrary, according to Investec,[26] South Africa stood to lose R264-billion in future income if the Bill was implemented in its current written form, representing a "significant impact on jobs in the mining sector and a serious impairment of shareholder value."[27] The uncertainty created by the Bill knocked R70-billion off the Johannesburg Stock Exchange in a week after the Bill was announced. For now, the industry has survived, but this may be short term. Trevor Manuel appears to be a very determined minister in getting his policies through, even the most unpopular ones. What can be deduced from his precedent of aggressive pursuit of policies is that by 2009, things may not fall in industry's favour again.

South Africa is not alone in charging a royalty for its mineral resources. Most countries with significant mineral resources impose such a charge. For instance, in June 2004, the Peruvian government introduced a similar Royalty Bill, which proposed increasing royalties from one to three percent. As a result, potential developers of the Las Bambas copper project pulled out.[28] South Africa's Anglo American Corporation and BHP Billiton were among the bidders. In May 2003, the government of Chile also introduced a Royalty Bill, which also "requires mining companies to make payments, which can be deducted from future income taxes."[29] The royalty is levied in addition to income tax but scores as a deduction, as it constitutes a deductible expense in the production of income.

The Royalty Bill strained the relationship between the mining industry and the ANC government. Furthermore, the Mining Empowerment Charter, which also forms part of the same Mineral and Petroleum Resources Development Act (Act 28 of 2002) requires that mining companies commit to ensuring that 26 percent of their assets are in 'previously disadvantaged,' that is, non-white, hands by 2012. The process is still ongoing under the auspices of BEE, an alternative to nationalization, which enriches politically connected black elites while marginalizing the poor to further despair. The Chamber has also made progress in meeting the requirements of new labor legislation discussed in the previous chapter, both regarding mineworkers and its management structure. For instance, for the first time, there are now black faces in the Chamber of Mines Executive Council. The question whether this is sufficient remains.

The mining industry in general has made significant investments in the country. As mentioned elsewhere, the Chamber of Mines committed the mining sector to an investment of R100 billion in capital projects for the period 2003–2007.[30] While there have been threats of litigation against South African mining companies for complicity with apartheid, the ANC government has diligently worked to discourage these moves. The argument has been that most of "these companies are now assisting in South Africa's development."[31] Overall, the relationship between the industry and the ANC government is good, but it is often strained by new polices, which are part of the reconstruction process. The point raised in Chapter Three is worth repeating; in early October 2003, the rand strengthened to 6.9 to US$1 and the mining industry warned that it might lay off as many as 70,000 mineworkers and halt up to R100 billion worth of capital investments. However, any major retrenchments would certainly attract government interest, but the fact that it has not happened when the rand was at its strongest level since 2002 is a reflection of the extent to which restructuring has succeeded in curtailing operating costs.

GEAR, RETRENCHMENTS AND ORGANIZED LABOR

The ANC now argues that international trends do not allow alternative growth path and GEAR was a compromise to save the fledging democracy by stabilizing the economy and avoiding a meltdown.[32] Emmanuel Wallerstein argues that Marxism-Leninism "as a strategy and an ideology has played out its historic role and has become marginal to the ongoing political economy of the world system."[33] The socialist hangover remains and in holding on to its allegiance to classical dogmas of socialism, despite its grotesque political and economic record, South Africa's left is firm on its avowedly Marxist line and awaits the resurrection of grand socialism, "presumably under the joint pressure of capitalist rationality and working-class struggle."[34] Whether this is possible on the basis of class appeals is irrelevant, but it is obviously at odds with realities of the contemporary international political economy. Internationally, the post-*perestroika* and *glasnost* socialist experiences in the modern international economic system have not survived in any form that is recognizable as socialist. While the inherent moral superiority of socialism once inspired millions, as its distortions became inevitable, social revolutions in the Marxist-Leninist recipe and the future of socialism itself have become increasingly impractical. Today, it is one thing to debate the dialectics of Marxism and the nuances of class struggle when in opposition. However, the responsibility to govern currently demands pragmatism and therefore radically different approaches altogether.

The constraints of pursuing socialist policies in the contemporary international political economy are properly understood. The ANC's recognition of this reality has meant drifting more towards the center of the political spectrum, if not to the right. While it can be argued that the ANC sold out to the capitalist agenda, the alliance partners (Cosatu and the SACP)—who must have been better informed—simply did not have any leverage against this course. The introduction of GEAR not only demonstrates the extent to which Cosatu and the SACP failed in influencing the ANC towards a more socialist direction, but more importantly, their diminishing role in policy formulation. One senior Cosatu interviewee told me, "we engage with the government and government has been shifting towards a somewhat more proactive approach on GEAR. We do not have alternative proposals and we continue to fight for them. We engage in Nedlac[35], the alliance and we go on strike."[36]

In particular, the core of the tensions between the ANC and Cosatu revolves around the privatization process that followed GEAR. Although government has shelved the privatisation drive, this is exactly where GEAR is responsible for job losses that have ensued since its inception. Advocates of privatization generally come from business and government and, in the GEAR period, largely from within the ANC itself. They argue that privatization will:

- Bring capital, technology and managerial expertise that the public sector lacks;

- Ensure efficient provision of high quality goods and services;
- Facilitate the spread of ownership to previously disadvantaged communities;
- Attract foreign direct investors that are essential for economic growth.

Conversely, the opponents of privatization—who are largely from the trade union movements and community organizations—are not convinced by these motivations. They argue that:

- The private sector will only invest where there are high levels of profit. This could mean that the goal of providing the service will change from meeting a need to making a profit;
- Privatization means troubles for workers (job losses, reduced wages and harsher working conditions) as companies cut costs to maximize profits;
- Privatization can weaken the unions, as many companies involved in privatization are non-union;
- The involvement of the private sector in the provision of services leads to an increase in user charges. This reduces access to service for the working class and the poor;
- Privatization may undermine accountability of those who provide a service. Private companies are mainly accountable to shareholders who are only concerned about profits.[37]

While Cosatu opposes privatization, it has also gained handsomely in the process by purchasing businesses with R62 million collected from union members, many of whom earn poverty wages, as part of a campaign to defend jobs.[38] This may have been prompted by the realization that there have been no tactical retreats. Instead, the ANC has pressed on with restructuring, including that of state owned entities that have caused severe job losses.[39] An example of such entities is Telkom, the fixed line telephone company that is partially privatized. Since 1994, it has reduced its labor force of 60,000 by half. In opposition, Cosatu supported by the SACP has gone on strike against privatization and job losses, but to no avail.

Part of the reason Cosatu's industrial protests are no longer such a formidable threat to the ANC government is that it has systematically been weakened by the very job losses, thus putting it in a subordinate position in relation to the ANC in the alliance. It would have been unthinkable, to antagonize the labor federation in the late 1980s. The job losses have meant that Cosatu support base has diminished significantly. The more vigorous the state pursues neo-liberal economics—privatization and the restructuring in the private sector, the frailer Cosatu becomes.

*   *   *   *   *

In its second central resolution (2003) on the state and future of the federation, Cosatu acknowledged its beleaguered position, " . . . we are operating under changed conditions of struggle in the context of consolidation of democracy and globalization."[40] It also acknowledged that capital continuously finds new ways of production and organizing work to bolster its profits. The resolution went on to argue that, "political democracy also places demands that we must develop new strategies and capacity to engage with complex new challenges . . . In short, we have to adapt our strategies and organization "or die," [my emphasis] to this changed reality." It emphasized its vision to retain the character of the federation as a transformative and revolutionary union movement committed to the national democratic revolution and the struggle for socialism:

> We want a federation that has strong affiliates capable of responding to demands in their own sectors. To that extent, we commit ourselves to building both the capacity of affiliates and the federation to respond to the overall challenges facing our movement and the needs of the working class. In the long run, a job creation industrial strategy is the most effective way to defend the labor movement.[41]

Thus, the revolution the federation talks about has to happen within before it can take place at the national level. Paradoxically, a revolution within would save a revolution at the national level. Ultimately, occasional threats by Cosatu to embark on industrial action—which have almost become a ritual—no longer have the intensity they had against the apartheid regime in the 1980s and early 1990s.[42] As Cosatu's General Secretary, Zwelinzima Vavi put it, "before 1994 workers could unite easily with farm workers, business people, students and intellectuals since we faced the same oppression."[43] The political transition, together with increasing space for pluralism and neo-liberal economic orthodoxy, has loosened the ties.

Restructuring and retrenchments in many of the sectors where Cosatu draws its affiliates has reduced its membership from roughly 1.8 million to 1.7 million in two years between 2000 and 2002. This trend can be attributed to the fact that blue-collar workers have largely dominated the federation—the ones who were on the receiving-end of apartheid's labor battering and are now discarded by the logic of neo-liberal economic attrition. The trend was essentially the same in Britain during its restructuring process. Susan George reminds us that Margaret Thatcher used privatization as a weapon to break the power of the trade unions. By destroying the public services, where unions were strongest, she was able to weaken them drastically. Thus, between 1979 and 1994 the number of jobs in the public sector in Britain was reduced from over 7 million to 5 million.[44]

The odds seem to be against the trade union movement. The increasingly acrimonious relationship with the ANC government and accelerating job losses serve to undermine Cosatu's voice.[45] The logic of the democratic social revolution is that over time, the working class would dominate the political arena numerically and ultimately vote themselves to power and legislate the end of capitalism and the establishment of a socialist society. Persuasive as this might have been, especially during the cold war, it has now become fundamentally flawed. Even where socialist parties were voted to power in the past few years, such as in Brazil, Ecuador, Venezuela, Bolivia and others, there is no record of legislating an end to capitalism. Instead, there is disinclination to embrace radical initiatives and therefore less vigorous pursuit of broad socio-economic development oriented objectives. What we have witnessed has, instead, been the resurgence of a diluted capitalist welfare state, certainly not one Keynes envisaged. This should be understood from the fact that the extent to which Keynesian welfare state has been implemented depended on the political strength of labor.[46]

Since the mid-1990s, instead of recruiting beyond its traditional frontiers to strengthen its support base in the face of hostile government macroeconomic policy, the labor movement has been climbing a greased pole by immersing itself in debilitating fights over economic policy. These fights only served to further entrench the divide within the alliance. The rhetoric seems to be changing, as an interviewee in Cosatu expressed to me:

> GEAR is no longer in place and the ANC also says so. Strong elements of it are still in place. For instance, the whole agreement with government to introduce sectoral strategies is new. They have relaxed monetary policy and cut interest rates. When people say that GEAR is in place, I am not too sure what that means . . . I would say the ANC has moved from a straight free market policy to a right wing social democratic policy. This is not exactly huge progress, but it is progress. To say that policy is exactly the same as it was five years ago is not true. I am not saying that the policy is what we want, but it is still like that.[47]

The result of this has been a brewing instability within the leadership of the federation to the detriment of the labor movement itself. Unabated, reductions in the number of members threaten the federation, as it increasingly operates on an ever-shrinking pool of funds. For instance, in April 2003, Cosatu's central committee reported that it was owed R4.9 million in affiliation fees, a situation that has put pressure on its organizational capacity.[48] These developments are further constraining Cosatu and limiting its influence within the tripartite alliance.

The Position of Labor after Transition

In the historical context of South Africa, Bhorat *et al,* points out that "over the past one hundred years, political influences on the South African labor market have been characterized by a plethora of legislation that was instrumental in maintaining, until the 1970s, a workforce strictly divided on the basis of race."[49] While the broad historical dimensions and origins of the cheap labor system in South Africa have been put into context, the legacy and structural realities of the system remain.

So far, evidence presented of South Africa's attempts to eradicate the imbalances of the past reinforces the belief that the "best intentions of governments are no guarantee of success or of the generous improvement of social equity and justice"[50] many South Africans desire. Amongst others, the most profound of these social equities is unemployment and limited employment opportunities, especially in the context of people's heightened optimism in the new political order. Or is/was it misplaced optimism? Although there were reasonable grounds for great expectations, in the first decade of freedom, 1994–2004, increasing unemployment threaten the promise of "a better life for all." In the same period, South Africa's major growth sectors have recorded positive increases in national economic output. Notwithstanding the fact that the country relies on these sectors to close the unemployment divide, they are actually shedding jobs at an alarming rate and this presents real challenges to the problem of job creation.

Overall responsibility for job creation rests on appropriate government policies. In the contemporary democratic political system, while this ultimately makes the ANC government responsible for an economy that has not created enough jobs, the current unemployment crisis must be understood as an outcome of the historical "cheap labor" policy. For now, however, to most analysts, GEAR remains the most convenient scapegoat. Be that as it may, rising levels of unemployment continue to threaten social stability. The reason for this, one interviewee told me, is that "politicians and business in particular wanted an economy that was reliant on market forces with decreasing state control."[52] In the process, GEAR compromised the ability of the state because it emphasized rolling back the state from being redistributionist and developmental.

By 2004, however, unemployment declined to 26 percent (the expanded definition remained at 36 percent). Still, the number of people out of work remained over five million, which may not be politically sustainable in most countries, but somehow South Africa manages. While the economy expanded by five percent in 2004, not enough jobs were created. For now, the figures are encouraging, but higher levels of economic growth and investments are needed. Conversely, if economic growth fails to create jobs, it may compromise government's pledge to halve poverty, unemployment and the eradication of informal settlements by 2014. It would also endanger the objective of meeting the Millennium Development Goals. For, in 2004, a third of South Africa's population lived on annual income of less than R3,000. Organized labor finds itself having to contend with the forces of neo-liberalism and defend its interests with diminishing resources. Caught off guard by its ANC ally's adoption of neo-liberal economic policies, there are feelings of disillusionment with the political establishment, especially over the political chicanery that led to the adoption of GEAR and subsequent job loses in the economy in general.

In the face of international economic sanctions, the apartheid economy grew through import substitution, relying on internal resources. However, the attainment of freedom meant reintegration into the international economy. According to an interviewee in the National Treasury, this reintegration necessitated diversifying the economy from agriculture, gold and the primary export commodities, and driving the economy to other areas such as manufacturing, textiles, telecommunications, financial services and vehicle assembly. This meant that those without the necessary skills required by these industries remain largely unemployed, as the industries that absorbed them in the past no longer require such a huge labor force. Put differently, the victims of apartheid have now become the victims of democracy's neo-liberal capitalism. Inevitably, for the poor and the destitute, democracy's notion of egalitarian redistribution is increasingly becoming a myth. Certainly, this does not increase people's levels of personal happiness and sense of social and economic well-being. For, there is a fallacy that economic growth equals development, which, as Amartya Sen argues:

> Requires the removal of major sources of unfreedom; poverty as well as tyranny, poor economic opportunities as well as systematic social deprivations. Sometimes the lack of substantive freedoms relates directly to economic poverty, which robs people of the freedom to

satisfy hunger; or to achieve sufficient nutrition, or to obtain remedies for treatable illness, or the opportunity to be adequately clothed or sheltered, or to enjoy clean water or sanitation facilities.[53]

Recent estimates by the Bureau of Market Research have projected that South Africa's population will grow by 6.1 percent from 45.3 million in 2001 to 48.1 million by 2006. Interestingly, the black population is expected to grow by seven percent from 35.1 million in 2001 to 37.6 million during the same period (this research seems to contradict projections of population reduction due to HIV/AIDS. However, there are no reliable statistics to reflect the actual number of people dying from the disease each year). If the economy continues on its path of job destruction, people's patience might wane. The ANC is certainly aware of this reality, which has prompted the need for the Growth and Development Summit discussed elsewhere. The most profound challenge is to eradicate unemployment by increasing the domestic investment portfolio. The business sector has already started to honour its commitment. For instance, as argued elsewhere, the Chamber of Mines committed the mining sector to an investment of R100 billion in capital projects for the period 2003–2007.[54] For its part, the ANC manifesto for the 2004 election outlined a commitment to invest an additional R100 billion in the next 10 years (2004–2014) to boost attempts aimed at growing the economy.

Between 1995 and 2002, the number of people employed increased from 9,557,185 to 11,157,818.[55] This represents 1,600,633 net new jobs. What is important to note is that this increase was much lower than the rate of population growth and also lower than the total number of people who lost their jobs during the same period. In the same vein, Alan Hirsch contends that "unemployment grew as the number of new jobs failed to keep up with the number of people liberated into the job market."[56] The ANC is committed to addressing this problem and according to its manifesto for the 2004 general elections, the practical steps for this objective were, amongst others:

A Growing Economy

- Ensuring low interest and low inflation rates, as well as low government debt so that more resources are spent on attacking poverty, building economic infrastructure and creating work opportunities;
- Through government and state-owned enterprises, invest more than R100-billion in improving roads, rail and air transport as

well as telecommunications and energy; encourage more investment in key economy sectors such as manufacturing, information
and communication technology, mining and business services so
as to further enhance economic competitiveness;

- Spending over R15 billion in facilitating broad-based Black Economic Empowerment which also benefits communities—including
youth, women and people with disabilities—as well as workers
and small businesses;
- Conduct research into the full impact of casualisation of labor
and outsourcing, and device ways of dealing with their negative
impact on workers and the economy as a whole.

Sustainable Livelihoods

- Create one million job opportunities through the Expanded Public Works Programme;
- Ensure that those who wish to start and sustain their small businesses, including youth and women, have access to credit, through
dedicated funding to support micro-loan financing, through further reforms to existing support agencies and through changes
being introduced in the financial system and institutions;
- Intensifying assistance to youth agencies to provide skills training
for employment and self-employment and ensure implementation
of the National Youth Service and help unemployed graduates to
get work skills;
- Complete the land restitution program and speed up land
reform, with 30 percent of agricultural land redistributed by
2014, combined with comprehensive assistance to emergent
farmers;
- Ensure involvement of communities in local economic development initiatives to provide work, build community infrastructure
and ensure access to local opportunities and also encourage the
emergence of co-operatives.

To ensure that all these objectives are met by 2009, the government
pledged to strengthen co-operation among economic partners, business,
trade unions and community organizations to implement the agreements
of the Growth and Development Summit, which are aimed at creating
work and fighting poverty. Government aims to forge stronger partnerships
across all sectors to deal with the challenges of economic redistribution,
fighting crime and corruption.

WITHER ALLIANCE? THE POLITICS OF GEAR

In South Africa, the trade union movement has been the traditional bastion of unwavering ANC support. This support has its roots in the pre-apartheid era and consolidated itself in the 1980s with the coalition of autonomous civil society organizations under the United Democratic Front banner, the subsequent rise of Cosatu and their explicit support of the ANC. Shortly after the 1994 elections, ostensibly on the basis of common goals and objectives of freeing the oppressed majority politically, the ANC-SACP formed a political alliance with Cosatu.[57] Cosatu and the SACP's discontent over GEAR's adoption is important to this analysis for the following reasons. First, for Cosatu, GEAR is retrogressive as it threatens its existence as a labor movement and with this, further reduction of its meaningful role in South Africa's reconstruction project. Essentially, neo-liberalism undermines the intensity of revolutionary fervor. It also reduces the bargaining achievements Cosatu has won for workers since its formation. While Cosatu fought successfully against apartheid, it is being humiliated by its own ally, the ANC, through policies that undermine its very existence.

Second, regarding the SACP, the concern is more ideological. While the ANC was denounced throughout the struggle as a communist front, the SACP is at pains to comprehend the ANC's enthusiastic embrace of unashamed neo-liberal market view of economics, antithetical to anything that resembles socialism. The significance of this trajectory rests in the overwhelming constraints of post cold war democratic and economic reconstructions under the hegemony of neo-liberalism and globalization. With this reality, the nuances and appeals of socialism are gradually losing their axiomatic grip on people's psyche. The neo-liberal embrace painfully reveal that long-standing ideals can be easily undermined by pragmatism and the need to conform to prevailing economic orthodoxy as determined by the structural realities of the distribution of power in the international political and economic matrix. It is not about doing what politicians believe in, but what would be viable given the circumstances.

On the basis of its alliance with Cosatu and the SACP, there are reasonable expectations for conformity and therefore ideological dissent is not inseparable from disloyalty. Overall, the converse attitude of many of those on the left, Cosatu and the SACP, is a deeply held ideological conviction in opposition to GEAR. Thus, GEAR became the fault line of rancorous debates within the tripartite alliance, with Cosatu and the SACP as unremitting voices of articulate criticisms.[58] The ANC government's inability to create sufficient jobs and the ideology behind GEAR has prompted the weakened camps of Cosatu and the SACP to go on the offensive in a struggle to defend their interests, thus threatening their alliance with the ANC. Both Cosatu and the SACP are bitter over the non-consultative policy-making processes that form the hallmarks of GEAR. Notwithstanding GEAR's achievements in stabilizing the economy, its merits are getting lost amid the vociferous cacophony of ideological dissent (See Table 5.2 below).

Moreover, the SACP finds itself under the overwhelming neo-liberal hegemonic influence of the ANC. Consequently, the problem for the SACP is the reality of having to deal with an old ally that has embraced an ideological and traditional enemy of socialism. In the aftermath of GEAR, the alliance constituted a union between two opposing forces, one overwhelmingly capitalist and imperialist, and the other socialist. Accordingly, the latter serves as an inconvenient fetter for the capitalist aspirations of the former. What is interesting to note is that the differences between the two regarding the political economy of the post-apartheid political arrangement have endured since exile. However, the two accommodated each other largely because it was agreed that the social question relating to the political economy of the new South Africa was to be addressed only after the national question of getting rid of the apartheid state had been effected. There was therefore little substance to separate them before 1994.[59]

The ANC relied on the SACP for intellectual tutelage which provided a robust ideological anchor for a sound political strategy. Today, the ANC's ideological commitment—as reflected in GEAR—runs contrary to the fundamental ideological premises of the SACP. Conversely, the ANC's enduring relationship with the SACP contradicts its newly found salvation in neo-liberal doctrine. What the ANC now needs is a strategy for the evolution of democracy and the market system in a way that would alleviate the plight of millions who are living in poverty. While there may be a contradiction in terms, towards this, the ANC has to rely on the SACP and Cosatu, not for ideological tutelage, but for control of the working class. Therefore, future political vision rather than *non-binding* pledges made during the struggle holds the ground. The ANC's alliance with the New National Party in the Western Cape was a clear testimony to this reality.

The ANC is no longer suffering the material and ideological deprivations that necessitated an alliance with the SACP. In the cold war deep freeze, as the ANC protests became militantly radicalized through an armed struggle, the alliance guaranteed substantial financial, ideological and military help from the Soviet Union. Colin Bundy summed up the distinct contributions made by the SACP to the ANC during this period:

- When the ANC went underground after its banning in 1961, the SACP could contribute a decade's experience of working and organising underground which was particularly important in the formation of MK (Mkhonto we Sizwe, Spear of the Nation, ANC's armed wing);

- The SACP provided a ready-made network of linkages to the USSR, Eastern Europe and sympathetic organizations in the West;

- The USSR and Eastern bloc countries were the major international supporters of the ANC, especially in the areas of supply of military equipment and training;

- It provided a significant input of intellectual support, guidance and sophistication to the ANC. This was revealed especially at the Morogoro Conference (Tanzania) where the ANC adopted many of the major theoretical constructions of the SACP, and;

- It played a major part in theorising the armed struggle and developing military strategy.[60]

However, all these came at a cost for the ANC during its liberation struggle, as its antagonists were easily able to dismiss it as a communist front.[61] The fraternal patronage of the cold war era and the days in exile appear to limit the ability of the SACP to break free of the ideological relics of the past. Disagreements over the adoption of neo-liberal policies and the endless labor haemorrhage have provided the necessary ferments for tensions, but not sufficient for a break-up in the alliance. The SACP-Cosatu's inability to dissuade the ANC from embracing neo-liberalism has, however, weakened the alliance. Essentially, policy matters have largely been taken out of the realm of debate and have become an issue for bureaucrats and consultants.

While the ANC has largely abandoned the ideals of socialism envisioned in the Freedom Charter as its main goal, the alliance has not pulled apart at the seams. The ties that bind the alliance persist, in part because of historical fraternity and opportunities in the government employment matrix, which reward Cosatu and SACP elite. For instance at one point, the ANC drew at least seven Cabinet Ministers from the SACP, two provincial premiers and 65 Members of Parliament. More importantly, the 'deployment and redeployment' of political leaders by the ANC, be they Cosatu or SACP members, has meant that potential "troublemakers" are either put out of sight or expelled from the party.[62] Depending on the dictates of the moment, they are largely redeployed within government or the party structure. Some of these potential dissidents have become successful businessmen/women, the main beneficiaries of BEE.

This shift has led SACP Secretary General, Blade Nzimade to go as far as accusing his own comrades—bourgeoisie Marxists holding shares—" . . . who think with their stomachs, and not their heads," for supporting privatization because they have vested economic interests in the schemes.[63] Verbal abuse also became common currency in exchanges within the alliance and the ANC's responses to criticisms of GEAR have not been restrained. Both Presidents Mandela and Mbeki have called Cosatu and the SACP: "liars," "revolutionary opportunists," "ultra left" and other labels. At its 9th national congress (September 16–19, 1997), Cosatu gave then President Nelson Mandela the opportunity to deliver the keynote address. He used it to rebuke trade union leaders, whom he accused of being "selfish" and "sectoral," bent on protecting their interests at the expense of the nation.[64] It was during a similar occasion, at the 10th congress (July 1–5, 1998) of the SACP, that Mandela castigated Cosatu and the SACP. He warned that "if Cosatu and the SACP leave the internal structures of the organization and go public, and not only attack what we consider a fundamental policy of the organization but ridicule it, they must be aware of the implications."[65]

The implications have not been forthcoming yet, but this language would have been unthinkable in the period before 1994 when the ANC was mobilizing all resistance groups to its fold. There was a well-founded fear—although its intensity fluctuates over time—of the alliance breaking up and both sides realize the potential consequences. The possibilities of the alliance breaking up in the near future are consistently narrowing as organized labor strength diminishes due to retrenchments. Speaking at the launch of the Millennium Labor Council in June 2000, Cosatu Secretary General Zwelinzima Vavi (also a member of the SACP), aptly, and in a brutally frank fashion, made the following statements:

> It is clear that trade-offs have to be made. But in our view such trade-offs should not result in a chicken-and-pig-breakfast relationship. In such a situation the chicken is asked to make a partial contribution by laying an egg while the pig has to sacrifice its life to make the bacon.[66]

In the July/August 1999 issue of its publication, *Umsebenzi* (Zulu for "employment"), the SACP argued for the rolling back of the market, and demanded a state-led development programme. It argued for state subsidies to be extended and an acceptance by the government that capitalism constitutes one of the biggest threats to South Africa's fledging democracy. As Jeremy Cronin, Deputy Secretary General of the SACP put it:

> GEAR was, essentially, based on Reserve Bank economic models, assisted by World Bank economists. Its fundamental assumption is that

macro-economic policy should be entirely devoted to stability and that growth and transformation will come from elsewhere.[67]

Cronin also pointed the disastrous consequences of GEAR, whose terms he insists, have to be seriously revised.

The ANC's hegemonic position within the alliance led Mbeki to suggest that the alliance was not cast in stone and could be broken up if this became necessary.[68] It is apparent, however, that the ANC has succeeded in making its recalcitrant junior partners toe the line and know their rightful place in the alliance. For instance, the strongly worded declaration of the 10th congress of the SACP in 1998 reaffirmed its commitment to the alliance, despite Mandela's assault. Some of the key resolutions of the Congress were continuing to build and strengthen the SACP as an autonomous formation within the context of the ANC-led alliance; building the ANC alliance and recognizing this as a "strategic imperative"; working tirelessly as Communists to ensure an overwhelming ANC victory in the 1999 elections; as well as rejecting the overall thrust of GEAR and reaffirming that a macroeconomic policy on its own is insufficient. While the appeals of communism as an ideology may not be dead, they are certainly in decline. The SACP's mass political constituency is relatively small and maintains a diminishing presence in the political landscape. Inevitably, its survival seems to depend largely on sustaining its alliance with the ANC. Every time the talk of severing ties with the ANC is mooted, there is a realization of the difficulties that the SACP might face.

Unlike the ANC, which has been able to shake off its socialist overtones, the demise of the Soviet Union and communist political hegemony in Eastern Europe have left the SACP at a rather severe disadvantage. Internationally, socialism is in disrepair. Even prodigious revisionist Marxist intellectual auxiliaries are traumatized by their inability to modify the dogmas of socialism as envisaged by Karl Marx, Frederich Engels and later polished and refined by Vladimir Lenin, to be discernible for contemporary realities. Notwithstanding this inability, socialism as practiced relied heavily on coercive brutality which contradicts democratic values. There was nothing appealing about Stalinism, although it was equated with a rather convoluted version of democracy.

The demise of the communist bloc has also cost the SACP the intellectual coherence that enabled it to provide tutelage to the ANC. The ANC was no longer interested in archaic dogmas either. Indeed, the ANC simply creamed off that intellectual leadership and recruited it to its Cabinet. This reality has reduced the socialist commitment of senior members of the SACP who are in Cabinet. They have often been the people vigorously driving the neo-liberal agenda in their respective portfolios. They have consistently justified their actions based on acceptance of the realities rather than ideological considerations. Ultimately, the SACP increasingly appears as a receptacle of disillusioned, recalcitrant eternal Marxists who ineffectually contest the ANC's rebirth in neo-liberalism, and whose nostalgia of socialist experiences elsewhere refuses to find solace within the new found faith.

The reluctance to recondition itself and continue instead to recount archaic dogmas has made the SACP leadership take a rather severe stance towards its own members who vigorously criticize its junior position in the alliance. The challenge for the ANC has been not to alienate Cosatu and the SACP to too great an extent as they still serve an important purpose, but only on terms and conditions determined by the ANC's hegemonic position within the alliance. In the process, despite trauma over the adoption of GEAR, Cosatu and the SACP still play an important role, but much less than they desire. Minimum consensus exists within the alliance, but the ANC has what amounts to some kind of veto power—an interdiction—which the junior partners do not have, and even if they disagree, they may not get away with it.

In trying to counter that veto power, Cosatu and the SACP often retreat to their cocoons when they cannot get their way within the alliance, then remobilize their support and vent their anger through industrial action. The downside of it is that most people have come to realize just how much they stand to loose in such industrial actions, and their intensity has significantly subsided from the overwhelming support throughout the 1990s. From the unemployed masses, most industries have secured a labor reservoir which substitutes formal labor at short notice in times of industrial action, much in the same way the gold mining industry has come to rely on sub-contracted labor. For instance, when hundreds of Airports Company South Africa workers (ACSA) went on strike in late October 2003, Charmaine Lodewyk, ACSA's group executive for communications was optimistic that the flight schedule would not be interrupted. As she puts it, "we have put in place contingency plans to ensure there are no disruptions to services and we expect operations to continue as normal."[69]

The symbiotic relationship within the alliance makes it difficult for Cosatu and the SACP to seriously rethink their positions for the obvious reason that the left's project is not to run away from political power, but as Roger Southall puts it, "using the access to that power to realize whatever progressive potentialities exist."[70] Although with increasingly limited influence, the SACP and Cosatu attempt to dilute and restrain the capitalist aspirations of the anti-socialist neo-liberal cadre. Forsaking the

ANC alliance would be a grave mistake. However, by remaining within the alliance, the SACP and Cosatu are increasingly accused of betraying the revolution and for complicity in and as co-directors of government's policies that sacrifice the poor on what John Saul referred to as "the altar of the neo-liberal logic of global capitalism."[71]

In what must have been a self-cleansing exercise, in July 2000, Dale McKinley, an SACP member and a freelance journalist was unceremoniously suspended by the SACP for attacking leaders of the tripartite alliance.[72] When the SACP was unbanned in 1990, half the central committee cathartically left the organization with the prediction that it would wither away. If Cosatu-SACP were to leave the alliance, they will certainly be accused of breaking the accord on which the very fabric of South Africa's successful transition is premised; the spirit of freedom, democratic consolidation, nation-building and the good intentions of government. For now, amongst others, these reasons have given Cosatu and the SACP leaders contemplating secession pause. They will remain locked in a bad marriage they dislike but dare not leave. However, possibilities that could disrupt the precarious equilibrium remain.

During the ANC's 51st Congress held at the University of Stellenbosch in December 2002 the ANC General Secretary Kgalema Motlante made it clear that, "if the ANC loses its left wing, it will not fly. . . . The ANC needs both its left wing and its right wing to be a well-balanced organization." He further argued that Cosatu and SACP play a vital role and it was essential to the democratic revolution that the alliance remained united. Cosatu and SACP answered the call. Cosatu's Secretary General Zwelinzima Vavi asserted, "breaking the alliance can never be in the interest of the ANC, the workers, the communists or the country."[73] To those who await the alliance's demise with architectural grand designs for the ruins or to compose obituaries, SACP's Secretary General, Blade Nzimande made it clear ". . . . to them we have a simple message, this is our government, this is our ANC and we will defend it."[74] Despite having transformed itself into a political party in the 1990s, the ANC still has all the hallmarks of a broad-church liberation movement that represents various social groups fighting oppression.

Organized labor cannot rival the overwhelming support the ANC currently commands from other constituencies apart from the working class. Cosatu and the SACP understand that a miscalculated break-up can be catastrophic. Populism alone based on a specific class appeal may not be sufficient to save Cosatu and the SACP at the ballot box. Their worst scenario may be a disappearance into the political wilderness. Donald Silke observed in 1996 that even "if the ANC were to shed a million voters to an alternative political home, its power would be more dented than damaged."[75] Inadvertently, GEAR saves the ANC at the political level. As Roger Southall points out:

> The ANC's effective conversion to neo-liberalism via GEAR has undercut much of the potential for opposition to it based on ideological grounds. The resort to criticism based upon pragmatic grounds—challenging the lack of overall performance, failure to deliver services, a reluctance to recognize and root out corruption—offers only limited opportunity for coalescence by the opposition around a common platform.[76]

De Klerk's decision to leave the Government of National Unity in 1996 to lead his party into unambiguous opposition bears testimony. This marked the beginning of the National Party's incremental disappearance from the political landscape. In light of all these factors, for now, Cosatu and the SACP are bound to remain in the alliance.

ADIEU POVERTY? THE ECONOMICS OF GEAR

After the first democratic elections in 1994, the ANC got 62.6 percent of the vote—the level of support that most governments throughout the world can only dream of. The 1996 Constitution further strengthened the ANC's power. For instance, the provision made by the Interim Constitution (upon which the 1994 elections took place), for the leader of the second largest party in parliament to become a Deputy President was discarded. Power was further consolidated when the Senate was abolished in favour of the National Council of Provinces, which gave the provinces more powers. What is important to note is that out of nine provinces, the ANC won outright majorities in six after the 1994 elections. While it failed to win in three, its power and influence in each was substantial. Because the 1996 Constitution was drafted at a time when the ANC had the upper hand in government, it was able to slacken most of the restrictive fetters that limited its room for manoeuvre during the initial negotiations before the transition. In summary, the 1996 Constitution was an attempt to shift the locus of power to the center and that has been successful as the Presidency holds the power to appoint and dismiss premiers.

In the 1999 national elections, most analysts plausibly expected the ANC support to decline from its 1994 levels. There were enough reasons for this plausibility because of alliance discontent over GEAR and job loses. However, holding to these expectations meant ignoring the achievements of the first five years of the ANC in power 1994–1999, in which it alleviated the plight of millions. According to its 1999 election manifesto, under the auspices of the RDP, the ANC government brought water to three million people; housed nearly three million people by building 750,000 houses; connected two million houses to the electrical grid; built or rehabilitated over 500 health clinics; transferred 220,000 hectares of land to 68,000 households; built over 10,000 new class rooms and connected three million telephone lines to the people.[77] By 2003 new statistics on land distribution reveal that about 800,000 hectares of land was returned to people who had lost theirs because of racially discriminatory laws. In total, about 700,000 people received about three million hectares of land through government's redistribution since 1994.[78] According to the ANC's manifesto for the 2004 general elections, delivery figures for social services have increased. The *Ten Year Review* re-emphasized the point that the government embarked on the course of implementing a programme to systematically dismantle apartheid and create a democratic society guided by the provisions of the RDP. To this effect, the Department of Social Development's expenditure on social grants rose from R10 billion in 1994 to R34.8 billion in 2003, reaching 6.8 million beneficiaries.[79]

Tertiary education enrolment increased from 150,000 in 1994 to 280,000 by 2003. With this development, general literacy increased from 83 percent in 1996 to 89 percent by 2001, and households having access to clean water increased from 60 percent in 1996 to 85 percent in the same year. This means that an additional nine million citizens or 3.7 million households now have access to clean water. The number of households with access to sanitation increased from 49 percent in 1994 to 63 percent in 2003. Households connected to the electricity grid increased from 32 percent in 1994 to 70 percent by 2001. In addition, between 1994 and 2003—1,985,545 million housing subsidies were approved, accounting for an expenditure of R24.22 billion.[80]

According to the Macro-Social Report (forthcoming), by 2005, the following had been achieved:

- Approximately 2.4 million housing subsidies were approved. During the same period, 1.74 million housing units were built for the poor;
- 3.5 million homes have been electrified since 1994, which translates to over 435,000 homes per annum;
- 47.5 million people (91 percent of the population) had access to improved water supply (although there was an embarrassing outbreak of waterborne diseases in Delmas and parts of KwaZulu-Natal);
- Basic sanitation infrastructure reached over 8.2 million people;
- There had been a successful formation of an integrated education system, even though there is a clear need for more resource allocation and capacity-building in poor areas;

- Nutrition and early childhood interventions had been established to improve results for children from poor backgrounds;
- Secondary school enrolment had reached 89 percent and primary school enrolment 104 percent.
- More than 10 million people were accessing social security grants (but it is questionable if this is economically sustainable); (The minister of Finance has warned that South Africa is in danger of becoming a nation too dependent on handouts from the state which in turn has a damaging effect on the entrepreneural spirit).
- The cumulative total number of land claims settled as at 31 December 2005 stood at 68,719. The cumulative number of beneficiaries reached 939,737. Land restored totals 1,006,959 hectares;

Notwithstanding these achievements, the battle against poverty is not being won.

*   *   *   *   *

The ANC's level of support further consolidated its dominant position in the South African political landscape. Despite the problems of GEAR and high levels of unemployment, for now opposition to the ANC can be likened to a proverbial fly trying to move a dunghill. However, in the light of continuing discontent over neo-liberal economics, it remains to be seen if the ANC will maintain electoral realignment in its political support in subsequent elections. So far, what is obvious is that despite discontent over GEAR, it has worked in collecting political kudos and in restructuring an economy that was in regression. The table below reflects this achievement:

Table 5.2. South Africa's Performance, 1980–1993 versus 1994–2000[81]

	1980–1993	1994–2000
Economic Growth	1% per annum	2.7% per annum
Real personal disposable income	Fell by 10.2%	Rose by 3.3%
Real gross capital formation	Fell by 2.4% per annum	Rose by 4.6% per annum
Import cover (weeks)	1980=21/1993=10	1994=10/2000=23
Weighted exchange rate	-7.6% per annum	-7.4% per annum
Net international capital inflows	-R41 billion	+R95 billion
Consumer price index (CPI) inflation	14%	7%
Government expenditure	27% of GDP	24% of GDP
Real unit labor costs	Rose by 9.5% per annum	Fell by 1.4% per annum

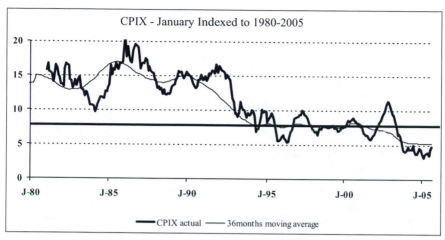

Figure 5.6. South Africa's Consumer Price Index, 1980–2005

Source: Bureau for Economic Research

In contrast with the period 1994–2000, the economy picked up from the negative indicators of the period 1980–1993. For instance, while real personal disposable income fell by 10.2 percent in the period 1980–1993, it grew by 3.3 percent in the period 1994–2000. The sanctions campaign of the 1980s led to a net international capital outflow of –R41 billion (a substantial amount in the exchange rate of R2.23 to the U.S. dollar). Conversely, in the period 1994–2000, net international capital inflow rose to +R95 billion. Consumer price inflation has also been brought down by half in the two periods, and these, of cause, are the positive offsets of GEAR. Recent statistics on CPIX fluctuations against set target since January 1980 show remarkable achievements:

When compared with the period 1980 to 1995, when inflation went out of control against set target, there have been marked improvements with greater domestic price stability. Inflation was brought below the target of roughly seven percent. In the fourth quarter of 2004, inflation even went below five percent. Total public debt fell from more than 60 percent of GDP in 1994 to about 19 percent by late 2004. There have been innovative new ways and in terms of economic growth rate, South Africa has experienced 10 years of continuous economic expansion, the longest upwards phase of the business cycle on record. As a result, South Africa has not approached the lenders of last resort, the International Monetary Fund and the World Bank to keep its budget balanced. This is an outcome of good financial and prudent regulation and management, which reduces the risk of systematic financial crisis. While the economy was in regression in the 1980, so far, South Africa's GDP growth rate has been as follows:

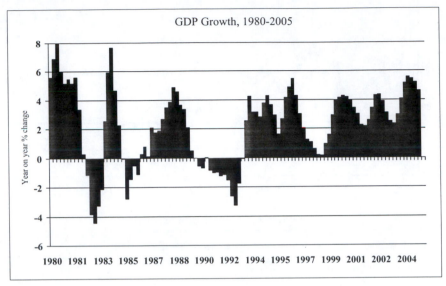

Figure 5.7. South Africa's GDP Growth, 1980–2005.

Source: Bureau for Economic Research

In contrast to the 1980s when the economy registered negative growth rates, even as much as -4 percent in 1982, since 1994, there have been positive economic growth rates of three percent on average. However, there was a slump in 1998 which can be attributed to the Asian financial crisis. Overall, the GDP growth trend since 1994 reflects marked improvements in macroeconomic stability and cultivates business and investor confidence. The economic growth rates achieved have not been sufficient to reduce rising unemployment rates—therefore unable to appease populists.

At a rate of three percent economic growth rate, it would take South Africa more than 20 years to double the economy. However, if South Africa's economy achieved the desired six percent growth rate (which is still insufficient to meet socio-economic demands), it would take roughly 12 years to double the size of the economy, and therefore, people's income. Certainly, if this is realized, it would increase the amount of resources available for redistribution and therefore alleviate the problem of unemployment, reduce poverty, accelerate transformation and increase fixed investment. Consumption led growth, not supply-side export driven will even take longer to double the economy. It is important to emphasize that doubling the economy in itself neither reduces poverty, nor address inequality. The figure below shows the time it takes to double the economy at different growth rates:

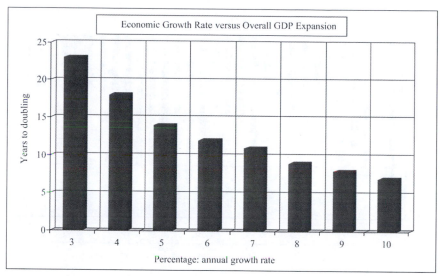

Figure 5.8. Economic Growth Rate versus Overall GDP Expansion.

Source: Chamber of Mines of South Africa

Before the ANC took over, the budget deficit was seven percent of the GDP in 1993 and the country barely had three weeks foreign exchange reserves, with a payment crisis looming.[82] However, by the end of 2005, the South African Reserve Bank had managed to build a substantial foreign reserve which stood at US$22 billion. Sanctions had worked their way into the economy as fiscal deficit stood at -5 percent of GDP by 1987. In 2000 and 2001, the budget deficit was reduced lower than one percent of GDP. An analysis of the budget deficit since 1975 shows the fluctuations. Overall, as the figure below shows, there have been remarkable achievements.

A stable macroeconomic framework is in place and its achievements must be underscored as precursor for sustainable economic growth and development of South Africa. However, this stable macroeconomic framework must equally dovetail with other interests, such as meeting people's basic socio-economic needs over time. Maximum possible efficiency has not been achieved and disturbing levels of inequalities persist. Meeting people's basic socio-economic needs is not beyond retrieval and burning questions on how to overcome the enduring consequences of apartheid—poverty—remain. For instance, in response to the "state of the nation debate" in February 2005, President Mbeki asked: "what should be done to accelerate the advance towards eradicating the many backlogs that undermine social integration?" These questions are important because

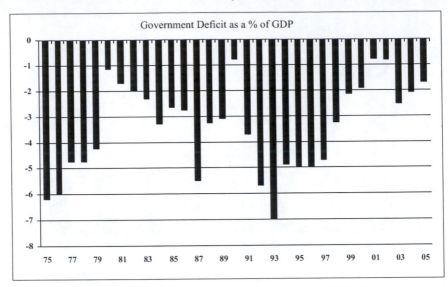

Figure 5.9. Government Deficit as a Percentage of GDP, 1975–2005

Source: Bureau for Economic Research

the poor and the destitute—almost one third of the population—feel left out of the benefits of positive economic performance.

The effects of neo-liberal policies on the poor have been the same even in advanced democracies. Susan George points that in Britain, during the 1980s, the top one percent of taxpayers received 29 percent of all the tax reduction benefits, with the result that a single parson earning half the average salary found his or her taxes had increased by seven percent, whereas a single person earning ten times the average salary received a 21 percent tax reduction. Similarly, in the United States in the same period, the top 10 percent of families increased their average family income by 16 percent, the top five percent increased theirs by 23 percent. However, for the poor Americans, the bottom 80 percent all lost something. The lower they were on the scale, the more they lost. The bottom 10 percent of Americans reached their nadir and lost 15 percent of their already meagre incomes.[83] For a country like South Africa with structurally embedded acute historical inequalities, corresponding figures may be far more disturbing.

* * * * *

While the country's macroeconomic fundamentals provide reasonable grounds for optimism—largely for middle-class consumerism—upsurges of sporadic service delivery protests that characterized South Africa's local government's landscape in the course of 2005, reflect the degree to which ordinary people who remain trapped in the vicious cycle of poverty feel left out and disillusioned, despite prudent macro economic management. Gunder Frank specified at least three features of capitalism, which collectively constitute the dominant cause of underdevelopment. It is necessary to outline the essence of these for a comprehensive understanding of the dynamic economic forces at play:

- The expropriation of surplus from the many and its appropriation by the few;
- The polarization of the capitalist system into metropolitan centers and peripheral centers (an application of Emmanuel Wallerstein's center periphery thesis, within the state and not the international level—my emphasis);
- The continuity of the fundamental structure of the capitalist system, which ensures the perpetuation of the first and second point (above), even while more superficial elements of this system are constantly changing.[84]

Widespread service delivery protests are an expression of popular discontent with the persistent structural violence of poverty, which exacerbates the stress and anxieties of daily life. Naturally, while government is useful and ought therefore to be accepted as a voluntary obligation, service delivery protests undermine the social contract between government and the citizenry. In French philosopher, Jean Jacques Rousseau dissection, service delivery protests undermine what he referred to as the *General Will*, that is, the source of legitimate authority, which resides with the collective will as contrasted with individual interests.[85]

It is the stubborn persistence of poverty which inevitably provides the necessary ferments for protests, especially when there is no legal recourse. Or is it too early to argue that service delivery protests debunk the customary formulation that orthodox macroeconomic policies cause short-term pain but long-term gains? Whatever the answer—the rhyme is perfect—but service delivery protests reflect the degree to which the promise of a "better life for all" has been frustrated by lack of optimal equilibrium between economic growth and adequate economic redistribution. Despite the legacy of acute historical inequalities, race, class and gender continue to determine access to economic privilege, with the rural poor, women in particular, bearing the brunt. Certainly, widespread service delivery protests are not an expression of the abundance of leisure, hope and confidence, but an exhibition of despair arising from feelings of being forsaken, perceived government's neglect and inadvertent, yet humiliating dereliction of duty.

Conspiracies explaining service delivery protests became a rather convenient scapegoat, but what is interesting is that service delivery protests take place at a time when economists, policy makers and politicians have become more optimistic about future prospects for accelerated economic development. Conversely, it is complicated to explain why service delivery protests did not take place in the late 1990s when economic growth was sluggish. Be that as it may, for individuals, lack of socio economic security reduces productive opportunities and increases physical and psychological ill being, despair and uncertainty, thus human security. Human security should be understood as a synthesis of advances of socio-economic provisions for the improvement of people's lives. In simple terms, human security means safety from chronic threats of hunger, disease, repression and protection from sudden and hurtful disruptions in the patterns of daily life, whether in homes or in communities.[86]

In his seminal study on the causes of rebellion and violent conflict, Ted Gurr has argued that general feelings of unrealized pent-up potential, uncertainty, despair and inability to acquire certain material conditions have a long-term effect on the collective psyche and on people perceptions. Relative deprivation as he puts it, that is, the difference between people's *value expectations* and their *value capabilities*, which in the South African context include, access to adequate sanitation, employment, housing and even adequate education, present a real dilemma. According to Ted Gurr:

> *Value expectations* refer to both present and future conditions. People ordinarily expect to keep what they have; they also generally have a set of expectations and demands about what they should have in the future, which is usually as much more than what they have at present. *Value expectations* are the goods and conditions of life to which people believe they are capable of getting and keeping. On the other hand, the *value capabilities* of a collectivity are the average value positions its members perceive themselves capable of attaining or maintaining. *Value capabilities* also have both present and future connotations. In the present, the *value capabilities* are represented by what people have actually been able to attain or have been provided by their environment: the *value position*. [87]

One's inability to escape these negative effects may lead to despair, frustration and its associated behaviour, mainly instigation to aggression. In this vein, psychological assumptions of the generic sources of human aggression assert that aggression is solely instinctive, that is, it is solely learned, or that it is an innate response activated by frustration. Deprivation disorient one's behaviour and triggers aggressive impulses and in the absence of avenues for expressing discontent, violent conflict becomes a displacement of such frustrations, sometimes leading to spontaneous uprisings or even revolution. Hopefully, feelings of despair and relative deprivations will subside as the benefits of economic growth trickle down through redistribution. So far, it has been the exact opposite. Redistribution may not be realized if the primacy of society over the system remains marginal and subordinate to market mechanisms—which are socially disembedded, but have nevertheless become the epicentre of economic, social and political matrix.

CONCLUDING REMARKS

This chapter attempted to dissect the central questions to this analysis. First is the position of the gold mining industry and its relationship with the ANC government after the transition, in particular the post GEAR period. The analysis shows that the gold mining industry successfully restructured into a globally competitive industry and demonstrates the extent to which that was achieved. When compared with Australia, Brazil, Canada, and the U.S., South Africa was the most expensive gold producer throughout the 1980s until the late 1990s. This was due to a combination of a variety of factors, among them, the engagement of a massive labor force.

The opening up of the economy, the restructuring process and the massive labor haemorrhage, allowed the industry to become the lowest-cost large-scale producer by 1999. The industry demonstrated a century-old maturity in resilience that has been the distinctive feature of its struggle with governments. The new mode of regulation—democracy—is working well and does not threaten the mode of accumulation, which is neo-liberal political economy. The analysis demonstrated how the mode of accumulation has made the industry so competitive against other major gold producers. While the ANC commands absolute control of the political apparatus, corporate South Africa wields hegemonic control over the economic apparatus. For now, majority control of the political apparatus coexists with minority control of the economy.

Restructuring has allowed the industry to stop the escalation in real production costs. As such, the gold mining industry was able to consolidate its activities in South Africa. Its management and work practices have evolved towards productivity and efficiency and, practices regarding human capital have changed. More importantly, as argued in Chapter Four, the industry has globalized its activities. On the basis of all these, it is fair to argue that the gold mining industry has averted a crisis that was sparked by over-reliance on favourably low productivity cheap labor policies. This did not have anything directly to do with GEAR, but with the imperative to remain in business and the challenges of competitiveness at a global level. Generally, the relationship between the mining industry and the ANC is good, but it is often strained by new government statutory provisions, especially the Royalty Bill introduced to give effect to the Minerals and Petroleum Resources Development Act, (No. 28 of 2002). While the ANC government introduces legislative measures that threaten the industry's existence, it simultaneously protects the industry from threats of litigious prosecution.

Second, the position of labor has been weakened after GEAR and the restructuring in the gold mining industry and the economy in general. The mining industry shed 200,000 jobs between 1994 and 2004. General unemployment levels of 40 percent are politically and socially unacceptable. It is labor that has borne the brunt of post-apartheid labor market restructuring. By bestowing authority on the market forces to determine the demand and supply mechanisms in the economy, GEAR directly assaults organized labor.

Third, the health status of the tripartite alliance between the ANC, Cosatu and the SACP is undermined by discontent over the ANC's adoption of neo-liberalism. However, despite disagreements, for Cosatu and the SACP, remaining within the ANC-led alliance for now appears to be the only viable alternative. For, if Cosatu and the SACP were to leave the alliance, they would be accused of breaking the accord on which the very stability of South Africa's democracy is premised, especially since the ANC relies heavily on Cosatu and the SACP to control the working class. Besides, the political system and its institutions are still fragile and therefore need further consolidation. More importantly the political landscape does not guarantee any future for Cosatu and the SACP outside the alliance. For some time to come, the alliance will remain in place largely on terms and conditions dictated by the ANC. Still, the scope both for consensus and disagreement exists.

The winners of South Africa's transition have been corporate South Africa and the ANC itself, while the impoverished majority and organized labor have become the losers. Along ideological grounds, organized labor, Cosatu and also the SACP (although they still sit in government) were caught off guard by the ANC's capricious ideological shifts. The two have largely failed in influencing the ANC against adopting neo-liberal economic policies. Corporate South Africa gained as the political changes brought the lifting of economic sanctions and an opportunity to globalize business operations. The ANC on the other hand achieved the liberation mandate by gaining political power and the control of government.

Conclusion
South Africa's Transition in Retrospect

In 1960, Ghana was the richest black African country. Now it is one of the poorest. At present, South Africa is the only country on the continent with the smallest hope of attaining First World status. What will it be in ten years' time? Possibly, a black dictatorship of unparalleled atrocity, a theatre of one of Africa's endless civil wars, an industrial scrapheap, beastly, bloody and bankrupt.[1]

Prior to South Africa's first democratic elections in 1994, analysts of all shades presented cynical dissections of what a black majority government could mean. A review of South Africa's transition reveals profound challenges to conventional thinking (as in the epigraph above) and most pessimistic analyses of Malthusian proportion that sought to present scenarios of the post-apartheid reconstruction. First was the peaceful transition itself that challenged conventional wisdom that projected a disorderly Congo-type re-enactment. More importantly, South Africa has so far managed to maintain peace within its racial mix. Second was the fear of political fracturing along black ethnic lines.[2]

These analyses ignored the fact that blacks could overcome divisions, and to focus on issues of common interest. The emergence of the National Union of Mineworkers and the 1987 strike bears witness to this ability. The analysis of black politics fracturing along ethnic fault lines underestimated the capacity of Africans to resolve their differences. So far, South Africa's young democracy has defied the kind of pessimism and stereotypes leveled on Africans as power custodians. Contrary to Johnson's projection, ten years of South Africa's democracy have been dominated by remarkable progress in reconstructing apartheid's architecture.

Unlike in Zimbabwe where British troops supervised the transfer of power, and Namibia where UN forces did the same, there was a relatively smooth internally managed transfer of power, an unusual phenomenon in the recent history of the continent. While the transition took place, challenges of reconstruction and economic redistribution remain. Despite its weaknesses, GEAR has managed to resuscitate the economy by reducing the fiscal deficit and national debt, bringing down inflation as well as lifting trade barriers, removing tariffs and import duties, and generally winning praise largely from mainstream economists and business interests, for establishing a sound macroeconomic base on which future prosperity can be built.[3] Legitimate questions on how that future prosperity would be shared remain.

As South Africa's transition took place after the cold war, most analysts predicted the ANC, Cosatu and the SACP alliance would disintegrate because the leftist ideals that inspired them had collapsed. What this tells us is that globalization, capitalism and neo-liberalism in particular, have had a serious impact on South Africa's transition. The tensions that emerged within the alliance have largely been ideological differences over the adoption of GEAR. It has also revealed the hegemonic power of capitalism in coercing a movement that had been overwhelmingly socialist to acquire a new conviction and policy orientation within a relatively short period of time. For now, despite ideological differences, the alliance has not disintegrated and for some time to come the ANC will continue to draw its strength from economic disparities between the racial divide. All these salient factors combined make it more complicated to analyze South Africa's transition.

*   *   *   *   *

Overall, in the first decade of democracy, 1994–2004, the ANC has made phenomenal progress in some areas, but at the same time, GEAR has had unintended consequences. While GEAR has been blamed for job losses, this case study of the gold mining industry has shown that, there is only indirect relation between the two. In general, South Africa's unemployment crisis should be seen as an outcome of economic restructuring in accordance with GEAR and a new labor regime based on the respect for human rights enshrined in the Constitution. It is an inevitable price of reversing centuries of imbalances.

Regarding the gold mining industry, this analysis makes the following four empirical points some of which support the theoretically approaches. FIRST, retrenchments in the gold mining industry were not linked to the introduction of GEAR. Downscaling in the gold mining industry has been taking place long before GEAR as an outcome of a crisis in the mode of regulation, which inevitably constrained the mode of accumulation. If anything—GEAR was ideologically suitable for a new mode of accumulation, for restructuring and international competition. This can be attributed to at least three factors: first, the rise in black unionism, which in addition to other factors, was the most prominent factor that caused the restructuring in the gold mining industry as old ways of working suddenly changed after persisting for the better part of a century.

After the 1987 NUM strike, job loses can be attributed to increasing union power and the restructuring process that ensued. For as Malherbe and Segal put it, "the union action contributed to the further rise of a third in unskilled wages between 1982 and 1998."[4] Second, the mining industry could no longer be insulated from the political and legislative changes that characterized the transition. For an industry that has been the driving force of the South African economy, its complicity with successive apartheid governments meant that it enjoyed privileges that were not extended to any other industry. It ran a parallel employment system outside the parameters of formal employment policies, even running a parallel immigration policy through the bilateral treaties. All these facilitated the gold mining industry's mode of accumulation. With the restructuring of the labor market, new challenges confronted the mining industry, gold in particular.

The imposition of new labor laws, amongst others, The Labor Relations Act of 1995, the Basic Conditions of Employment Act of 1997 and the Employment Equity Act of 1998, exacerbated job losses in the gold mining industry. Overall, instead of encouraging employers to hire, the new labor laws imposed stringent requirements which protected workers. While these statutory provisions were enthusiastically welcomed by organized labor, they were perceived by business and investors as being in conflict with the spirit of GEAR because of the increased labor market regulation. The legislation demanded an element of responsibility, requiring employers to implement new work practices at a time when industries, the gold mining industry in particular, were more concerned about cutting production costs and the need to be competitive at the global level.

Third, has been a slump in the gold price. By 1999, the price of gold fell below US$260 an ounce. This price slump destroyed the margins of an industry whose profits are not only predicated, but sometimes even hedged on high gold prices. As a result, by the late 1990s half the shafts in the South African gold mining industry were making a loss. This exerted pressure on the mining industry to curtail production costs in order to produce an ounce below the market unit price. This led to reduction in mine labor, which still accounted for 56 percent of total costs of operating a gold mine by 2004. The reduction in mine labor has also helped the gold mining industry to save escalating cost of running the hostels. However, apart from reducing working costs, for the Chamber of Mines the retrenchments also served to undermine the bargaining power of the NUM.

*   *   *   *   *

SECOND, the future of the gold mining industry is no longer dependent on the availability of a cheap, docile and exploitable labor pool, but on career mining consisting of a smaller, well-trained and better-paid labor force. The idea is to achieve maximum productivity with a minimum labor force. This was achieved in five ways; first, the industry closed marginal and unproductive mines, which it resuscitates when the gold price rises, making the margins between production costs and profits reasonable. Second, the industry has been relying on the sub-contracted component of labor, which is not unionized and therefore cheaper. Third, the industry has been hedging its future gold production when the gold price is favourable. This means that fluctuations in gold price do not affect productivity since it is the production of gold that has been paid in advance.

Fourth, the gold industry has been selling some of its closed shaft to consortiums of Black Economic Empowerment that largely mine gold using contract labor since their long-term production is always uncertain as it depends on the gold price. Fifth, the gold mining industry has been resorting to reprocessing old mine dumps as new gold refining techniques can salvage at least one gram of gold per ton. Advances in electronics, physics and chemistry have cumulatively made reduction plants, where the mineral is extracted from the mineral-bearing rock, more efficient. For instance, at the Rand Refinery, improved computerized Electrolytic Refining method now refines gold to 99.99 percent fineness. In addition, bacteria are now used to assist in the extraction of gold from certain types of gold bearing rock through a process known as bioleaching, which was pioneered in South Africa.

THIRD, by reducing the total labor force by two thirds, the industry restructured itself to become the lowest cost gold producer in the world. In the process, the traditional mining house has been destroyed and replaced by holding companies, among them, Billiton and Anglo-American. For instance, AngloVaal has split into three groups focusing on mining, consumer goods and engineering. Technology, lower labor turn out and restructuring helped reduce production costs. This was important because South Africa's gold is of such low grade that the gold mining industry would not have been able to compete with Australia, Canada and the United States at a global level in the absence of "cheap labor" policies under the new democratic political order.

The restructuring has enabled the industry to focus on assessing international trends, costs and opportunities of exploration outside South Africa. In this regard, today, South African mining companies own and operate mines in Australia, Brazil, China, Ghana, Mexico, Mongolia, Namibia, Tanzania and the USA. In addition to globalising their operations, mining houses have also diversified. For instance, Billiton and Gencor divested from their paper, oil and consumer interests though an unbundling process.

FOURTH, regarding organized labor, despite the advent of democracy and new representation, the enforcement of a rather strict form of neo-liberalism, has gradually reduced its bargaining position. The labor movement's alliance with the ANC has not alleviated its predicaments brought by neo-liberal economics. While they had benign intentions, new labor laws inadvertently undermined the populist aspirations of the left. Furthermore, politically contentious issues such as HIV/AIDS should also be taken into consideration when analysing current job losses. As the economy moves further away from a "cheap labor" system to a professional, skilled and better-paid workforce, those without the necessary skills required by industries will remain unemployed. The industries that absorbed unskilled labor in the past no longer require such a huge labor force. Put differently, the true victims of apartheid have now become the victims of democracy's neo-liberal capitalism. This reality has caused tensions within the ANC-led alliance. However, while the reduction in labor force has served to undermine organized labor, for some time to come the alliance will continue.

*   *   *   *   *

The second set of conclusions focus more specifically on evidence to the theoretical approaches to this analysis. Chapter Two summarized the history of the South African gold mining industry through an analysis of how the industry forged an alliance with the state to establish a mode of regulation necessary to facilitate its accumulation strategies. It demonstrated how this accumulation strategy diligently served the interests of the gold mining industry. After Union in 1910, the state enacted a series of legislative instruments to guarantee that the mines got the "cheap labor" they wanted. Amongst other legislation, the Land Act of 1913; the Apprenticeship Act of 1922; Colour Bar Act and the Urban Areas Act (1923); the Industrial Conciliation Act (1924) and the Wage Act of 1925 formed the pillars of these policies.

After the National Party came to power in 1948, the period of high apartheid, 1960–1973 successfully entrenched the state's hegemonic positions over African resistance politics. However, it was this suppression of black voices, which eventually undermined the mode of regulation. For instance, while the ANC was banned, avenues for voicing discontent included, amongst others, a militant student movement informed by black consciousness. As African protests against apartheid, both industrial and political, turned violent, this resulted in a fundamental disequilibrium which undermined the very foundations of the mode of regulation and accumulation forged after the Boer War. The search for a new regime of accumulation and mode of regulation led to clandestine ANC-capital negotiations since the late 1970s.

Chapter Three analysed the restructuring process that took place in the gold mining industry, prior to and after the transition. It demonstrated the extent to which capital succeeded in advocating a favourable accumulation strategy, namely, the neo-liberal market framework, with a subsequent mode of regulation—democratic compromise. Under the new mode of regulation, the industry was able to globalize its operations, invest abroad and compete at the international level. This could not be achieved under the sanctions campaign and international isolation during apartheid. Clearly, the entire system, political and economic matrix had to be overhauled. The chapter demonstrates how the industry prepared itself for the new mode of accumulation, well in advance. The central argument is that the industry shifted from reliance on the "cheap labor" system and restructured itself in preparation for competitiveness at the global level. This new mode of accumulation was the only lifeline for corporate South Africa. If there was an alternative to acquiring a new mode of accumulation without universal franchise, black people could have remained bracketed—just as they have been throughout.

Chapter Four is a reflection on the transition. It discussed the new mode of regulation, democratic post-apartheid South Africa under the leadership of the ANC. It analysed how the ANC shifted from largely socialist leanings to neo-liberalism under pressure from both internal capital and the reality of neo-liberal hegemony internationally. It demonstrates how the ANC's ideological conviction changed from one extreme to the other within a relatively short period of time and how it became a champion of neo-liberalism. The analysis revealed some of the profound challenges facing South Africa in the post-cold war reconstruction, that is, how to balance the need for fiscal conservatism with the need for social justice. Economically (by technical calculations), GEAR works for capital and the middle class, but social issues remain contentious. South African capital projected scenarios, which provided valuable insights of what was required for long-term profit maximization. Black Economic Empowerment became part of the strategy worked out in the 1980s to get rid of apartheid and have non-racial capitalism. It has also become part of the compromise for the ANC's adoption of neo-liberal policies.

Chapter Five analyzed the position of the gold mining industry post-apartheid. It assessed the extent to which the mining industry has restructured through a comparison with other major gold producers; Australia, Canada and the U.S. The comparison revealed the pace in which South Africa's gold mining industry adjusted its operations in the absence of "cheap labor" to compete with other major gold producers. The analysis focused on the following central questions: first, the position of the gold mining industry and its relationship with the new ANC government after the transition. The mode of regulation is working well and sustains the mode of accumulation.

Second, is the position of labor after GEAR. The chapter argues that GEAR threatens the existence of organized labor, thus reducing its meaningful role in South Africa's reconstruction. It also reduces the bargaining achievements Cosatu has won for workers since its formation. While Cosatu fought successfully against apartheid, it is being humiliated by its own ally, the ANC through policies that undermine its very existence—the evidence is overwhelming. By failing to create jobs, GEAR has not been an antidote, as labor markets have shut the most vulnerable citizens out of jobs. While the economy has recovered from its regression trajectory, the failure to create sufficient jobs to cut into the disturbing levels of unemployment will continue to have retrogressive effect on South Africa's social landscape. For, inequality, crime and poverty in South Africa are driven by the lack of wage income. On the part of the ANC, failure to create jobs is certainly an inadvertent, yet humiliating dereliction of duty.

Third, is the hegemonic ideological struggle in the tripartite alliance between the ANC, Cosatu and SACP after GEAR. The analysis reveals the constraints of post-cold war democratic and economic reconstructions under the hegemony of neo-liberalism and globalization. One of the hard lessons for South Africa and for other countries in political transition is that it is one thing to debate the dialectics of Marxism or the nuances of class struggle when in opposition. Once faced with the real task of governing, economic pragmatism becomes inevitable. It was also through the ballot box that left leaning political parties came to power in Argentina, Brazil, Chile, Ecuador, Uruguay and Venezuela as a counterpoint to unpopular neo-liberal economics. However, long-standing ideals can be easily undermined by the demands to conform to the prevailing economic orthodoxy and the distribution of power in the international political economy. It is important to reiterate that it is not about doing what politicians believe in, but what would work given the circumstances.

Notes

NOTES TO THE FOREWORD

1. Wilmot G. James, 1992. *Our Precious Metal: African Labour in South Africa's Gold Industry* Bloomington, Cape Town and London: Indiana University Press, David Philip & James Currey.

NOTES TO THE INTRODUCTION

1. Chamber of Mines, 2003, p. 19, Annual Report, Chamber of Mines, Johannesburg.
2. *South Africa's Yearbook,* 2005. pp. 459, Government Communication and Information Service (GCIS), Pretoria.
3. Government Communication and Information Service (GCIS), 20003. pp. 157–158, *South Africa Year Book,* GCIS, Pretoria.
4. *Mail and* Guardian, March 9–15, 2001, as quoted in Terreblanche, S. 2003. p. 66, *A History of Inequality in South Africa, 1652–2002,* University of Natal Press, Pietermaritzburg.
5. *Ibid.*
6. See Chamber of Mines *Annual Reports,* 1994–1995, 1996–1997, 1998–1999 and 1999–2000, Chamber of Mines, Johannesburg.
7. *Ibid.*
8. *South Africa Year Book,* 2000, p. 267, Government Communication and Information Service, Pretoria.
9. According to the South African Institute of Race Relations, 2001, p. 222, poverty income varies according to household size—the larger the household, the larger the income required to keep its members out of poverty. Poverty income levels range from R551 for one individual to R2, for a household of eight members or more per month.
10. Statement of the president of the African National Congress, Nelson Mandela, at his inauguration as President of the Democratic Republic of South Africa, Union Buildings, Pretoria, May 10, 1994.

11. Friedman, S. 2004. p. 185, "An Act of the Will: Manuel and the Politics of Growth," in Parsons, R. (ed.), *Manuel's Markets and Money: Essays in Appraisal*, Double Storey Books, Cape Town.

NOTES TO CHAPTER ONE

1. Stephen Gelb as quoted in O'Meara, D. 1996. p. 425, *Forty Lost Years: The Apartheid State and the Politics of the National Party, 1948–1994*, Ravan, Johannesburg and Ohio University Press, Athens.
2. Berman, B. 1990. p. 12, *Control and Crisis in Colonial Kenya: The Dialectic of Domination*, James Currey, London; Heinemann, Kenya and Ohio University Press, Athens.
3. *Ibid.*, pp. 14–15.
4. *Ibid.*, p. 12.
5. See Crush, J., and C. Tshitereke, 2001. p. 50. "Contesting Migrancy: The Foreign Labor Debate in Post-1994 South Africa," *Africa Today*, Volume 48, Number 3. See also Jeeves, A. 1995, "Migrant Labor and the State under Apartheid, 1948–1999," in Cohen, R. (ed.) *The Cambridge Survey of World Migration*, Cambridge University Press, Cambridge.
6. Berman, B. 1990. p. 12.
7. *Ibid.*
8. See for instance, Bond, P. 2000, *Elite Transition: From Apartheid to Neo-Liberalism in South Africa,* University of Natal Press, Pietermaritzburg. Gelb, D. (ed.) 1991, *South Africa's Economic Crisis*, David Philip, Cape Town. Habib, A., D. Pillay, and A. Desai, 1998, "South Africa and the Global Order: The Structural Conditioning of a Transition to Democracy," *Journal of Contemporary African Studies*, Volume 16, Number 1. Macro-Economic Research Group, 1993, *Making Democracy Work: A Framework for Macroeconomic Policy in South Africa*, Center for Development Studies, Bellville. And Wood, E. 2000, *Forging Democracy from Below: Insurgent Transitions in South Africa and El Salvador*, Cambridge University Press, Cambridge.
9. For a discussion, see O'Meara, D. 1996. pp. 421–489.
10. *Ibid.*, p. 428.
11. O'Meara, D. 1996. p. 428.
12. *Ibid.* p. 429.
13. Minowa, M. 2001, "Japanese Capitalism in Crisis: A Regulationist Interpretation," (A book Review) in *Asia-Pacific Development Journal*, Volume 8, Number 1.
14. Wilson, F. 2001. p. 103, "Minerals and Migrants: How the Mining Industry has Shaped South Africa," *Daedalus, Journal of the American Academy of Arts and Sciences*, Winter.
15. Miliband, R. 1977. p. 124, *Marxism and Politics*, Oxford University Press, Oxford.
16. Tickel, A., and J. Peck, 1992. p. 192, "Accumulation, Regulation and the Geographics of post-Fordism: Missing Links in Regulationist Research," *Progress in Human Geography*, Volume 16, Number 2.

17. *Ibid.*, p. 192.
18. See Greenberg, S. 2002. p. 4, "Land Reform and Transition in South Africa," Paper presented to the Ford Foundation Environment and Development Affinity Group in Cape Town, Rand Afrikaans University, June 7.
19. Yudelman, D. 1984. *The Emergence of Modern South Africa: State, Capital, and the Incorporation of Organized Labor on the South African Gold Fields, 1902–1939*, David Philip, Cape Town and Johannesburg.
20. *Ibid.*, p. 7.
21. Crush, J., A. Jeeves and D. Yudelman, 1991. p. 10, *South Africa's Labor Empire: A History of Black Migrancy to the Gold Mines*, Westview Press, Boulder, Colorado and David Philip, Cape Town.
22. Government Communication and Information Service (GCIS) 2005. p. 38, *South Africa Year Book,*. GCIS, Pretoria.
23. Hertzog defined civilized labor as "all work done by people whose standard of living conforms to the standard of living generally recognized as decent from a white person's point of view." Uncivilized labor was defined as "work performed by persons whose goal is restricted to the mere necessities of life in accordance with the ideas of undeveloped and savage people." For a discussion, see, Muller, C.F.J. 1993. p. 415, *500 Years: A History of South Africa*, Third edition, revised and illustrated, Van Schaik, Pretoria.
24. Truth and Reconciliation Commission, 1998, Section 63, as quoted in Crush, J., and C. Tshitereke, 2001. p. 51.
25. Giddens, A. 1985. pp. 8–10, *The Nation State and Violence*, Cabridge University Press, Cambridge.
26. Berman, B. 1990. p. 27.
27. *Ibid.*, p. 28.
28. *Ibid.*, p. 21.
29. See Reader's Digest, 1988. p. 454, *Illustrated History of South Africa: The Real Story*, Reader's Digest, Cape Town.
30. *Ibid.*
31. O'Meara, D. 1996. p. 429.
32. *Ibid.*
33. Berman, B. 1990. p. 30.
34. Botha, P.W. August, 15, 1985. "Rubicon speech," delivered at the Durban City Hall. See "http://www.anc.org.za" (accessed, October 15, 2004).
35. Rile, E. 1991. p. 173, *Major Political Events in South Africa, 1948–1990*, Fact on File, Oxford University Press, Oxford.
36. In Kenya, Berman argues that *formal co-optation*, the creation of essentially powerless but visible offices and agencies, was used to create *the illusion of access and influence* in order to maintain the *reality of state power and control* over the African population; while *informal co-optation*, the unofficial and often covert provision of access to ostensibly independent state agencies, helped sustain the *appearance of state autonomy* and obscure the *reality of direct settler influence*. Berman, B. 1990. pp. 33–34.
37. For a discussion on the South African military, see Seegers, A. 1996. *The Military in the Making of Modern South Africa*, Tauris Academic Studies, I.B. Tauris Publishers, London and New York.

38. See Greenberg, S. 2002. p. 4.

39. Macroeconomic Research Group, 1993. *Making Democracy Work: A framework for Macroeconomic Policy in South Africa*, Center for Development Studies, Belleville.

40. Marais, H. 1999. p. 150, *South Africa Limits to Change: The Political Economy of Transformation*, Zed Books, London, Cape Town University Press.

41. *Ibid.*, p. 74.

42. Robinson. V. 2004, "Strangers in a new land," reported that the poor whites problem that was so prevalent in the 1930s is rearing its head again. White unemployment had nearly doubled since 1995. Today, 430,000 whites, out of a total population of 4,5 million are too poor to live in traditional white areas and 90,000 are in a rearguard survival struggle. Of these, 305,000 are Afrikaners and 215,000 are English speaking. The *Mail and Guardian* July 9–15.

43. *Ibid.*

44. Berman, B. 1990. p. 30.

45. Andrew, M. 1994. p. 61, "Labour, the Keynesian Welfare State, and the Changing International Political Economy," in Stubbs, R. and G. Underhill, *Political Economy and the Changing Global Order*, McClelland and Stewart, Toronto.

46. Hunt, D. 1989. p. 26, *Economic Theories of Development: An Analysis of Competing Paradigms*, Harvester Wheatsheaf, London.

47. According to the South African Communist Party's (SACP) "Contemporary Struggles and the National Democratic Revolution," globalization and neoliberalism are castigated for destroying social democracy. However, a revival of social democracy in European countries in the 1990s is seen as a beacon of hope for South Africa's painful transition. See: Netshitenzhe, J. 2000, "National Democratic Revolution and Class," *African Communist*, Number 154, Second Quarter, South African Communist Party, Johannesburg.

48. Milner, H. 1998, p. 122, "International Political Economy: Beyond Hegemonic Stability," *Foreign Policy*, Spring.

49. For a comprehensive discussion, see Schumpeter, J.A. 1943, *Capitalism, Socialism and Democracy*, Allen and Unwin, London. See also *Business Cycles: A Theoretical, Historical, and Statistical Analysis of the Capitalist Process*, 1939. Volume 2; and *History of Economic Analysis*, 1954.

50. Gray, J. 1998. p. 196, *False Dawn: The Delusions of Global Capitalism*, Granta Books, London.

51. Rostow, W. 1960, *The Stages of Economic Growth: A Non-Communist Manifesto*, Cambridge, Cambridge University Press.

52. On this note, see Waltz, K. 2000. p. 14, "Structural Realism after the Cold War," *International Security*, Volume 25, Number 1.

53. Keet, D. 1999. p. 5, *Globalization and Regionalization—Contradictory Tendencies: Counteractive Tactics or Strategic Possibilities*, Foundation for Global Dialogue, Occasional Paper Number 18, Braamfontein, Johannesburg.

54. See Mkandawire, T., and C. Soludo, 1998. p. 41, *Our Continent, Our Future: African Perspectives on Structural Adjustment*, IDRC—Ottawa, CODESRIA—Dakar.

55. Strange, S. 1985. p. 235, "Protectionism and World Politics," *International Organization*, Volume 39, Number 2. Liberals have always insisted on limiting the power of the state. For instance, Edmund Burke declared that "it is in the power of the state to prevent much evil; it can do very little positive good." Thomas Paine's, eloquent pamphleteer for the American Revolution (of which Burke approved), wrote in his "Common Sense" that "Government, even in its best state, is but a necessary evil" and generations of Americans almost ritualistically repeated Thomas Jefferson's advice that government is best that governs least. See *Britannica Encyclopedia Multimedia Edition*, 1999 under *Liberalism*.

56. Cerny, P. 2000. p. 302, "Political Globalization and the Competition State," in Stubbs, R., and G. Underhill, (eds.) *Political Economy and the Changing Global Order*, McClelland and Stewart, Toronto.

57. Sally, R, 1994. p. 166, "Multinational Enterprises, Political Economy and Industrial Theory," *Review of International Political Economy*, Volume 1, Number 1.

58. Wade, R. 1992. p. 272, "East Asia's Economic Success: Conflicting Perspectives, Partial Insights, Shaky Evidence," *World Politics: A Quarterly Journal of International Relations*, Volume 44.

59. George, S. 2001. p. 11, "A Short History of Neoliberalism: Twenty Years of Elite Economics and Emerging Opportunities for Structural Change," in Bello, W., N. Bullard and K. Malhotra, (eds.), *Global Finance: New Thinking on Regulating Speculative Capital Markets*, Zed Books, London.

60. *Ibid.,* p. 1.

61. See George, S. 1999. "Public Institutions and Civil Society, Citizenship and Solidarity: An Area of Confrontation?" Paper presented at the Parliamentarians—NGOs Conference, Strasbourg, May 28–02 June.

62. See Holsti, K. 1985. p. 66, *The Dividing Discipline: Hegemony and Diversity in International Theory*, Allen and Unwin, London.

63. See George, S. 2000. She gives an example of Oskar Lafontaine, the former German Finance Minister whom the *Financial Times* called an "unreconstructed Keynesian," who was consigned to this hell for daring to propose higher taxes on corporations and tax cuts for ordinary families.

64. Williamson, J. 2000. p. 1, "What should the World Bank think about the Washington Consensus?" *The World Bank Research Observer*, Volume 15, Number 2, pp. 251–264.

65. Washington Institute for International Economics, 1990, "What Washington Means by Policy Reform," in Williamson, J. ed., *Latin American Adjustment: How Much Has Happened?* Washington Institute for International Economics, Washington.

66. While the blueprint may look attractive, in essence, "privatization" of public assets means government's willingness to alienate or surrender the product of decades of work by thousands of people, transferring it to large private holders. Equally, "deregulation" of public assets means a government's willingness to give up its sovereignty for the benefit of transnational corporations and financial market operators.

67. Escobar, A. 1995. p. 58, *Encountering Development: The Making and Unmaking of Third World*, Princeton University Press, New Jersey.
68. See Rist, G. 1997. p. 1, *The History of Development: From Western Origins to Global Faith*, Zed Books, London and New York.
69. Crush J. 1995, "Introduction: Imagining Development," in Crush, J. *Power of Development*, Routledge, London and New York.

NOTES TO CHAPTER TWO

1. See Callinicos, L. 1994. p. 22, *A People's History of South Africa, Volume One: Gold and Workers 1886–1924*, Ravan Press, Johannesburg.
2. There is a debate on whether the labor system that was established was coercive or whether the need to earn money on the part of Africans and the new consumer culture enticed them into wage employment. For instance, see James, W. 1992, *Our Precious Metal: African Labor in South Africa's Gold Industry, 1970–1990*, Indiana University Press, Bloomington and Indiana. Jeeves, A., and D. Yudelman, 1986, "New Labor Frontiers for Old: Black Migrants to the South African Gold Mines, 1920–85," *Journal of Southern African Studies*, Volume 13, Number 1. See also Harries, P. 1986, "Capital, State, and Labor on the 19th Century Witwatersrand: A Reassessment," *South African Historical Journal*, Volume 18. Harries, P. 1994, *Work, Culture and Identity: Migrant Laborers in Mozambique and South Africa, 1860–1910*, Heinemann, Portsmouth. Mawby, A. 2000, *Gold Mining and Politics—Johannesburg, 1900–1907: The Origins of the Old South Africa*, Lewinston, Queenston. Simons, J., and R. Simons, 1983, *Class and Colour in South Africa, 1850–1950*, International Defense Aid Fund for Southern Africa, London. Macnad, R. 1987, *Gold: Their Touchstone—Goldfields of South Africa 1887–1987*, Jonathan Ball Publishers, Johannesburg.
3. Macnad, R. 1987. pp. 33–34.
4. Jacobsson, D. 1936. p. 149, *Fifty Golden Years of the Rand 1886–1936*, Faber and Faber, London.
5. Leyds, G. 1964. p. 245, *A History of Johannesburg: The Early Years*, Nasionale boekhandel, Cape Town.
6. *Ibid.*
7. Innes, D. 1984. p. 72, *Anglo-American and the Rise of Modern South Africa*, Heinemann, London.
8. Richardson, P., and J.J. Van-Helten, 1980. p. 26, "The Gold Mining Industry in the Transvaal, 1886–1899," in Warwick, P. (ed.) *The South African War: The Anglo-Boer War 1899–1902*, Longman, London.
9. Innes, D. 1984. p. 58.
10. Terreblanche, S. 2003. p. 68, *A History of Inequality in South Africa, 1652–2002*, University of Natal Press, Pietermaritzburg.
11. According to Smith, I. 1996. p. 47, between 1886 and 1899 some 75, 000 people emigrated from Britain to South Africa and many of them were Cornish tin-miners. See *The Origins of the South African War, 1899–1902*, Longman, London and New York.

12. For a discussion, see, Clark, N., and W. Worger, 2004. p. 25, *South Africa: The Rise and Fall of Apartheid*, Longman, London.

13. Levy, N. 1978. p. 205, "Problems of Acquisition of Labor for the South African Gold Mining Industry: The Asian Labor Alternative and the Defense of the Wage Structure," Center for Southern African Studies, University of York.

14. The Chamber of Mines 13th Annual Report, 1902. p. XL, Chamber of Mines, Johannesburg.

15. Jeeves, A. 1974. p. 15, "The Control of Migratory Labor in the S.A. Gold Mines in the Era of Kruger and Milner, *Journal of African Studies*, Volume 2, Number 1.

16. Chamber of Mines 14th *Annual Report*, 1903. p. XLV, Chamber of Mines, Johannesburg.

17. The need to control the supply side of labor led to the establishment of reserves in the form of villages near the mines where, as John Hays Hammond, an American engineer who was then advising Rhodes in the 1890s put it, "boys could live with their wives and families." Initially, the idea had been discarded because mine owners feared the political consequences arising from the work force they would have created from such arrangements. See Sampson, A. 1978. p. 50.

18. James, W. 1992. p. 2.

19. Lionel Phillips as quoted in Harries, P. 1986. p. 28.

20. See Butler, J. 1964. p. 231, (the title was not readable) *Boston University Papers in African History*, Volume 1, Boston University Press, Boston Massachusetts. For a discussion, see also Davies, R. 1979. *Capital, State and White Labor in South Africa, 1900–1960*, Harvester Press, Brighton.

21. James, W. 1992. p. 18.

22. Wilson, F. 1972. p. 148, *Migrant Labor*, South African Council of Churches, SPRO-CSA, Johannesburg.

23. Jeeves, A. 1975, has estimated that the death rate among Africans on the mines in the early years was roughly between 80 and 100 per thousand workers per annum.

24. Allen, V.L. 1992. p. 229, *The History of Black Mineworkers in South Africa Volume One: The Techniques of Resistance*, The Moor Press, National Union of Mineworkers, Johannesburg.

25. Although the Chamber of Mines despised independent contractors, preferring a system where they determined all conditions of service, they were to reconsider their position much later, as post-apartheid laws demanded uniformity across the labor market.

26. Richardson, P. 1982. p. 10, *Chinese Mine Labor in the Transvaal*, Macmillan Press, London and Basingstoke. He also points out "the most successful attempts to reduce costs came through the reduction of unskilled labor turnover, the rationalization of administrative costs and the spread of investment funds."

27. Harries, P. 1986. "Capital, State, and Labor on the 19th Century Witwatersrand: A Reassessment," *South African Historical Journal*, Volume 18.

28. Jeeves, A. 1975. p. 127.

29. Jeeves, A. 1985. p. 255, *Migrant Labor in South Africa's Mining Economy: The Struggle for the Gold Mines Labor Supply,* McGill-Queen's University Press, Kingston and Montreal, Witwatersrand University Press, Johannesburg.

30. Obviously, loss of labor through medical rejection was wasteful and to overcome the hurdle of the ban on tropical recruiting, the Chamber of Mines even underwrote the expansion of colonial medical services in Bechuanaland and the other High Commission Territories. It provided modest grants-in-aid to support the training of paramedical staff and the establishment of mobile clinics. This was partly to improve the chronically poor health of the target population; numbers of whose males would now have to meet the medical standard established by the WNLA for mine recruits. Mining is hard work and the WNLA obviously preferred men with the physique of an American football player. For a discussion, see also Jeeves, A., and D. Yudelman, 1986. p. 110.

31. For a discussion, see Jeeves, A., and D. Yudelman, 1986. p. 108–115.

32. *Ibid.*

33. In the early years of production, 1887–1889, the Chamber of Mines estimates the unrecorded production of the mining industry at 42,000 oz.; this, together with the recorded production, brings the total to 642,804 oz. for the three years. See also, Watermeyer, G.A., and Hoffenberg, S.N. 1932. p. 4, *Witwatersrand Mining Practice,* The Transvaal Chamber of Mines, Gold Producer's Committee, Chamber of Mines, Johannesburg.

34. Government took a decision to expatriate the Chinese Miners, For a discussion, see Jeeves, A. 1985. p. 254. See also Richardson, P. 1982. *Chinese Labor in the Transvaal.* MacMillan Press, London.

35. Chamber of Mines, 2001, *Statistical Tables,* Chamber of Mines, Johannesburg.

36. Levy, N. 1978. p. 59, "Problems of Acquisition of Labor for the South African Gold Mining Industry: The Asian Labor Alternative and the Defense of the Wage Structure," Center for Southern African Studies, University of York.

37. *Ibid.* Government harassment for taxes pushed people to the point were they even had to sell their children in prearranged marriages in order to benefit by the *lobola* cattle in advance on marriage. Others even committed suicide to avoid a prison sentence for tax evasion.

38. Report of the South African Native Affairs Commission, 1903–1905, Government Printer, Pretoria.

39. Innes, D. 1984. p. 67.

40. Mamdani, M. 1996. p. 227, *Citizen and Subject: Contemporary Africa and the Legacy of Late Colonialism,* James Currey, London and David Philip, Cape Town.

41. See Barker, B. *et al,* 1988. p. 316, *Illustrated History of South Africa,* 1988, Reader's Digest, Cape Town.

42. Nkomo, S. 1985. p. 84, "Migrant Labor Economic Theory and National Development Policy: The Case of South Africa and Lesotho," Ph.D. Thesis, (unpublished), University of Delaware.

43. From the outset, the purpose of the reserves, Mbeki, G. 1964. p. 67, explained, was to provide a source of "cheap labor" for white agriculture, mining and industry. On the one hand, the reserves have also served as factories for the production of migrant workers, while on the other they have proved suitable grounds for the physical wrecks whom industry discarded in the same way as cane fibre is thrown away after is juice has been extracted. For a discussion, see *South Africa: The Peasants' Revolt*, International Defense and Aid Fund for Southern Africa, London.

44. Allen, V. 1992. p. 214.

45. For a full discussion on the "Push-Pull theory," see Wilson, F. 1972. *Migrant Labor*, South African Council of Churches, SPRO-CSA, Johannesburg.

46. See Arrighi, G. 1973, p. 182–183, "Labour Supplies in Historical Perspective: A Study of the Proletarianization of the African Peasantry in Rhodesia," In Arrighi, G. and Saul, J. (eds.) *Essays on the Political Economy of Africa*, Monthly Review Press, New York and London.

47. Jeeves, A. 1986. p. 73, "Migrant Labor and South African Expansion, 1920–1950," *South African Historical Journal*, Volume 18.

48. Crush, J., A. Jeeves and D. Yudelman, 1991. p. 11, *South Africa's Labor Empire: A History of Black Migrancy to the Gold Mines*, Westview Press, Boulder and David Philip, Cape Town.

49. Jeeves, A. 1986. p. 87–88.

50. Data provided by the Chamber of Mines, Johannesburg.

51. The issue here is not whether the "civilized policy" served the interests of white miners, but to acknowledge that it was designed to do just that, its failures are outside the scope of this analysis.

52. Muller, C.F.J. 1993. p. 415, *500 Years: A History of South Africa*, Third edition, revised and illustrated, Van Schaik, Pretoria.

53. Guelke, A. 1974. p. 100, *Apartheid and the Labor Market*, Center for Southern African Studies, York University.

54. Lipton, M. 1985. p. 5.

55. See James, W.G. 1992. p. 2, *Our Precious Metal: African Labor in South Africa's Gold Industry, 1970–1990,* Indiana University Press, Bloomington and Indiana.

56. Mamdani, M. 1996. pp. 218–284, *Citizen and Subject: Contemporary Africa and the Legacy of Late Colonialism*, James Currey, London and David Philip, Cape Town.

57. Lipton, M. 1985. p. 35.

58. Muller, C.F.J. 1993. p. 418.

59. O'Meara, D. 1983. p. 237, *Volkskapitalisme: Class, Capital and Ideology in the Development of Afrikaner-Nationalism 1934–1948*, Ravan Press, Johannesburg.

60. Bhorat, H. *et al*, 2001. p. 3, *Fighting Poverty: Labor Markets and Inequality in South Africa*, University of Cape Town Press, Cape Town.

61. Chamber of Mines, 2001. *Statistical Tables*, Chamber of Mines, Johannesburg.

62. Although the component of labor that increased was largely foreign, however, South Africans still made a significant percentage of the labor force.

63. McKinley, D. 1997. p. 5, *The ANC and the Liberation Struggle: A Critical Political Biography*, Pluto Press, London and Chicago.
64. For a discussion, see Davis, M. 1987, *Apartheid's Rebels: Inside South Africa's Hidden War*, Yale University Press, New Haven.
65. See Kempton, D. 1989. p. 153, *Soviet Strategy Towards Southern Africa: The National Liberation Movement Competition*, Praeger, New York.
66. Davis, M. 1987. p. 4.
67. McKinley, D. 1997. p. 11.
68. After all, the deputation approach was what the leaders thought was the answer, and therefore, it was top down. When it failed, they reverted to consolidating their presence within the workers, the peasants and others.
69. Holland, H. 1989. p. 60, *The Struggle: A History of the African National Congress*, Grafton Books, London.
70. In retrospect, the cause that the ANC pursued from then onwards can be attributed to the militancy of the Youth League. It is interesting that it was under the leadership of mainly Youth League founders that the ANC ultimately achieved its goals.
71. Jeeves, A., and D. Yudelman, 1986. p. 117.
72. Under the Nkomati Accord, the two governments undertook to respect each other's sovereignty and to remove groups who were planning attacks against the state. The Mozambique authorities followed up by closing ANC camps, seizing its arms, cutting off supplies, and restricting it to ten representatives in Maputo. For a discussion, see Barber, J. 2004. p. 22.
73. Crush, J., and W. James, 1991. p. 302, "Depopulating the Compounds: Migrant Labor and Mine Migrancy in South Africa," *World Development*, April.
74. Terreblanche, S. 2003. p. 73, *A History of Inequality in South Africa, 1652–2002*, University of Natal Press, Pietermaritzburg.
75. Crush, J., A. Jeeves and D. Yudelman, 1991. p. 24.
76. Wilson, F. 1972. p. 141.
77. James. W. 1992. p. 34.
78. *Ibid.*, p. 265.
79. James, W. 1992. pp. 93–94, *Our Precious Metal: African Labor in South Africa's Gold Industry, 1970–1990*, Indiana University Press, Bloomington and Indiana.
80. O'Meara, D. 1996. p. 273, *Forty Lost Years: The Apartheid State and the Politics of the National Party, 1948–1994*, Ravan, Johannesburg and Ohio University Press, Athens.
81. See Lang, J. 1986. pp. 455–474, *Bullion Johannesburg—Men, Mines and the Challenges of Conflict*, Jonathan Ball, Johannesburg.
82. See Crush, J., A. Jeeves and D. Yudelman, 1991. p. 177, *South Africa's Labor Empire: A History of Black Migrancy to the Gold Mines*, Westview Press, Boulder and David Philip, Cape Town.
83. At the time the NUM was formed, P.W. Botha was also introducing some cosmetic political reforms in light of increasing black discontent with apartheid. However, some of these reforms further alienated blacks. For

instance, following the passing of a new Constitution, the Tricameral par-
liament-separate representative chamber for whites, coloured and Indians,
to legitimize the apartheid sate without real compromises on the relative
power position of Afrikaners. Although coloureds and Indians boycotted
the Tricameral parliament, the point worth noting is that they were represented and black were not. This development further antagonized the
already resentful Africans and turned them against Indians and coloureds
for accepting political representation at their expense.

84. *Ibid.*, p. 179.

85. Speech to the South African Institute of Race Relations by Cyril Ramaphosa, SAIRR press release, July 31, 1985.

86. See Brunt, S. 1987. "A South African Experience—a British Miner's view
of the South African Mining Industry," National Union of Mineworkers,
Sheffield.

87. Crush, J. 1989. p. 8, "Migrancy and Militance: The Case of the National
Union of Mineworkers of South Africa," *African Affairs*, Volume 88, pp.
5–24.

88. Southall, R. 1986. pp. 195–9, "Migrants and Trade Unions in South Africa
Today," *Canadian Journal of African Studies*, Volume 20, Number 5.

89. James, W. 1992. p. 91.

90. In 1978, the "Frontline States" formed the Southern African Development
Coordination Conference (SADCC) in order to end economic dependence
on South Africa. In the same year, Denmark, Norway and Sweden established bilateral trade relations and prohibited new investment in South
Africa. In the 1980s, call for sanctions also came from the Commonwealth,
with only British Prime Minister, Margaret Thatcher holding off economic
sanctions. In 1984, 49 U.S. companies pulled out of South Africa; another
50 followed suite in 1985. At the beginning of 1985, Citibank declared
that it would make no new loans to the South African government for the
foreseeable future. For a discussion on sanctions, see Clark, N., and W.
Worker, 2004. *South Africa: The Rise and Fall of Apartheid*, Longman,
London. See also Nerys, J. 2000. "The Campaign Against British Bank
Involvement in Apartheid South Africa," *African Affairs*, Volume 99, pp.
415–433. Nossal, K.R. 1994. *Rain Dancing: Sanctions in Canadian and
Australian Foreign Policy*, University of Toronto Press, Toronto. Crawford,
N., and A. Klotz. 1999. *How Sanctions Work: Lessons from South Africa*,
International Political Economy Series. St. Martin's Press, New York.

91. This broader anti-apartheid movement picked up steam in the early 1980s
when a constellation of loosely allied, largely black, political structures that
challenged apartheid emerged. These were, amongst others, churches, trade
unions and civic organizations whose common purpose and objectives culminated in the formation of the United Democratic Front (UDF) in 1983.
The UDF was an extra-parliamentary umbrella body composed of more
than 550 affiliated trade unions, community organizations, religious, sport,
students movement and other organizations in order to coordinate resistance to government's proposed constitutional amendments and power-
sharing. This development was the largest anti-apartheid movements since

the banning of the ANC in 1960. The militancy of the UDF is reflected in the fact that in November 1984, it coordinated black boycotts of the local council's elections. It was largely in response to successes of the UDF in organizing black resistance that P.W. Botha imposed a State of Emergency on July 28, 1985.

92. The paranoia that gripped the state led to the securitization of non-existential threats. The government expanded the South African Police Service (SAP) complement from 34,271 in 1981 to 68,000 by 1987. The police budget increased from R954 million in 1975 to R2,496 billion in 1987. The reason blacks resorted to political protest was that they had neither legal nor political recourse and could only resort to protest politics as a means of voicing their discontent. See Flynn, L. 1992. p. 249, *Studded with Diamonds and Paved with Gold: Miners, Mining Companies and Human Rights in Southern Africa*, Bloomsbury, London. See also Blumenfeld, J. (ed.) 1987. *South Africa in Crisis*, Croom Help, London and New York.

93. For detailed discussion, see Crush, J. 1989. "Migrancy and Militance: The Case of the National Union of Mineworkers of South Africa," *African Affairs*, Volume 88, pp. 5–24.

94. Flynn, L. 1992. p. 250, *Studded with Diamonds and Paved with Gold: Miners, Mining Companies and Human Rights in Southern Africa*, Bloomsbury, London.

95. See Chamber of Mines, 2003. *Statistical Tables*, Chamber of Mines, Johannesburg.

96. Even where there was an embargo, sanctions were sometimes circumvented. For instance equipment was often exported through intermediaries in roundabout ways to avoid announcement of the origin of the goods. Such tactics were also used in fruit exports from South Africa. One was to send the consignment to Swaziland and then re-sell it to European or U.S. importers, now labelled "Packaged in Swaziland." For a full discussion on how apartheid South Africa used circuitous routes to undermine sanctions see, Landgren, S. *Embargo Disimplemented: South Africa's Military Industry*, Stockholm Institute for Peace Research (SIPRI), Oxford University Press, Oxford.

97. Crush, J., A. Jeeves and D. Yudelman, 1991. p. 1.

NOTES TO CHAPTER THREE

1. Segal, N., and S. Malherbe, 2000, p. 34.

2. See Chamber of Mines, 2003, *Statistical Tables*, Chamber of Mines, Johannesburg. (Please note that this table is for Chamber of Mines gold mines only).

3. Segal, N., and S. Malherbe, 2000, p.1, "A Perspective on the South African Mining Industry in the 21st Century," The Graduate School of Business, University of Cape Town.

4. Chamber of Mine's Memorandum to the National Treasury on the Draft Minerals and Petroleum Royalty Bill, 2002, p. 30.

5. Although Russia is also a major gold producer, I could not find comparative statistics.

6. Chamber of Mines, 2001. p. 6, *Annual Report, 2000–2001*, Chamber of Mines, Johannesburg.

7. On September 22, 2003, during an International Monetary Fund conference, a meeting of central bankers took place in Dubai to discuss a new deal that would cover subsequent future sale of gold by central banks. Measures discussed were implemented in 2004. Thus, the fate of the Washington accord—known formerly as the Central Bank Gold Agreement—has helped to push the bullion price to a six-and-a-half-year peak. The old deal, limiting central bank gold sales to 400 tons a year for five years, expired in September 2004. Following this news, a London Bullion Market Association survey argued that a rise in central bank gold sales to an average of 484 tons a year could be easily absorbed if the buoyant gold price remains. See *Business Report*, "Central Bankers to forge new Gold Deal next year," September 22, 2002.

8. Pogue, T. E. 2000. "An Overview of Producer Services in the Mining Industry in South Africa," Development Policy Research Unit, Working Paper Number 00/35, University of Cape Town.

9. For instance, in September 2003, Canada restarted its nuclear power reactor at Pickering, Ontario. During the same period, Iran continued to insist on the right to develop nuclear power in order to meet its growing demand for electricity. Already running two nuclear power reactors, South Africa's utility, Eskom, is commencing construction of pebble bed nuclear power reactors, and the list of potential international customers continues to grow.

10. The Second World War was ended with the use of nuclear bombs. At the time, British Prime Minister Winston Churchill asked his South African counterpart, Jan Christian Smuts, to investigate if there were any uranium deposits in South Africa. With hundreds of mines countrywide, it was discovered that there were significant deposits of uranium on the Witwatersrand. This was hailed as a strategic discovery since South African production could then outstrip that of Canada and the Congo—the Allies' suppliers during World War II. During the 1950s, production reached the level of 6,000 tons annually—all of it marketed to the U.S. and the U.K. under agreements dating back to the immediate postwar period. See, Crocker, C. 1981. p. 56, *South Africa's Defense Posture: Coping with Vulnerability*, Sage Publications, Beverly Hills.

11. Moolman, E. 2003. p. 16, *An Econometric Analysis of Labor Demand at an Industry Level in South Africa*, Trade and Industrial Strategies (TIPS), Johannesburg.

12. New management include the recruitment of Mr. Mzolisi Diliza—recruited for reasons that have more to do with broader process of Black Economic Empowerment. In interviews with the National Union of Mineworkers in Johannesburg, it was pointed out that his appointment has not meant a good step forward for the industry as he serves the interests of capital. More aptly, "a person like Diliza has done nothing, but we hope to make

progress in the bargaining council." Interview with mineworkers, July 14, 2003, Johannesburg.

13. Interviews with mineworkers, July 14, 2003, Johannesburg.
14. Interview with an executive of the Chamber of Mines, February 12, 2003, Johannesburg.
15. See http://www.mbendi.co.za/orgs/cb33.htm (accessed October 15, 2003).
16. Godsell, B. "Focus on Value and Growth," AngloGold presentation at the Denver Mining Investment Forum October 03, 2002.
17. A feasibility study done in August 2003 stated Cerro Corona could produce 147,000 ounces of gold and 65-million pounds of copper per year, with total cost of US $212 an ounce of gold and 48 cents per pound of copper. Cerro Corona, expected to come into production by mid-2006, has total reserves of 2.39 million ounces of gold and 397,000 tons of copper. Shone, H. "Gold Fields buys Peru project," *The Sunday Times*, December 21, 2003.
18. Bain, J. "Gold Fields enters mine venture in China," *Business Day*, December 24, 2003.
19. Interview with a Cosatu official, July 25, 2003, Johannesburg.
20. National Union of Mineworkers interviews, July 14, 2003, Johannesburg. One interviewee argued that, "we have been accorded new opportunities to bargain for medical aid for mineworkers, social services that benefit miners." For one who has been with the National Union of Mineworkers since 1986, and has therefore witnessed the transformation process first hand, there has indeed been remarkable progress but there are other areas where the industry is dragging its feet.
21. The debate on the hostel or compound system was more vibrant in the 1990s. For comprehensive discussion, see Ramphele, M. 1993. *A Bed Called Home: Life in the Migrant Labor Hostels of Cape Town*, David Philip, Cape Town; Mamdani, M. 1996. *Citizen and Subject: Contemporary Africa and the Legacy of Late Colonialism*, James Currey, London, David Philip, Cape Town; Crush, J., and W. James, 1991. "Depopulating the Compounds: Migrant Labor and Mine Migrancy in South Africa," *World Development*, April.
22. Barons, C. "So many questions: An interview with Gwede Manthashe," *Sunday Times*, August 3, 2003.
23. Lipton, M. 1985. p. 111, *Capitalism and Apartheid South Africa, 1910–84*, Gower publishing, Aldershot.
24. Chamber of Mines, Annual Report, 2001–2002, p. 8, Chamber of Mines, Johannesburg.
25. James, W. 1992. p. 18.
26. Bridge, S. "Chamber leads royalty fight," *Business Report*, May 10, 2003.
27. Baxter, R., and S. Jones, 2002. p. 84, "Transformation in the 1990s," in Jones, S. *The Decline of the South African Economy*, Edward Elgar, Cheltenham and Northampton.
28. Chamber of Mines, 2001. pp. 3–4, *Statistical Tables*, Chamber of Mines, Johannesburg.

29. South Africa does have other smaller gold producers outside of the Witwatersrand in the form of Archaean greenstone belts. The main gold producing greenstone belts are the Barberton greenstone belt and the Kraaipan greenstone belt. The Barberton greenstone belt is situated in the Mpumalanga province, just north of Swaziland. The Kraaipan belt is located west of Johannesburg, near Kuruman. Other smaller belts exist in the Northern Province, but have been worked sporadically.

30. *Business Report*, "Ashanti's Midas Touch," August 23, 2003.

31. Interview with a National Union of Mineworkers official, Johannesburg, July 14, 2003. It appears as though GEAR is simply dismissed for its ideological commitment rather than based on a comprehensive evaluation and analysis of its performance.

32. Interview with a Cosatu official, July 25, 2003, Johannesburg.

33. Strange, S. 1987. p. 568, "The Persistent Myth of Lost Hegemony," *International Organization*, Volume 41, Number 4.

34. Chamber of Mines, 2005, *Statistical Tables*, Chamber of Mines, Johannesburg. Note that figures in this table include non-Chamber gold mines.

35. Idson, T. 2001. p. 280, "Skill-biased Technical Change and Trends in Employer Size Effects," in Polachek, S. (ed.), *Worker Wellbeing in a Changing Labor Market*, Research in Labor Economic, Volume 20, State University of New York, Binghamton.

36. See Seidman, G. 1995. p. 176, "Shafted: The Social Impact of Downscaling in the OFS Goldfields," in Crush, J., and W. James, *Crossing Boundaries: Mine Migrancy in a Democratic South Africa*, IDRC, Ottawa and IDASA, Cape Town.

37. Chamber of Mines, The Importance of Gold Mining in South Africa, http://www.bullion.org.za/bulza/educatn/nbgold98.htm (visited, August 08, 2003).

38. This rate of job losses has weakened the position of both the NUM and Cosatu as its membership dropped by six percent from roughly 1.8 million to 1.7 million between 2000 and 2002. The NUM lost more than 130,000 affiliates between 1994 and 2001. See also *Business Day*, "Labor's challenges," April 16, 2003.

39. Mamdani, M. 1996, pp. 218–284, has referred to hostel system as 'the rural in the urban' but there are no real distinctions between the mining hostels and sprawling townships that characterize South Africa. If anything, they coexist with each other in the same geographic place with townships servicing the everyday needs of hostel dwellers. For a full discussion, see Mamdani, M. 1996, *Citizen and Subject: Contemporary Africa and the Legacy of late Colonialism*, David Philip, Cape Town.

40. See also Wilson, F. 1996. p. 323, "Human Capital Formation and the Labor Market in South Africa," *American Economic Review*, Volume 82, pp. 322–5.

41. See African National Congress, 1994, *Reconstruction and Development Programme*, Umanyano Publications, Johannesburg.

42. See Chamber of Mines *Annual Report*, 2000–2001. p. 8.

43. Interview with a union official, National Union of Mineworkers, Johannesburg, July 14, 2003. The interviewee further stressed, "I do not think

the job losses come as a result of GEAR but as the industry tries to reshape itself in the face of new opportunities outside the country."

44. See Gastrow, P. 2001, *Theft from South African Mines and Refineries: The Illicit Market for Gold and Platinum,* Institute for Security Studies, Pretoria and Cape Town.

45. Chamber of Mines, (undated), p. 12. *The Contribution of the Mining Industry to Sustainable Development in South Africa,* Chamber of Mines, Johannesburg.

46. Smith, R. 1996. p. 45, *The Origins of the South African War 1899–1902,* Longman, London and New York.

47. Segal, N., and S. Malherbe, 2000, p. 27.

48. *Ibid.,* p. 95.

49. For a discussion on dumps rehabilitation, See Mphephu, N.F., "Rehabilitation of Tailing Dams on the Central Rand, Johannesburg," unpublished paper, Center for Applied Mining and Exploration Geology, University of the Witwatersrand.

50. Interview with a Chamber of Mines senior official, February 12, 2003, Johannesburg.

51. Chamber of Mines, *Mining News,* November 2003, p. 3, Chamber of Mines, Johannesburg.

52. The substitution of capital for labor can be attributed to the growing impact of HIV/AIDS, which has hit the mining industry. Interestingly, a Chamber of Mines commissioned study by the University of Cape Town Business School revealed that the first miners in South Africa to test HIV-positive were three men at a copper mine in Messina in 1989. In 1992, an AIDS policy was developed and agreed to by the major unions. In the long term, continuous engagement of miners with HIV/AIDS posed its own risks as a result of absenteeism. The swift reduction in labor force could also be attributed to the fear that the gold mining industry could be statutorily compelled to provide medical care for thousands of miners who may be infected with the virus in the largely single-sex compound dormitories where 71 percent of miners were still accommodated. For a discussion, see Segal, N., and S. Malherbe, 2000, "A Perspective on the South African Mining Industry in the 21st Century," The Graduate School of Business, University of Cape Town.

53. Interview with a Chamber of Mines senior official, February 12, 2003, Johannesburg.

54. Segal, N., and S. Malherbe, 2000, p. 6.

55. AECI is a South African explosives company. In the 1930s, it introduced ammonium nitrate based explosives as a substitute for nitro-glycerine. With these developments, South African production moved to the forefront of explosives technology. These developments were driven by the production needs of South African gold mines. After World War II, the demand of mining at depth level led to the innovative new explosive 'Dynagel' for use in damp conditions. In the 1960s the "PPAN" explosive was developed. This explosive had a better-controlled blast, a longer shelf life and better conditions in damp conditions than its predecessors. AECI started fusehead

production for electric detonators in 1971. It supplies detonators and initiation devices to South African mines. *Ibid.*, p. 94.

56. SASOL started the production of explosives in 1984. As an owner of various collieries, SASOL had direct experience in mining. Further, it was producing nitrates and was looking for way of beneficiating these products. Since starting to produce explosives it has aggressively captured market share within South Africa, as well as expanding abroad. SASOL Mining Explosives (SMX) achieved a turnover of R667 million in 1999. SMX strategy is based on technological innovation. SASOL has patented a process by which microspheres of gas can be incorporated into porous ammonium nitrates. This significantly improves the efficiency and performance of the explosives. On the basis of this technology, SASOL currently exports explosives (more than 100,000 tons in 1997). It is also expanding its production offshore. It opened a plant in Manitoba, Canada in 1999. SASOL also supplies detonators and initiation devices to the South African mining industry. *Ibid.*, p. 94.

57. Segal, N., and S. Malherbe, 2000, p.10.

58. See also Davies, R., and J. Head, 1995. p. 204, "The Future of Mine Migrancy: Trends in Southern Africa," In Crush, J., and W. James (eds.), *Crossing Boundaries: Mine Migrancy in a Democratic South Africa*, IDRC, Ottawa and IDASA, Cape Town.

59. South African Reserve Bank, 2004. p. 4, *Quarterly Bulletin: September,* South African Reserve Bank, Pretoria.

60. Government Communication and Information Service, *South Africa's Year Book, 2003/2004, 2004*, p. 161. Government Communication and Information Service, Pretoria.

61. South African Reserve Bank, 2004. p. 5, *Quarterly Bulletin: June,* South African Reserve Bank, Pretoria.

62. Bhorat, H. 2003. p. 3, "The Post-Apartheid Challenge: Labor Demand Trends in the South African Labor Market, 1995–1999," Development Policy Research Unit, University of Cape Town.

63. Jacobs, S., and J. Faull, "The ANC is Betraying its History," *Sunday Times,* April 27, 2003.

64. Mabanga, T. "Outlook Fair for Mining," *Mail and Guardian*, February 7 to 13, 2003.

65. Bridge, S. "Mbeki critical of mine management," *Business Report*, October 12, 2003.

66. Bridge, S. "Crisis threatens 70 000 mine jobs," *Business Report* October 10, 2003.

67. Unpublished Data: Chamber of Mines Economics Division

68. Mabanga, T. "Outlook fair for mining," *Mail and Guardian*, February 7—13, 2003.

69. Crush, J. *et al*, 1999, *Undermining Labor: Migrancy and Sub-contracting in the South African Gold Mining Industry*, Migration Policy Series Number 15, Southern African Migration Project, Queen's University at Kingston.

70. While there are good reasons for reforming the South African labor market, it has however been argued that government has not adequately

considered the economic consequences; that is, the cost increasing effects of these laws. Firms have therefore responded to legislation by using a wide range of techniques such as subcontracting, outsourcing and temporary labor practices," See also Hofmeyr, J. 2001. p. 2, "The case for flexibility in South Africa's labor market," University of Natal Durban, paper presented at the *Work 2001 Conference*, Johannesburg.

71. Labuschane, G., and E. Muller, 1993. p. 48, "Population and Migration in Southern Africa in the 1990s," *Politicon*, Volume 20, Number 1. McDonald, D. *et al*, 1998. p. 33, points out that in Mozambique, official remittances in the form of "deferred payment" from Mozambican workers in South African mines alone make up 55 percent of the non-aid budget of the Mozambican government and is an essential part of the household budged of most miner's families. See *Challenging Xenophobia: Myth and Realities about Cross Border Migration in Southern Africa*, 1998, Policy Paper Number 7, Southern African Migration Project, IDASA, Cape Town and Queen's University, Kingston.

72. Crush, J. *et al*, 1999. p. 10.

73. A study by Jeanne Esselaar of the Division of Economics at the University of Natal has outlined why firms outsource and the reasons organized labor oppose the practice. For a full discussion, see Esselaar, J. 2002, "The Debate over Outsourcing in South Africa: Evidence from a Case Study," Division of Economics, University of Natal, Durban. See also Segal, N., and S. Malherbe, 2000. "A perspective on the South African Mining Industry in the 21st Century," The Graduate School of Business, University of Cape Town.

74. National Union of Mineworkers interview, July 14, 2003, Johannesburg. An interviewee pointed out that sub-contracting undermines the social gains of organized labor and insisted that sub-contractors must comply with the current labor laws.

75. National Union of Mineworkers interview, July 18, 2003. Interestingly, the interviewee remained confident that the number of miners would increase as the mining industry is, in his words, "opening up" with black business tapping into the sector. However for the interviewee, the disappointing performance of people like Mzolisi Diliza, Chief Executive of the Chamber of Mines does not leave much room for optimism. On the contrary, interviews with mineworkers themselves reveal a different picture. When I asked them on their prospects for employment in the next 10 years, their response was, "there will not be more employment opportunities, but the current labor force will be retained," National Union of Mineworkers interview, July 14, 2003, Johannesburg.

76. Miners' interview, National Union of Mineworkers, July 8, 2003, Johannesburg. Of interest is that miners understand better the causes of their job losses.

77. *Ibid*.

78. Bhorat, H., Lundall. P., and S. Rospabe, 2002. p. 47, "The South African Labor Market in a Globalizing World: Economic and Legislative Considerations," Development Policy Research Unit and the International Labor Organization.

79. See also Rosenthal, J. "The Savage Side of Industry's Saviour," *Business Report*, September 17, 1999.

80. See Chamber of Mines *Statistical Tables*, 2005 and the Department of Labor, *Mining Statistics*, 2005, Pretoria. Additional statistics on sub-contracted labor from the National Union of Mineworkers.

81. Tshitereke, C. 1998. p. 76, *Debate on the Contract Labor Migrant System in South Africa—1990–1998*, Unpublished Masters Thesis, University of Stellenbosch.

NOTES TO CHAPTER FOUR

1. Nelson Mandela as quoted in Bond, P. 2000. p. 13, *Elite Transition: From Apartheid to Neo-liberalism in South Africa*, University of Natal Press, Pietermaritzburg, Pluto Press, London.

2. Marais, H. 1999. p. 146, *South Africa Limits to Change: The Political Economy of Transformation*, Cape Town University Press, Rondebosch.

3. Torres, L. 1998. p. 174, *Labor Markets in Southern Africa*, Fafo-report 257, Institute for Applied Social Science.

4. For full discussion on restructuring the South African labor market, see Standing, G., J. Sender, and J. Weeks, 1996. The total comes to 90 percent and one can only speculate that the remaining 10 percent consist of those who are self employed in the informal sector.

5. Statistics South Africa, *Census 1996*, Statistics South Africa, Pretoria.

6. Williams, P. 1999. p. 147, "Reflections on the 'new' South Africa," *African Affairs*, Volume 98, Number 392.

7. Saul, J.S. 2002. p. 1, "Cry for the Beloved Country: The Post Apartheid Denouement." (while doing research, I had access to the original unedited version of the paper, which was subsequently published, however, the two versions are different) in Jacobs, S., and R. Calland (eds.) *Myth, Ideology and the Politics of Thabo Mbeki*, University of Natal Press, Pietermaritzburg.

8. Weeks, J. 1998. p. 795, "Stuck in low GEAR? Macroeconomic Policy in South Africa, 1996–1998," *Cambridge Journal of economics*, Volume 23, pp. 795–811.

9. Edwards, C. 1998. p. 49, "Financing Faster Growth in South Africa: The Case for Reforming the Financial Sector," *Transformation*, Volume 35, University of Natal, Durban.

10. African National Congress, 1955. p. 2, *The Freedom Charter*, African National Congress, Johannesburg.

11. Michie, J., and V. Padayachee, 1998. p. 632, "Three Years After Apartheid: Growth, Employment and Redistribution?" *Cambridge Journal of Economics*, Volume 22, Number 5, September.

12. Arnold, M. 1992. p. 15, "Engaging South Africa After Apartheid," *Foreign Policy*, Number 87, pp. 139–156.

13. Mandela, N.R. 1991. J.H. Heinz company foundation distinguished lecture, University of Pittsburgh, Soldiers and Sailors Memorial Hall, December 6.

14. See, Mandela, N.R. 1997. p. 2, "A Vision for Africa," address at the world economic forum, southern Africa economic summit, May 21, Harare.

15. Bond, P. 2000. p. 16. *Elite Transition: From Apartheid to Neo-liberalism in South Africa*, University of Natal Press, Pietermaritzburg, Pluto Press, London. Elite transition in the sense that transition did not affect every sphere of life. For instance, the political elite changed, but the economic power remains largely in the hands of white owned conglomerates.

16. For a discussion on Ethiopia and its resistance of IMF imposed structural adjustment conditions, see Stiglitz, J. 2002. pp. 23–52, *Globalization and its Discontents*, Norton, New York.

17. See Michie, J., and V. Padayachee, 1998. p. 624.

18. See also Kelly, M.V. 1993. *Financial Institutions in South Africa*, Juta Press, Johannesburg; Bond, P. 2000. p. 72; Marais, H. 1999. p.92, p.133.

19. Interview with an ANC-SACP Member of Parliament, Cape Town, August 22, 2003.

20. Webster, E., and E. Glenn, 1999. pp. 21–22, "Lessons for South Africa: Unions, Democracy, and Economic Liberalization, *Working USA* —September/October.

21. Gray, J. 1998. p. 204. *False Dawn: The Delusions of Global Capitalism*, Granta Books, London.

22. See Marais, H. 2001. "The Logic of Expediency: Post-Apartheid shifts in Macro Economic Policy," in Jacobs, S., and R. Calland (eds.) *Myth, Ideology and the Politics of Thabo Mbeki*, 2002, University of Natal Press, Pietermatritzburg.

23. See Bond, P. 1996. "The Making of South Africa's Macro-Economic Compromise" in Maganya, E. (ed.), *Development Strategies in Southern Africa*, IFFA, Johannesburg.

24. Escobar, A. 1995. p. 128, *Encountering Development: The Making and the Unmaking of the Third World*, Princeton University Press, Princeton, New Jersey.

25. See, Marais, H. 1999. p. 152, *South Africa Limits to Change: The Political Economy of Transformation*, Zed Books, Cape Town University Press.

26. *Ibid* .

27. See Webster, E., and G. Adler, 1999. pp. 88–89.

28. During this period, the South African economy was dominated by a group of conglomerates, the four largest of which controlled 83 percent of the companies listed on the Johannesburg Stock Exchange (JSE, the tenth largest stock exchange in the world in the late 1980s) prior to the end of apartheid.

29. Macroeconomic Research Group, 1993. *Making Democracy Work: A framework for Macroeconomic Policy in South Africa*, Center for Development Studies, Belleville.

30. Marais, H. 1999. p. 127, *South Africa Limits to Change: The Political Economy of Transformation*, Zed Books, Cape Town University Press.

31. Bond, P. 2000. p. 39.

32. Naidoo, R. 2003. "The Union Movement in South Africa's Transition, 1994–2003, National Labor Economic and Development Institute (NALEDI), unpublished paper.

33. Roux, A. 2000. p. 151. *Everyone's Guide to South African Economy,* Zebra Press, Rivonia.

34. Marais, H. 1999. p. 157.

35. See Murray, M 1994. p. 18, *The Revolution Deferred: The Painful Birth of Post-Apartheid South Africa,* Verso, London and New York.

36. Mandela, N. 1991. J.H. Heinz company foundation distinguished lecture, University of Pittsburgh, Soldiers and Sailors Memorial Hall, December 6.

37. Wittenberg, M. 1997. p. 176, "Growth, demand and redistribution: Economic debate, rhetoric and some food for thought," in Michie, J., and V. Padayachee (eds.), *The Political Economy of South Africa's Transition: Policy Perspectives in the Late 1990s,* Dryden Press, London.

38. Weeks, J. 1998. p. 796, "Stuck in low GEAR? Macroeconomic Policy in South Africa, 1996–1998," *Cambridge Journal of Economics,* Volume 23, pp. 795–811.

39. African National Congress, 1994. *Reconstruction and Development Program: A Policy Framework.* Section 1.1.1, Umanyano Publications, Johannesburg.

40. Lester, A., E. Nel, and T. Binns, 2000. p. 248, *South Africa, Past Present and the Future: Gold at the End of the Rainbow?* Longman, London.

41. *Reconstruction and Development Program,* 1994. p. 22.

42. *Ibid.,* 1994. p. 1.

43. See Southall, R. 2003. p. 62, "The State of Party Politics: Struggles within the Tripartite Alliance and the Decline of Opposition," In Daniel, D., Habib, D., and R. Southall, *State of the Nation: South Africa, 2003–2004,* Human Sciences Research Council, Pretoria.

44. See also Moll, T. 1991. p. 313, "Growth Through Redistribution: A Dangerous Fantasy," *The South African Journal of Economics,* Volume 59, Number 3.

45. Barberton, C. 1995. p. 24, *Prioritizing Prioritization in Government,* Public Information Center, IDASA, Cape Town.

46. The weaknesses of macroeconomic populism rest on the denial of trade-offs: the implicit belief that a wide range of desirable welfare objectives can be met at once through rises in nominal government spending. See also Ffrench-Davis, R. 1976. p. 110, "Policy Tools and Objectives of Redistribution," in Foxley, A. (ed.) *Income Distribution in Latin America,* Cambridge University Press, Cambridge.

47. See Calitz, E. 1997. pp. 328–330, "Aspects of the Performance of the South African Economy," *The South African Journal of Economics,* Volume 65, Number 3. For a discussion, see also Dornbusch, R. and S. Edwards (eds.). 1991. *Macroeconomic Populism in Latin America,* Chicago University Press, Chicago and London.

48. Natrass. N. 1994 as quoted in UNDP's Development Report, 2005. pp. 34, *Overcoming Underdevelopment in South Africa's Second Economy,* United

Nations Development Programme, Development Bank of Southern Africa and the Human Sciences research Council, Johannesburg.

49. For a discussion, see Cornia, G.A. 2006, "Potential and Limitations of Pro-Poor Macroeconomics: An Overview," in Cornia, G.A. (ed.). *Pro-Poor Macroeconomics: Potential and Limitations*, Macmillan, London.

50. Mandela, N. 1991. J.H. Heinz Company Foundation distinguished lecture, University of Pittsburgh, Soldiers and Sailors Memorial Hall, December 6.

51. Kentridge, M. 1993. p. 5, *Turning the Tanker: The Economic Debate in South Africa*, Center for Policy Studies, Johannesburg.

52. Lester, A., E. Nel, and T. Binns, 2000. p. 251, *South Africa, Past Present and the Future: Gold at the End of the Rainbow?* Longman, London.

53. See Southall, R. 2003. p. 62.

54. Bhorat, H. 2002. p. 2. *et al*, also argue that soon after the transition, the international community needed clear signals concerning economic policy direction of the new government, and domestic policy makers produced a set of policy stances, encapsulated under the Growth Employment and Redistribution. See, "The South African Labor Market in a Globalizing World: Economic and Legislative Considerations," Development Policy Research Unit, University of Cape Town, Rondebosch, Paper commissioned by the International Labor Organization.

55. Although both reports of the Labor Market Commission to investigate the development of a comprehensive labor market policy (1996) and the ILO commissioned study by Standing *et al,* contradicted much of the thinking behind GEAR.

56. Stiglitz, J. 2002. p. 35.

57. Frank, A.G. 1969, "The Development of Underdevelopment," reprinted in Wilber C.K., and Jameson, K.P. 1992, p. 107, *The Political Economy of Development and Underdevelopment,* McGraw-Hall, London and New York.

58. Interview with a Cosatu official, July 25, 2003, Johannesburg.

59. See Marais, H. 2001. "The Logic of Expediency: Post-Apartheid Shifts in Macro Economic Policy," in Jacobs, S., and R. Calland (eds.) *Myth, Ideology and the Politics of Thabo Mbeki*, 2002, University of Natal Press, Pietermatritzburg.

60. For a discussion on the East Asian economic crisis, see, Chang, H. *et al,* 1998. "The Asian Crisis: Introduction," *Cambridge Journal of Economics,* Volume 22, pp. 649–652. Iraj Abedian, Chief Economist of Standard Bank of South Africa has, however, pointed out that South Africa's inability to attract Foreign Direct Investment, which was a problem, became a benefit as those countries whose economies were heavily dependent on Foreign Direct Investment were hit the worst. See also Lamont, J. "Feeding off the Fruits of Austerity," *Financial Times,* November 26, 2001.

61. Following the crisis, the South African equity markets suffered an initial decline of 22 percent in dollars but then recovered to the equivalent of 15 percent loss with the Johannesburg Stock Exchange showing greater resilience than other emerging stock markets. However, as the Asian crisis took hold, the South African stock market with a capitalization of US$245

billion moved to the top of the investible indices for emerging markets. See Arnold, G. 2000, *The New South Africa*, Macmillan and St. Martin's press, London and New York.

62. COSATU, 1997. p. 22, "A Programme for the Alliance," *African Communist*, Volume 146, Number 1.

63. See: Economic Policy in the Alliance: A Central Committee Discussion Document, South African Communist Party, Third Quarter, 1997.

64. See the Department of State Expenditure and Treasury 1996, The *Growth Employment and Redistribution, a Macroeconomic Strategy*, Department of State and Expenditure, Pretoria.

65. Michie, J., and V. Padayachee, 1998. p. 626.

66. Bruggemans, C. 2003. p. 63, *Change of Pace: South Africa's Economic Revival*, University of the Witwatersrand Press, Johannesburg.

67. Interview with a Cosatu official, Johannesburg, July 25, 2003.

68. Mandela, N. 1964, Statement during the Rivonia Trial, 1963–1964.

69. IMF, *South Africa—Selected Economic Issues*, 1996. p. 84, IMF Staff Country Report Number 96, Volume 4, IMF, Washington D.C.

70. Naidoo, R. 2000. "The Impact of Socio-economic restructuring on the Working Class and the Challenges Facing Them," paper presented at the Harold Wolpe Forum, University of Cape Town, August 17.

71. Mills, G. 2003. "South Africa's Greatest Challenge is to Transform and Grow the Economy," *Mail and Guardian*, August 8–14. See also, ANC Election Manifesto 2004, "A people's contract to create work and fight poverty," African National Congress, Johannesburg.

72. Sparks, A. 2003. p. 16, *Beyond the Miracle: Inside the New South Africa*, Jonathan Ball Publishers, Johannesburg.

73. Innocenti, N.D. "Feeding Off the Fruits of Austerity," *Financial Times*, November 26, 2001.

74. Hone, H. "AngloGold, GoldFields defy the odds and deliver," *Sunday Times*, August 3, 2003.

75. Chamber of Mines interviews, February 12, 2003, Johannesburg.

76. Letsie, L.E. 2003. as quoted in UNDP's Development Report, 2005. pp. 31–32: *Overcoming Underdevelopment in South Africa's Second Economy*, United Nations Development Programme, Development Bank of Southern Africa and the Human Sciences Research Council, Johannesburg.

77. Sparks, A. 2003. p. 220, *Beyond the Miracle: Inside the New South Africa*, Jonathan Ball Publishers, Johannesburg.

78. Bhorat, H. *et al*, 2001. p. 5.

79. *Ibid*.

80. Bolin, L. "Foreign investors still hesitant about South Africa," *Sunday Times*, November 03, 2003.

81. South African Reserve Bank, 2002. p. 22, *Annual Report*, South African Reserve Bank, Pretoria.

82. In India, foreign investment provided a more nurturing environment for domestic entrepreneurs. In the process, India has managed to spawn a number of companies that now compete internationally with the best that Europe and the United States have to offer. Moreover, many of these firms

are in the most cutting-edge, knowledge-based industries—software giants Infosys and biotechnology. See, Hunag, Y., and T. Khanna, 2003. "Can India Overtake China," *Foreign Policy Magazine,* September/October, Carnegie Endowment for Peace, Massachusetts.

83. Van Rensberg, T. 1999. "A Critical Assessment of Primary Listings of South African Companies in Offshore Stock Exchanges," paper presented to the TIPS Annual Forum at Glenburn Lodge, Muldersdrift, September 19–22. These companies still maintain secondary listings in the Johannesburg Securities Exchange. None of these companies have terminated any of their operations in the geographic area of South Africa, leaving the aggregate size and potential growth of the gross domestic product largely unaffected. It is speculated that the likely expansion of offshore listed companies may give South Africa extra impetus to economic growth in the future. Walters, S., and J.W. Prinsloo, 2002. p. 71, "The Impact of Offshore Listing on the South African Economy," *South African Reserve Bank Quarterly Bulletin,* September.

84. Interview with a senior Cosatu official, July 25, 2003, Johannesburg.

85. Carmody, P. 2002. p. 263, "Between Globalization and (post) Apartheid: The Political Economy of Restructuring in South Africa," *Journal of Southern African Studies*, Volume 28, Number 2.

86. Mabanga, T. "Ventures into the interior," *Mail and Guardian*, January 30 to February 05, 2004.

87. Carmody, P. 2002. p. 265.

88. Lourens, C. "Nigeria tops SA for direct U.S. investment," *Business Day*, January 29, 2004.

89. http://earthtrends.wri.org/searchable_db/index.cfm   (accessed   June   14, 2004).

90. Chamber of Mines interviews, February 12, 2003, Johannesburg.

91. See Christiansen, H., and A. Bertrand, 2003. "Trend and Recent Trends in Foreign Direct Investment," Directorate for Financial, Fiscal and Enterprise Affairs, OECD.

92. Rodrick, D. 2003. "On Road to Nowhere with Neo-liberal Economics," *Business Day*, October 17, 2002.

93. Mbeki, T. 2003. Responses to Question from MPs in the National Assembly, 5 May, Parliament, Cape Town.

94. Robinson, V. "What the social partners want," *Mail and Guardian*, May 9–15, 2003.

95. Agreement reached at the Growth and Development Summit, June 7, 2003.

96. Interview with an ANC-SACP Member of Parliament, August 22, 2003. He further argues that investors have, for instance, not gone to Zambia, even though they like economic policies there.

97. Lester, A., E. Nel, and T. Binns, 2000. p. 246, *South Africa, Past Present and the Future: Gold at the End of the Rainbow?* Longman, London.

98. George, S. 2001. p. 10, "A Short History of Neo-liberalism: Twenty Years of Elite Economics and Emerging Opportunities for Structural Change," in

Bello, W., N. Bullard and K. Malhotra, (eds.), *Global Finance: New Thinking on Regulating Speculative Capital Markets,* Zed Books, London.

99. Marais, H. 1999. pp. 170–171.

100. Strydom, P. 2002. p. 46, "Macroeconomic Policy, 1970–2000," in Jones, S. (ed.) *The decline of the South African Economy*, Cheltenham, UK and Northampton, USA.

101. South African Institute of Race Relations, 1998. p. 399, *South Africa Survey 1998–1999*, South African Institute for Race Relations, Johannesburg.

102. Jacobs, S., and J. Faull, "The ANC is Betraying its History," *Sunday Times,* April 27, 2003.

103. Van Zyl, J. "The Great GDP Myth: Economic 'Localization' is Key to Jobs Crisis," *Mail and Guardian,* June 6–12, 2003.

104. Cosatu, 2000. p. 86, *Accelerating Transformation: First Term Report of Cosatu Parliamentary Office*, Cosatu, Johannesburg.

105. Interview with a senior Cosatu official, July 25, 2003, Johannesburg.

106. Parsons, R. 2004. p. 10, "Setting the Scene," in Parsons, R. (ed), *Manuel's Markets and Money: Essays in Appraisal*, Double Storey Books, Cape Town.

107. *Ibid* ., p. 10.

108. *Ibid* .

109. Roux, A. 2004. p. 17, "Getting into GEAR," in Parsons, R. (ed), *Manuel's Markets and Money: Essays in Appraisal*, Double Storey Books, Cape Town.

110. Fedderke, J. "Focus on the Unemployed Rather than Labor Aristocracy," *Mail and Guardian,* June 6–12, 2003.

111. Table from Maziya, M. 2001. p. 205, "Contemporary Labor Market Policy and Poverty in South Africa," in Bhorat, H. *et al, Fighting Poverty: Labor Markets and Inequality in South Africa*, University of Cape Town Press, Rondebosch.

112. *Ibid* ., p. 30.

113. Interview with a senior NUM official, July 14, 2003, Johannesburg.

114. Interview with a Chamber of Mines official, February 12, 2003, Johannesburg.

115. Government Communication and Information Services, 2000, *South Africa Year Book*, p. 234. Government Communication and Information Services, Pretoria.

116. Interview with a former Director General of the National Treasury, August 25, 2003, Stellenbosch.

117. Carmody, P. 2002. p. 255, "Between Globalization and (post) Apartheid: The political Economy of Restructuring in South Africa," *Journal of Southern African Studies*, Volume 28, Number 2.

118. African National Congress, 2004. Election Manifesto: The Ten-Year Review, African National Congress, Johannesburg.

119. Lamont, J. "Pace of Change is Undermining Old Uncertainties," *Financial Times,* November 26, 2001.

120. Makgetla, N. "Growth Path Keeps Jobless in Despair," *Business Day*, September 5, 2003.

121. Frank further argued that analogously to the relations between development and underdevelopment on the international level, the contemporary underdeveloped institutions of the co-called backward or feudal domestic areas of an underdeveloped country are no less the product of the single historical process of capitalist development than are the co-called capitalist institutions of the supposedly more progressive areas. See Frank, A.G. 1969, "The Development of Underdevelopment," reprinted in Wilber C.K., and Jameson, K.P. 1992, p. 108–109, *The Political Economy of Development and Underdevelopment,* McGraw-Hall, London and New York.

122. Jacobs, S., and J. Faull, "The ANC is Betraying its History," *Sunday Times,* April 27, 2003.

123. Simon, J. *et al,* "Estimating the Impacts of AIDS on Business in South Africa," paper presented at the Boston University African Studies Seminar, April 10, 2001.

124. Lamont, J. 2001. "Pace of Change is Undermining Old Uncertainties," *Financial Times,* November 26.

125. Berman, B. 1990. p. 30. *Control and Crisis in Colonial Kenya: The Dialectic of Domination,* James Currey, London; Heinemann, Kenya and Ohio University Press, Athens.

126. Department of Trade and Industry, *Annual Report, 2001–2002,* Government Printer, Pretoria.

127. *Business Day,* "Jobless growth," October 29, 2002. In his study, Haroon Bhorat of the University of Cape Town's Development Research Unit contests the argument of a jobless growth in favor of a more friendly "poor employment growth." He, however, acknowledges that the economy has experienced growth rates with less labor. What is important to note is that restructuring process is taking place in all spheres of the economy so as to reduce inefficiencies. In government, as he put it, "the intention has been to reduce the size of the public sector wage bill. . . . And the result of this extensive and rapid public sector restructuring has been significant employment losses within the sector." Bhorat, H. 2003. p. 6, "The Post-Apartheid Challenge: Labor Demand Trends in the South African Labor Market, 1995–1999," Development Policy Research Unit, University of Cape Town.

128. Fedderke, J. "Higher Pay Means Fewer Jobs," *Mail and Guardian*, May 16–22, 2003. Certainly, the cost of labor has a negative impact on employment. The ILO commissioned study by Standing *et al,* 1996, pointed out that reducing labor costs would help boost employment. The GEAR document also refers to the importance of "wage moderation" and called for a national social agreement that ensures that wage and salary increases do not rise more than productivity growth. See also Barker, F. 1999. p. 189, *The South African Labor Market: Critical Issues for Renaissance,* J.L. van Schaik, Pretoria.

129. Greater Johannesburg Metropolitan Council—World Bank Partnership, *Constraints to Growth and Employment in South Africa,* 2000.

130. An interview with former Department of Labor official: Department of Labor interviews, July 22, 2003, Pretoria.

131. In particular, Nkrumah makes the following points about neo-colonialism: it continues to actively control the affairs of the newly independent state. In most cases neo-colonialism is manifested through economic and monetary measures. For example the neo-colonial territories become the target markets for imports from the imperial centre(s). While neo-colonialism may be a form of continuing control by a state's previous formal colonial master, new actors may also subject the state to imperial power. These new actors include imperial hegemons and the international financial and monetary institutions. See Nkrumah, K. 1965. *Neo-Colonialism: The Last Stage of Imperialism*, Thomas Nelson and Sons, London.

132. Baker, F. 2003. "The Impact of Labor Legislation on the Performance of the Labor Market," in Finnemore, M., and R. Van Rensberg, *Contemporary Labor Relations,* Butterworth, Johannesburg.

133. See Rist, G. 1997. p. 1, *The History of Development: From Western Origins to Global Faith*, Zed Books, London and New York.

NOTES TO CHAPTER FIVE

1. Chamber of Mines, 2001. *Statistical Tables,* Chamber of Mines, Johannesburg.

2. Chamber of Mines, 2003. p. 12, *Annual Report*, Chamber of Mines, Johannesburg.

3. In August 2005, Fitch Ratings became the third major international agency to upgrade South Africa's foreign credit ratings in 2005, following upgrades by Moody's and Standard and Poor's. See Government Communication and Information Service (GCIS) *South Africa Year Book*, 2005. p. 172, GCIS, Pretoria.

4. See Itano, I. "Central bank in South Africa is expected to cut key rate," *New York Times,* September 10, 2003.

5. DRD announced in early October 2003 that 2,700 mineworkers would definitely be retrenched at its Harties operation in the North West Province. While the company compounds the national unemployment crisis, it is also planning to buy Australian assets with up to US$100 million, *Independent Online*, October 10, 2003.

6. Chamber of Mines of South Africa, *Mining News*, September 2003.

7. National Union of Mineworkers Interviews, July 14, 2003, Johannesburg.

8. Shone, H., and R. Stovin-Bradford, "Commodity prices keep miners on check," *Sunday Times*, September 28, 2003.

9. Godsell, R. Interview with Alec Hogg, Johannesburg, February 14, 2003. See http//www.anglogold.co.za/

10. For AngloGold's successes, see *Annual Report*, 2002, AngloGold, Johannesburg.

11. GoldFields, 3003. *Annual Report*, GoldFields of South Africa, Johannesburg.

12. Chamber of Mines Interviews, July 29, 2003, Johannesburg.

13. *Chamber of Mines Annual Report* 2003, p. 18, Chamber of Mines, Johannesburg. The summit, as argued in Chapter Four, consisted of government, labor and business working together towards the provision of investment necessary for economic growth and job creation.

14. Interview with a Chamber of Mines official, Johannesburg, July 29, 2003,.

15. Terreblanche, S. 2003. p. 56, *A History of Inequality in South Africa, 1652–2002*, University of Natal Press, Pietermaritzburg.

16. *Ibid.*

17. O'Meara, D. 1996. p. 425, *Forty Lost Years: The Apartheid State and the Politics of the National Party, 1948–1994*, Ravan, Johannesburg and Ohio University Press, Athens.

18. Interview with a Chamber of Mines executive, February 12, 2003, Chamber of Mines, Johannesburg.

19. Bridge, S. "Change on revenue instead of profit still bothers mining sector," *Business Report*, February 19, 2004.

20. Bridge, S. "Chamber leads royalty fight," in *Business Report*, May 10, 2003.

21. *Ibid.*

22. *Bloomberg*, "Treasury to review rate on gold mining sales," as re-printed in *Business Report*, March 26, 2004.

23. National Treasury, Press Statement on the Mineral and Petroleum Royalty Bill, March 20, 2003.

24. *Business Report*, "Investec welcomes move on mining royalties," February 19, 2004. See also Loxton, L. "State on slow but global path to more holistic tax regime for mining, oil sectors," *Business Report*, June 9, 2004.

25. *Bloomberg*, "Treasury to review rate on gold mining sales," as re-printed in *Business Report*, March 26, 2004.

26. Investec is a South Africa registered company and listed in the Johannesburg Stock Exchange. Its core areas of activity are; investment banking and principal transactions, corporate banking and interest rate activities and private client group and asset management.

27. *Ibid.*

28. Jimena, J. "The royalty cools the Las Bambas bidding," *Canadian Mining Journal*, June 16, 2004. BHP-Australia Merged with South African gold mining companies.

29. Jimena, J. "Mining royalty news: Chile, Peru eye high metal prices," *Canadian Mining Journal*, May 5, 2004.

30. Chamber of Mines, 2003. p. 18, *Annual Report*, Chamber of Mines, Johannesburg.

31. Hennop, J. 2004, "New apartheid lawsuit is launched," *Business Day*, June 21, 2004.

32. Ebrahim, S. 2002. p. 50, "Defend, Advance and Consolidate the Alliance," *South African Labor Bulletin*, Volume 26, Number 2.

33. Wallerstein, I. 1991. p. 84, *Geopolitics and Geoculture: Essays on the Changing World-System*, Cambridge University Press, Cambridge.

34. *Ibid.*

35. National Economic Development and Labor Council, Nedlac.
36. Interview with a Cosatu official interview, Johannesburg, July 25, 2003.
37. International Labor Resource Group, Workers World News, September 1999, p. 1–2. "Privatization: Can it deliver?" Woodstock, South Africa.
38. It is not clear which businesses Cosatu bought, but See http://www.wsws.org/articles/2000/nov2000/sa-n14.shtml (accessed October 20, 2003).
39. For now, there is a moratorium on the privatization of the transport utility, Transnet, and the South African Airways. This may be attributed to Jeremy Cronin's (Deputy Secretary General of the SACP) chairmanship of the Transport Committee in the South African Parliament.
40. See Second Resolution of the Central Committee, 2003, Cosatu, Johannesburg.
41. *Ibid.*
42. "Cosatu's last major strike did not live up to expectations and it subsequently backtracked on its flirtation with anarchic social movements that seek to challenge the ANC," reported in the *Sunday Times*, October 5, 2003.
43. "Hard Labor Facing Union Federation," *Business Day*, September 1, 2003. There are many explanations for the waning unity within the labor movement. The Black Economic Empowerment could be one, as more and more blacks are drawn into the boardrooms of big business, they work against Cosatu's initiatives.
44. George, S. 2000. p. 12, "A Short History of Neo-Liberalism: Twenty Years of Elite Economics and Emerging Opportunities for Structural Change," in Bello, W., N. Bullars and K. Malhora, (eds.), *Global Finance: New Thinking on Regulating Speculative Capital Markets*, Zed Books, London.
45. *Business Day*, "Labor's Challenges," April 16, 2003.
46. Andrew, M. 1994. p. 62, "Labour, the Keynesian Welfare State, and the Changing International Political Economy," in Stubbs, R. and G. Underhill, *Political Economy and the Changing Global Order*, McClelland and Stewart, Toronto.
47. Interview with Cosatu official, July 25, 2003, Johannesburg.
48. Petros, N. "Hard Labor Facing Union Federation," *Business Day*, September 1, 2003.
49. Bhorat, H. *et al*, 2001. p. 3, *Fighting Poverty: Labor Markets and Inequality in South Africa*, University of Cape Town Press, Cape Town.
50. Berman, B. 2003. p. 21, "Capitalism Incomplete: State, Culture and the Politics of Industrialization," in Tetty, J., K. Puplampu and B. Berman, (eds.) *Critical Perspectives on Politics and Social Economic Development in Ghana*, African Social Studies Series, Brill, Leiden and London.
51. Jacobs, S., and J. Faull, "The ANC is Betraying its History," *Sunday Times*, April 27, 2003.
52. Interview with a former senior employee with the Department of Labor, July 26, 2003, Brooklyn, Pretoria.
53. Sen, A. 1999. p. 3, *Development as Freedom*, Alfred A. Knopf, New York.
54. Chamber of Mines, 2003. p. 18, *Annual Report*, Chamber of Mines, Johannesburg.

55. African National Congress. 2004. Election Manifesto 2004: "A people's contract to create work and fight poverty," African National Congress, Johannesburg.

56. Hirsch, A. 2004. p. 1, "South Africa's Development Path and the Government's Programme of Action," Paper presented at the DBSA/HSRC/UNDP conference on "Overcoming underdevelopment in South Africa's second economy," Pretoria, 28–29.

57. For a discussion on the origins of the ANC-SACP alliance, see for instance Evaratt, D. 1991. "Alliance Politics of a Special Type: The Roots of the ANC/SACP Alliance 1950–1954," *Journal of Southern African Studies,* Volume 18, Number 1.

58. Tom Lodge points out that the differences between the ANC and Cosatu in particular have always existed since the ANC was unbanned in 1990. As he puts it, "Cosatu complained of ANC unilateralism in its decision to suspend the guerrilla war in August 1990 and its advocacy at the beginning of 1991 of an all-party congress which should negotiate the route to a constituent assembly." See Lodge, T. 2003. p. 21, *Bus Stop for Everyone: Politics in South Africa,* (From Mandela to Mbeki), David Philip, Cape Town, and James Currey, London.

59. See, Evans, G. 1996. p. 252, "South Africa in Remission: The Foreign Policy of an Altered State," *Journal of Modern African Studies,* Volume 34, Number 2.

60. Colin Bundy as quoted in Hoare, S. 1991. p. 12, "SACP faces critical challenges," In *Democracy in Action,* February/March, Journal of the Institute for Democracy in South Africa—IDASA.

61. See Dubow, S. 2000. p. 72, *The African National Congress,* Sutton Publishing, Gloucestershire.

62. For instance, in September 1996, former Transkei leader General Bantu Holomisa, who was credited for allowing Umkhonto we Sizwe—Spear of the Nation, the ANC military wing—bases in the Transkei, was absorbed into the ANC in the post 1994 elections. He was given a Cabinet position as Deputy Minister of Environmental Affairs. However, his testimony to the Truth and Reconciliation Commission alleged that Sol Kerzner had donated money to the ANC, and the ANC forced President Mandela to make a confession to that allegation. After a disciplinary hearing he was dismissed from the party and therefore from parliament for bringing the party into disrepute.

63. Mathiane, M. "Nzimande Warns of Lack of Open Debate," *Business Day,* January 31, 2000.

64. *Business Day,* "ANC alliance has trouble meeting," August 25, 2000.

65. Adapted from: http://www.woza.co.za/news/sacpgearo.htm (accessed, October 20, 2003).

66. Vavi, Z. 2000, "Speech at the Millennium Labor Council," Cosatu, Johannesburg.

67. Jeremy Cronin in the *Mail & Guardian,* June 10–17, 1998.

68. Lodge, T. 1999. p. 113, *South African Politics Since 1994,* David Philip, Cape Town.

69. Nxumalo, F. "Deadlock prolongs ACSA strike," *Business Report*, October 31, 2003.

70. See Southall, R. 2003. p. 63, "The State of Party Politics: Struggles within the Tripartite Alliance and the Decline of Opposition," In Daniel, D., Habib, A., and R. Southall, *State of the Nation: South Africa, 2003–2004*, Human Sciences Research Council, Pretoria.

71. Saul, J.S. 2002. "Cry for the Beloved Country: The Post Apartheid Denouement," in Jacobs, S., and R. Calland (eds.) *Myth, Ideology and the Politics of Thabo Mbeki*, University of Natal Press.

72. South African Press Association, Press Release, August 16, 2000.

73. For both quotes, see Manusamy, S. "Alliance calls a truce on eve of conference: ANC, Cosatu and SACP bosses say they want unity after months of public feuding," *The Sunday Times*, December 15, 2002.

74. "Alliance needed more than ever: SACP," South African Broadcasting Corporation, December 17, 2003.

75. Silke, D. "Is there process to political realignment?" *Cape Times*, November 9, 1996. For instance, the formation of the United Democratic Movement in September 1997 did not in any way threaten the relative position of the ANC in the voting booths.

76. Southall, R. 1998. p. 169.

77. African National Congress, 1999. p. 3, "ANC 1999 Election Manifesto," African National Congress, Johannesburg.

78. *Pretoria News*, "Land returned to 700 000 South Africans," November 26, 2003.

79. African National Congress, 2004, *Ten-Year Review*, African National Congress, Johannesburg.

80. *Ibid*.

81. See Roux, A. 2002. p. 170, *Everyone's Guide to the South African Economy*, Zebra Press, Cape Town.

82. Naidoo, R. 2003. "The Union Movement in South Africa's Transition, 1994–2003, National Labor Economic and Development Institute (NALEDI), Unpublished paper.

83. See George, S. 1999. "Public Institutions and Civil Society, Citizenship and Solidarity: An Area of confrontation?" Paper presented at the Parliamentarians—NGOs Conference, Strasbourg, May 28–02 June.

84. Hunt, D. 1989. p. 173, *Economic Theories of Development: An Analysis of Competing Paradigms*, Harvester Wheatsheaf, London.

85. For a discussion, see Rousseau, J., 1973, *The Social Contract and Discourses*, Macmillan, London; see also Locke, J., 1960, *Two Treatises of Government*, Cambridge University Press, Cambridge, see also Thomas Hobbes, 1960, *Leviathan*, New York.

86. United Nations Development Programme 1994, *Human Development Report*, Oxford University Press, New York, p. 22.

87. For a discussion, see Gurr, T. 1970, pp. 24–27, *Why Men Rebel*, Princeton University Press, Princeton New Jersey. See also, J. Burton (ed.) 1990. *Conflict: Human Needs Theory*, St. Martin's Press, London. See also Wolfenstein,

V. 1967, *The Revolutionary Personality: Lenin, Trotsky, Gandhi*, Princeton University Press, Princeton.

NOTES TO THE CONCLUSION

1. Johnson, P. 1994, "De Klerk has Engineered a Suicide Leap into Universal Suffrage," *The Spectator*, April 30.
2. See Giliomee, H., and L. Schlemmer, 1994, "Overview: Can South African Democracy Become Consolidated," in Giliomee, H., and L. Schlemmer (eds.) *The Bold Experiment: South Africa's New Democracy*, Halfway House. Also, Lijphart, A. 1985, *Power-Sharing in South Africa*, Institute for International Studies, Berkeley, and Horowitz, D.L. 1991. *A Democratic South Africa? Constitutional Engineering in a Divided Society*, Berkeley.
3. See Sparks, A. 2003. pp. 3–4.
4. Segal, N., and S. Malherbe, 2000, p. 34, "A perspective on the South African mining industry in the 21st century," The Graduate School of Business, University of Cape Town.

Bibliography

BOOKS

African National Congress. 2000, *Together Speeding up Change: Fighting Poverty and Creating a Better Life for All*, African National Congress, Johannesburg.
———. 1994. *Reconstruction and Development Program*, Umanyano Publications, Johannesburg.

Allen, T. and A. Thomas. 2000. *Poverty and Development into the 21st Century*. Completely revised (eds.), Open University Press, New York.

Allen, V.L. 1992. *The History of Black Mineworkers in South Africa*. Keighley: Moor Press.

Arnold, G. 2000. *The New South Africa*, Macmillan and St. Martin's Press, London and New York.

Arrighi G. and J. Saul. (eds.) 1973. *Essays on the Political Economy of Africa*, Monthly Review Press, New York and London.

Ashforth, A. 1990. *The Politics of Official Discourse in Twentieth-Century South Africa*. Oxford Studies in African Affairs, Oxford University Press, Oxford.

Barber, J. 2004. Mandela's World: International Dimension of South Africa's Political Revolution, 1990–1999, James Currey, London.

Barker, F. 1999. *The South African Labour Market: Critical Issues for Renaissance*, J.L. van Schaik, Pretoria.

Barberton, C. 1995. *Prioritizing Prioritization in Government*, Public Information Center, Idasa, Cape Town.

Barker, B. *et al*, 1988. *Illustrated History of South Africa*, 1988, Reader's Digest, Cape Town.

Baxter, R. and S. Jones. 2002. "Transformation in the 1990s," in Jones, S. *The Decline of the South African Economy*, Edward Elgar, Cheltenham and Northampton.

Berman, B. 1990. *Crisis and Control in Colonial Kenya: The Dialectic of Domination*, James Currey, London; Heinemann, Kenya and Ohio University Press, Athens.

Biko, S. 1978. *I Write What I Like*, Heinemann, Berkshire.

Bond, P. 2000. *Elite Transition: From Apartheid to Neoliberalism in South Africa.* University of Natal Press, Pietermaritzburg.

———. 1996. "The Making of South Africa's Macro-Economic Compromise" in Maganya, E. (ed.) *Development Strategies in Southern Africa,* IFFA, Johannesburg.

Bhorat, H. *et al,* 2001. *Fighting Poverty: Labour Markets and Inequality in South Africa,* University of Cape Town Press, Cape Town.

Bruggemans, C. 2003. *Change of Pace: South Africa's Economic Revival,* University of the Witwatersrand Press, Johannesburg.

Buell, R. 1928. *The Native Problem in Africa,* The Macmillan Company, New York.

Burton, J. 1990. *Conflict: Human Needs Theory,* St. Martin's Press, London.

Butler, J. 1964. (the title was not readable) *Boston University Papers in African History,* Volume 1, Boston University Press, Boston Massachusetts.

Callinicos, L. 1994. *A People's History of South Africa, Volume One: Gold and Workers* 1886–1924, Ravan Press, Johannesburg.

———. 1981. *Gold and workers, 1886–1924,* Johannesburg; Ravan Press.

Cerny, P. 2000. "Political Globalization and the Competition State," in Stubbs, R. and G. Underhill, (eds.) *Political Economy and the Changing Global Order,* McClelland and Stewart, Toronto.

Chabal, P. and J.P. Daloz. 1999. *Africa Works: The Political Instrumentalization of Disorder,* African Issues, Oxford, Indiana University Press, Bloomington.

Clark, N. and W. Worger, 2004. *South Africa: The Rise and Fall of Apartheid,* Longman, London.

Cornia, G.A. (ed.) 2006. *Pro-Poor Macroeconomics: Potential and Limitations,* Macmillan, London.

Cosatu, 2000. *Accelerating Transformation: First Term Report of Cosatu Parliamentary Office,* Cosatu, Johannesburg.

Cox, R.W. *et al.* 1974. *The Anatomy of Influence: Decision Making in International Organization,* Yale University Press, New Haven.

Crawford, N. and A. Klotz. 1999. *How Sanctions Work: Lessons from South Africa,* International Political Economy Series, St. Martin's Press, New York.

Crocker, C. 1981. *South Africa's Defense Posture: Coping with Vulnerability,* Sage Publications, Beverly Hills.

Crush, J. 1987. *The Struggle for Swazi Labour, 1890–1920,* McGill-Queen's University Press, Kingston and Montreal.

———. and C.H. Ambler. (eds.) 1992. *Liquor and Labor in Southern Africa,* Ohio, Ohio University Press, Athens; University of Natal Press, Pietermaritzburg.

———. 1994. *Power of Development.* Routledge, New York

———. 1995. *Labour Migrancy in Southern Africa Prospects for Post-apartheid Transformation,* Southern African Labour Monographs, 3/95, Rondebosch: University of Cape Town, Labour Law Unit.

———. and W.G. James. (eds.) 1995. *Crossing Boundaries Mine Migrancy in a Democratic South Africa;* IDASA; IDRC, Cape Town, Ottawa, Ontario.

———. 1997. *Covert Operations: Clandestine Migration, Temporary Work and Immigration Policy in South Africa,* Southern African Migration Project, Queen's University at Kingston.

————. *et al* 1999. *Undermining Labour Migrancy and Sub-contracting in the South African gold Mining Industry*. Migration Policy Series, Number 15. Idasa, Cape Town.

————. and V. Williams. (eds.) 1999. *The New South Africans Immigration Amnesties and their Aftermath*, Southern African Migration Project, Idasa, Cape Town and Queen's University at Kingston.

Daniel, D., A. Habib and R. Southall. 2004. *State of the Nation: South Africa, 2003–2004*, Human Sciences Research Council, Pretoria.

Davidson, B., J. Slovo and A. Wilkinson. (eds.) 1976. *Southern Africa: The New Politics of Revolution*, Penguin, Harmondsworth.

Davies, R. 1979. *Capital, State and White Labor in South Africa, 1900–1960*, Harvester Press, Brighton.

Davis, M. 1987. *Apartheid's Rebels: Inside South Africa's Hidden War*, Yale University Press, New Haven.

Department of State Expenditure and Treasury 1996, *The Growth Employment and Redistribution, a Macroeconomic Strategy*, Department of State and Expenditure, Pretoria.

De Vletter, F. 1998. *Sons of Mozambique: Mozambican Miners and Post-Apartheid South Africa*, Southern African Migration Project, Queen's University at Kingston.

Dornbusch, R. and S. Edwards (eds.) 1991. *Macroeconomic Populism in Latin America*, Chicago University Press, Chicago and London.

Dubow, S. 2000. *The African National Congress*, Sutton Pocket Histories, Sutton.

Dugard, J. (ed.), 1992. *The Last Years of Apartheid: Civil Liberties in South Africa*, Ford Foundation, New York.

Duncan, D. 1995. *The Mills of God the State and African Labour in South Africa, 1918–1948*, Witwatersrand University Press, Johannesburg.

Du Toit, J. 1998. *The Structure of the South African Economy*, ABSA Bank, Southern Book Publishers.

Escobar, A. 1995. *Encountering Development: The Making and Unmaking of the Third World*, Princeton, Studies in Culture/Power/History, Princeton: Princeton University Press, Princeton.

Ffrench-Davis, R. 1976. "Policy Tools and Objectives of Redistribution," in Foxley, A. (ed.) *Income Distribution in Latin America*, Cambridge, Cambridge University Press.

Flynn, L. 1992. *Studded with Diamonds and Paved with Gold: Miners, Mining Companies and Human Rights in Southern Africa*, Bloomsbury, London.

Forgas, D. 1988. *The Antonio Gramsci Reader*, Lawrence and Wisehard, New York.

Gastrow, P. 2001. *Theft from South African Mines and Refineries: The Illicit Market for Gold and Platinum*. ISS Monograph Series, Number 54. Institute for Security Studies, Pretoria

George, S. 2000. "A Short History of Neo-Liberalism: Twenty Years of Elite Economics and Emerging Opportunities for Structural Change," in Bello, W., N. Bullard and K. Malhotra, (eds.), *Global Finance: New Thinking on Regulating Speculative Capital Markets*, Zed Books, London.

Giddens, A. 1985. *The Nation State and Violence*, Cabridge University Press, Cambridge.

Giliomee, H.B., L. Schlemmer, and S. Hauptfleisch (eds.) 1994. *The Bold Experiment South Africa's New Democracy*, Southern Publications, Johannesburg.

Government Communication and Information Service (GCIS) *South Africa Year Book*, 2000. GCIS, Pretoria.

———. 2005, *South Africa Year Book*. GCIS, Pretoria.

Gramsci, A. 1977. *Prison Notebooks* (Quaderni del Carcere) extracts as translated and commented by James, J. Fontana Modern Masters Series, London.

Grange, G.H. 1985. "Emerging Planning and Safety in the South African Mining Industry," Paper presented at the 21st International Conference of Safety in Mines Research Institute, Sydney 21–25 October 1985, In Green, A.R. (ed.) *Safety in Mines Research*, A.A. Balkema, Rotterdam, Boston.

Gray, J. 1998. *False Dawn: The Delusions of Global Capitalism*, Granta Books, London.

Greater Johannesburg Metropolitan Council—World Bank Partnership, 2000. *Constraints to Growth and Employment in South Africa*.

Green, T. and J. Gay. 1997. *Riding the Tiger: Lesotho Miners and Permanent Residence in South Africa*, Southern African Migration Project, Queen's University at Kingston.

Greenberg, S. 1980. *Race and State in Capitalist Development: South Africa in Comparative Perspective*, Ravan Press, Johannesburg.

Grey, P.C. 1919. *The Development of the Gold Mining Industry on the Witwatersrand 1902–1910*, Ravan Press, Johannesburg.

Grundy, K.W. 1991. *South Africa Domestic Crisis and Global Challenge*, Dilemmas in World Politics, Westview Press, Boulder.

Guelke, A. 1999. *South Africa in Transition: The Misunderstood Miracle*, International Library of African Studies, v.10. Taurus, London.

Gurr, T. 1970. *Why Men Rebel*, Princeton University Press, Princeton New Jersey.

Hauss, C. and M. Smith. 2000. *Comparative Politics: Domestic Responses to Global Challenges: A Canadian Perspective*, Nelson Thomson Learning, and Scarborough.

Hettne, B. 1995. *Development Theory and the Three Worlds*, Longman, London.

Hobson, J. A. and G. P. Gooch. 1972. *The War in South Africa: Its Causes and Effects*, Garland Library of War and Peace, Garland Pub, New York.

Hoile, D. 1986. *Understanding Sanctions*, International Freedom Foundation, London.

Holland, H. 1989. *The Struggle: A History of the African National Congress*, Grafton Books, London.

Holsti, K. J. 1985. *The Dividing Discipline: Hegemony and Diversity in International Theory*, Allen and Unwin, Boston.

Horowitz, D.L. 1991. *A Democratic South Africa? Constitutional Engineering in* a Divided Society, Berkeley.

Hunt, D. 1989. *Economic Theories of Development: An Analysis of Competing Paradigms*, Harvester Wheatsheaf, London.

IMF, *South Africa—Selected Economic Issues*, 1996. IMF Staff Country Report Number 96, Volume 4, IMF, Washington D.C.

Innes, D. 1984. *Anglo-American and the Rise of Modern South Africa*, Heinemann, London.

Jacobs, S. and R. Calland. (eds.) 2002. *Myth, Ideology and the Politics of Thabo Mbeki*, University of Natal Press, Pietermaritzburg.

Jacobsson, D. 1936. *Fifty Golden Years of the Rand 1886–1936*, Faber and Faber, London.

James, W.G. 1992. *Our Precious Metal: African Labour in South Africa's Gold Industry, 1970–1990*, David Philip, Cape Town, James Currey, London, Indiana University Press, Cape Town, London and Bloomington.

Jeeves, A. 1985. *Migrant Labour in South Africa's Mining Economy: The Struggle for the Gold Mines' Labour Supply, 1890–1920*, McGill-Queen's University Press, Kingston, Witwatersrand University Press, Johannesburg.

————. and M. Fraser. 1977. *All that Glittered: Selected Correspondence of Lionel Phillips, 1890–1924*. Oxford University Press, Cape Town, New York.

Jeppe, C. 1946. *Gold Mining on the Witwatersrand, Volume II*, Transvaal Chamber of Mines, Cape Times, Cape Town.

Jones, S. (ed.) 2002. *The Decline of the South African Economy*, Cheltenham, U.K. and Northampton, USA.

Kahn, B. 1996. *Exchange Control Liberalization in South Africa*, Idasa, Pretoria and Cape Town.

Keet, D. 1999. *Globalization and Regionalization—Contradictory Tendencies: Counteractive Tactics or Strategic Possibilities*, Foundation for Global Dialogue, Occasional Paper Number 18, Braamfontein, Johannesburg.

Kelly, M.V. 1993. *Financial Institutions in South Africa*, Juta Press, Johannesburg.

Kempton, D. 1989. *Soviet Strategy Towards Southern Africa: The National Liberation Movement Competition*, Praeger, New York.

Kentridge, M. 1993. *Turning the Tanker: The Economic Debate in South Africa*, Center for Policy Studies, Johannesburg.

Keynes, J.M. 1940. *How to Pay for the War: A Radical Plan for the Chancellor of the Exchequer*, Macmillan, London.

Kilmiste, A. 2000. "Socialist Models of Development," in Allen, T., and A. Thomas, *Poverty and Development into the 21st Century*, Open University Press, Oxford.

Kline, B. 1997. *Profit, Principle and Apartheid, 1948–1994*, The Edwin Mellen Press, Lewiston.

Landgren, S. 1989. *Embargo Disimplemented: South Africa's Military Industry*, Stockholm International Peace Research Institute (Sipri), Oxford University Press.

Lang, J. 1986. *Bullion Johannesburg: Men, Mines and the Challenge of Conflict*, Jonathan Ball Publishes, Johannesburg.

Le May, G.H.L. 1965. *British Supremacy in South Africa 1899–1907*, Clarendon Press, London.

Lester, A., E. Nel, and T. Binns. 2000. *South Africa, Past Present and the Future: Gold at the End of the Rainbow?* Longman, London.

Levy, N. 1993. *The Foundations of the Cheap Labour System in the South African Gold Mining Industry, 1887–1906*, Boston Spa, Wetherby, West Yorkshire, United Kingdom: British Library, Document Supply Centre.

Leyds, G.A. 1964. *A History of Johannesburg the Early Years*, Nasionale Boekhandel, Cape Town

Leys, C. 1996. *The Rise and Fall of Development Theory*, EAEP, Nairobi, Indiana University, Bloomington.

Lijphart, A. 1985. *Power-sharing in South Africa*, Policy Papers in International Affairs, Number 24. Berkeley: Institute of International Studies, University of California.

Lipton, M. 1985. *Capitalism and Apartheid South Africa, 1910–84*, Aldershot, Hants., Gower/M.T. Smith, London.

Lodge, T. 2002. *Politics in South Africa from Mandela to Mbeki*, David Philip, Cape Town, James Currey, London. Indiana Universtiy Press, Bloomington.

———. 1999. *South African Politics since 1994*, David Philip, Cape Town.

———. 1983. *Black Politics in South Africa since 1945*, Ravan, Johannesburg.

MacEwan, A. 1999. *Neo-liberalism or Democracy? Economic Strategy, Markets, and Alternatives for the 21st Century*, Zed. books, London, Pluto Press, New York.

Macnad, R. 1987. *Gold: Their Touchstone—Goldfields of South Africa 1887–1987*, Jonathan Ball Publishers, Johannesburg.

Macroeconomic Research Group (MERG). 1993. *Making Democracy Work: A Framework for Macroeconomic Policy in South Africa*, Center for Development Studies, Belleville.

Magubane, B. 1996. *The Making of a Racist State: British Imperialism and the Union of South Africa, 1875–1910*, Africa World Press, Trenton.

Mamdani, M. 1996. *Citizen and Subject: Contemporary Africa and the Legacy of Late Colonialism*, Princeton Studies in Culture/Power/History, Princeton, David Phillip, Cape Town, J. Currey, London.

Mandela, N. 1994. *Long Walk to Freedom: The Autobiography of Nelson Mandela*, Little Brown, Boston.

Marais, H. 2001. *South Africa Limits to Change: The Political Economy of Transition*, London, Cape Town: Zed Books, University of Cape Town Press, Cape Town.

Marais, J.S. 1961. *The Fall of Kruger's Republic*, Clarendon Press, Oxford.

Mawby, A.A. 2000. *Gold Mining and Politics Johannesburg, 1900–1907: The Origins of the Old South Africa*, African Studies: African Studies, Edwin Mellen Press New York.

Mbeki, G. 1964. *South Africa: The Peasants' Revolt*, International Defence and Aid Fund for Southern Africa, London.

McKinley, D. 1997. The ANC and the Liberation Struggle: A Critical Political Biography, Pluto Press, London and Chicago.

Miliband, R. 1977. *Marxism and Politics*, Oxford University Press, Oxford.

Mkandawire, T. and C. Soludo. 1998. Our *Continent, Our Future: African* Perspectives on Structural Adjustment, IDRC—Ottawa, CODESRIA—Dakar.

Moodie, T.D. 1975. *The Rise of Afrikanerdom Power, Apartheid, and the Afrikaner Civil Religion*, Perspectives on Southern Africa, 11. University of California Press, Berkeley.

———. and V. Ndatshe. 1994. *Going for Gold: Men, Mines, and Migration: Perspectives on Southern Africa*, Witwatersrand University Press, Johannesburg.

Moolman, E. 2003. *An Econometric Analysis of Labour Demand at an Industry Level in South Africa,* Trade and Industrial Strategies (TIPS), Johannesburg.

Moorson, R. 1986. *The Scope for Sanctions: Economic Measures Against South Africa*, Catholic Institute for International Relations, London.

Muller, C.F.J. 1993. *500 Years: A History of South Africa*, Third edition, revised and illustrated, Van Schaik, Pretoria.

Murray, C. 1981. *Families Divided: The Impact of Migrant Labour in Lesotho*. African Studies Series, Cambridge University Press, Cambridge.

Murray, M.J. 1994. *Revolution Deferred: The Painful Birth of Post-Apartheid South Africa*, Verso, New York.

Nkrumah, K. 1965. *Neo-Colonialism: The Last Stage of Imperialism*, Thomas Nelson and Sons, London.

Nossal, K.R. 1994. *Rain Dancing: Sanctions in Canadian and Australian Foreign Policy*, University of Toronto Press, Toronto.

O'Meara, D. 1996. Forty Lost Years: The Apartheid State and the Politics of the National Party, 1948–1994, Ravan Press, Johannesburg and Ohio University Press, Athens.

———.1983. *Volkskapitalisme: Class, Capital and Ideology in the Development of Afrikaner-Nationalism 1934–1948*, Ravan Press, Johannesburg.

Packard, R.M. 1990. *White Plague, Black Labor Tuberculosis and the Political Economy of Health and Disease in South Africa*, University of Natal Press, London: James Currey, Pietermaritzburg.

Pakenham, T. 1993. *The Boer War*, Jonathan Ball, Johannesburg.

Parsons, R. 2004. (ed.) *Manuel's Markets and Money: Essays in Appraisal*, Double Storey Books, Cape Town.

Paton, B. 1995. *Labour Export Policy in the Development of Southern Africa*, Macmillan in association with the Institute of Social Studies, London.

Polachek, S. (ed.) 2001. *Worker Wellbeing in a Changing Labour Market*, Research in Labour Economic, Volume 20, State University of New York, Binghamton.

Polanyi, K. 1957. *The Great Transformation*, Rinehart, New York.

Porter, A.N. 1980. *The Origins of the South African War: Joseph Chamberlain and the Diplomacy of Imperialism, 1895–99*, Manchester University Press, Manchester.

Posusney, M.P. and L.J. Cook. 2002. *Privatization, Labor Responses and Consequences in Global Perspective*, Edward Elgar Publishers, Northampton.

Przeworski, A. 1991. *Democracy and the Market: Political and Economic Reforms in Eastern Europe and Latin America*, Cambridge University Press, Cambridge.

Ramphele, M. 1993. *A Bed Called Home: Life in the Migrant Labour Hostels of Cape Town*, David Philip, Cape Town.

Richardson, P. 1982. *Chinese Mine Labour in the Transvaal*. Atlantic Highlands, Macmillan, London.

Rile, E. 1991. *Major Political Events in South Africa, 1948–1990*, Facts on File, Oxford and New York.

Rist, G. 1997. *The History of Development: From Western Origins to Global Faith*, Zed Books, London and New York.

Rostow, W.W. 1960. *The Stages of Economic Growth a non-Communist Manifesto*, Cambridge University Press, Cambridge.

Roux, A. 2000. *Everyone's Guide to South African Economy*, Zebra Press, Rivonia.

Sampson, A. 1987. *Black and Gold Tycoons, Revolutionaries and Apartheid*, Hodder and Stoughton, London.

Schaeffer, R. 1997. *Power to the People: Democratization Around the World*, Westview Press, Harper Collins Publishers.

Scholtz, G.D. 1948. *Die Oorsake van die Twede Vryheidsoorlo, 1899–1902*, Voortrekker Pers, Beperk.

Schumpeter, J.A. 1943. *Capitalism, Socialism, and Democracy*, Allen and Unwin, London.

Seegers, A. 1996. *The Military in the Making of Modern South Africa*, Tauris Academic Studies, I.B. Tauris Publishers, London and New York.

Sen, A. 1999. *Development as Freedom*, Alfred A. Knopf, New York.

Shimoni, G. and G. Shimoni. 2003. *Community and Conscience: The Jews in Apartheid South Africa*, The Tauber Institute for the Study of European Jewry Series: Tauber Institute for the Study of European Jewry Series (Unnumbered). David Philip, Cape Town.

Simons, J. and R. Simons. 1983. *Class and Colour in South Africa, 1850–1950*, International Defense Aid Fund for Southern Africa, London.

Simkins, C. and H.B. Giliomee. 1999. *The Awkward Embrace One-party Domination and Democracy*, Tafelberg, Cape Town. Centre For South African Politics, Stellenbosch.

Smith, I. 1996. *The Origins of the South African War, 1899–1902*, Longman, London and New York.

South African Institute of Race Relations, 1998. *South Africa Survey 1998–1999*, South African Institute for Race Relations, Johannesburg.

South African Reserve Bank, 2002. *Annual Report*, South African Reserve Bank, Pretoria.

Southall, R. 2003. *The State of Democracy in South Africa*, Frank Cass and Company, Dublin.

Sparks, A.H. 2003. *Beyond the Miracle: Inside the New South Africa*, Jonathan Ball Publishers, Johannesburg and Cape Town.

Standing, G., J. Sender, and J. Weeks. 1996, *Restructuring the Labour Market: The South African Challenge*, an ILO Country Review, International Labour Office, Geneva.

Statistics South Africa, *Census 1996*. Government Printer, Pretoria.

Stiglitz, J.E. 2002. *Globalization and its Discontents*, Norton, New York.

Strange, S. 1996. *The Retreat of the State the Diffusion of Power in the World Economy*, Cambridge Studies in International Relations Cambridge, University Press, Cambridge.

———. 1974. "IMF: Monetary Managers" in Cox, R.W. *et al. The Anatomy of Influence: Decision Making in International Organization*, Yale University Press, New Haven.

Stubbs, R. and G. Underhill. 1994. *Political Economy and the Changing Global Order*, McClelland and Stewart, Toronto.

Terreblanche, S. 1993. *A History of Inequality in South Africa, 1652–2002*, University of Natal Press, Pietermaritzburg.

Tetty, J., K. Puplampu and B. Berman, (eds.) 2003. *Critical Perspectives on Politics and Social Economic Development in Ghana*, African Social Studies Series, Brill, Leiden and London.

Thomas, A. 1997. *Rhodes: The Race for Africa*, Penguin Books, London.

Torres, L. 1998. *Labour Markets in Southern Africa*, Fafo-report 257, Institute for Applied Social Science, Johannesburg.

United Nations Development Programme, 1994. *Human Development Report*, Oxford University Press, Oxford and New York.

United Nations Development Programme, 2005. *Overcoming Underdevelopment in South Africa's Second Economy*, United Nations Development Programme, Development Bank of Southern Africa and the Human Sciences research Council, Johannesburg.

Van der Horst, S. 1942. *Native Labour in South Africa*, Oxford University Press, Oxford.

Van Onselen, C. 1982. *Studies in the Social and Economic History of Witwatersrand, 1886–1914*, Longman, London and New York.

Wallerstein, I. 1991. *Geopolitics and Geoculture: Essays on the Changing World-System*, Cambridge University Press, Cambridge.

———. 1984. *The Politics of the World Economy, the States, the Movements, and the Civilizations: Essays*. Studies in Modern Capitalism, Cambridge University Press, Cambridge.

Warwick, P. 1980. *The South African War the Anglo-Boer War, 1899–1902*. Longman, Harlow, Essex.

Watermeyer, G.A. and S.N. Hoffenberg. 1932. *Witwatersrand Mining Practice*, The Transvaal Chamber of Mines, Gold Producer's Committee, Chamber of Mines, Johannesburg.

Wilber C.K. and K.P. Jameson. 1992, p. 107, *The Political Economy of Development and Underdevelopment*, McGraw-Hall, London and New York.

Williamson, J. 1990. (ed.), *Latin American Adjustment: How Much Has Happened?* Washington Institute for International Economics, Washington.

Wilson, F. 1972. *Labour in the South African Gold Mines, 1911–1969*, African Studies Series, Cambridge University Press, Cambridge.

———. 1972. *Migrant Labour*. Johannesburg: Published jointly by the South African Council of Churches and SPRO-CAS, Johannesburg.

Wittenberg, M. 1997. "Growth, demand and redistribution: Economic debate, rhetoric and some food for thought," in Michie, J. and V. Padayachee (eds.), *The Political Economy of South Africa's Transition: Policy Perspectives in the Late 1990s*, Dryden Press, London.

Wolfenstein, V. 1967. *The Revolutionary Personality: Lenin, Trotsky, Gandhi*, Princeton University Press, Princeton.

Young, R. 2002. *Music, Popular Culture Identities*. Critical Studies (Amsterdam, Netherlands), Volume 19. Rodopi, Amsterdam.

Yudelman, D. 1983. *The Emergence of Modern South Africa: State, Capital, and the Incorporation of Organized Labor on the South African Gold Fields, 1902–1939*, Greenwood Press, Westport, Connecticut.

JOURNAL ARTICLES AND UNPUBLISHED MATERIAL

Andreasson, S. 2002. "Neoliberalism and the Creation of Virtual Democracies in the Global South," Unpublished paper, Department of Political Studies, Arizona State University.

Arnold, M. 1992. "Engaging South Africa After Apartheid," *Foreign Policy*, Number 87, pp. 139–156.

Baker, F. 2003. "The Impact of Labour Legislation on the Performance of the Labour Market," in Finnemore, M. and R. Van Rensberg, *Contemporary Labour Relations*, Butterworth, Johannesburg.

Berman, B. 1998. "Ethnicity, Patronage and the African State: The Politics of Uncivil Nationalism," *African Affairs*, Volume 97, Number 388.

———. 1994. "African Capitalism and the Paradigm of Modernity: Culture, Technology and the State," *African Capitalists in African Development*, pp. 235–261, Lynne Rienner Publishers, London.

———.1991. "Nationalism, Ethnicity and Modernity: The Paradox of the Mau Mau," *Canadian Journal of African Studies*, Volume 25, Number 2. pp. 181–206.

Bhagwati, J. 1998. "The Capital Myth," *Foreign Affairs*, Volume 77, Number 3.

Bhorat, H. 2003. "The Post-Apartheid Challenge: Labour Demand Trends in the South African Labour Market, 1995–1999," Development Policy Research Unit, University of Cape Town.

———. with Lundall, P. and S. Rospabe. 2002. "The South African Labour Market in a Globalizing World: Economic and Legislative Considerations," Development Policy Research Unit and the International Labour Organization.

———. 2002. "The South African Labour Market in a Globalizing World: Economic and Legislative Considerations," Development Policy Research Unit, Paper commissioned by the International Labour Organization.

Brunt, S. 1987. "A South African Experience—a British Miner's view of the South African Mining Industry," National Union of Mineworkers, Sheffield.

Calitz, E. 2002. "Structural Economic Reform in South Africa: Some International Comparisons," *The South African Journal of Economics*, Volume 70, Number 2.

———. 2003. "Economic Policy: Exploring the Independence of South Africa," *Journal of Studies in Economics and Econometrics*, Volume 27, Number 2.

———. 1997. "Aspects of the Performance of the South African Economy," *The South African Journal of Economics*, Volume 65, Number 3.

Cammack, D.R. 1990. "The Rand at War, 1899–1902: The Witwatersrand and the Anglo-Boer War," *Perspectives on Southern Africa*, Volume 44.

Carmody, P. 2002. "Between Globalization and (post) Apartheid: The Political Economy of Restructuring in South Africa," *Journal of Southern African Studies*, Volume 28, Number 2.

Chamber of Mine's Memorandum to the National Treasury on the Draft Minerals and Petroleum Royalty Bill, 2002.

Chamber of Mines of South Africa. 1988. *Facts and Figures*, Chamber of Mines, Johannesburg.

———. 1988. *The South African Mining Industry: Fact and Figures*, Chamber of Mines of South Africa, Johannesburg.

Chang, H. *et al.* 1998. "The Asian Crisis: Introduction," *Cambridge Journal of Economics,* Volume 22, pp. 649–652.

Chirwa, W.C. 1998. "Aliens and Aids in Southern Africa: The Malawi-South Africa Debate," *African Affairs*, Volume 96, Number 386.

Christiansen, H. and A. Bertrand. 2003. "Trend and Recent Trends in Foreign Direct Investment," Directorate for Financial, Fiscal and Enterprise Affairs, OECD.

Crush, J. and C. Tshitereke. 2001. "Contesting Migrancy: The Foreign Labour Debate in Post-1994 South Africa," *Africa Today*, Volume 48, Number 3.

———. and C. Tshitereke. 1999. "Hidden Treaties: South Africa's Bilateral Labour Agreement with its Closest Neighbors," Unpublished report, Southern African Migration Project, Queen's University, Kingston.

———. and W. James. 1991. "Depopulating the Compounds: Migrant Labour and Mine Migrancy in South Africa," *World Development*, Volume 19. Issue 4. pp. 301–316.

———. 1989. "Migrancy and Militance: The Case of the National Union of Mineworkers of South Africa," *African Affairs*, Volume 88, pp. 5–24.

Ebrahim, S. 2002. "Defend, Advance and Consolidate the Alliance," *South African Labour Bulletin*, Volume 26, Number 2.

Edwards, C. 1998. "Financing Faster Growth in South Africa: The Case for Reforming the Financial Sector," *Transformation,* Volume 35, University of Natal, Durban.

Evans, G. 1996. "South Africa in Remission: The Foreign Policy of an Altered State," *Journal of Modern African Studies*, Volume 34, Number 2.

Evaratt, D. 1991. "Alliance Politics of a Special Type: The Roots of the ANC/SACP Alliance 1950–1954," *Journal of Southern African Studies,* Volume 18, Number 1.

Harries, P. 1986. "Capital, State, and Labour on the 19th Century Witwatersrand: A Reassessment," *South African Historical Journal*, Volume 18.

Hunag, Y. and T. Khanna. 2003. "Can India Overtake China," *Foreign Policy Magazine,* September/October, Carnegie Endowment for Peace, Massachusetts.

George, S. 1999. "Public Institutions and Civil Society, Citizenship and Solidarity: An Area of Confrontation?" Paper presented at the Parliamentarians—NGOs Conference, Strasbourg, May/June.

Godsell, B. "Focus on Value and Growth," AngloGold presentation at the Denver Mining Investment Forum October 03, 2002.

Griffith, R. 1991. "The South African Military: The Dilemma of Expanded Influence in Decision-Making," *Journal of Asian and African Studies*, XXVI 1–2.

Guelke, A. 1974. "Apartheid and the Labour Market," Center for Southern African Studies, York University.

Halliday, F. 1991. "International Relations: Is there a New Agenda?" *Journal of International Studies*, Volume 20, Number 1, pp. 57–72.

Herbst, J. 2003. "Analyzing Apartheid: How Accurate were U.S. Intelligence Estimates of South Africa, 1948–1994? *African Affairs*, Volume 102, pp. 81–107.

Hirsch, A. 2004. "South Africa's Development Path and the Government's Programme of Action," Paper presented at the DBSA/HSRC/UNDP conference on "Overcoming underdevelopment in South Africa's second economy," Pretoria, 28–29.

Hofmeyr, J. 2001. "The Case for Flexibility in South Africa's Labour Market," University of Natal Durban, paper presented at the *Work 2001 Conference*, Johannesburg.

Hogendorn, J. 1987. "Migrant Labour in South Africa's Mining Economy 1924–1955." *Journal of Economic History*, Volume 47.

International Labour Resource Group, Workers World News, September 1999. "Privatization: Can it deliver?" Woodstock, South Africa.

Jeeves, A. and D. Yudelman. 1986. "New Labour Frontiers for Old: Black Migrants to the South African Gold Mines, 1920–1985," *Journal of Southern African Studies*, Volume 13, Number 1.

Jeeves, A. 1971. *Rand Capitalist and Transvaal Politics, 1892–1899*, Ph.D. Thesis, (unpublished), Queen's University at Kingston, Ontario.

———. 1974. "The Control of Migratory Labour in South Africa: Gold Mines in the Era of Kruger and Milner," *Journal of African Studies*, Volume 2, Number 1.

———. 1986. "Migrant Labour and South African Expansion, 1920–1950," *South African Historical Journal*, Volume 18.

Johnson, P. 1994. "De Klerk has Engineered a Suicide Leap into Universal Suffrage," *The Spectator*, April 30.

Labuschane, G. and E. Muller. 1993. "Population and Migration in Southern Africa in the 1990s," *Politicon*, Volume 20, Number 1.

Leger, J. 1992. "Occupational Disease in South African Mines—a Neclected Epidemic?" *South African Medical Journal*, Volume 81, pp. 197–201.

Lester, A., E. Nel and T. Binns. 2000. "South Africa's Current Transition in Temporal and Spatial Context," *Antipode*, Volume 32, Number 2.

Levy, N. 1978. "Problems of Acquisition of Labour for the South African Gold Mining Industry: The Asian Labour Alternative and the Defence of the Wage Structure," Center for Southern African Studies, University of York.

Litvak, L. *et al.* 1978. "South Africa; Foreign Investment and Apartheid," Institute for Policy Studies, Washington D.C.

Major Report of the Transvaal Labour Commission. 1903. (Appendinx to the Annual Report of the Transvaal Chamber of Mines, Johannesburg.

Mandela, N.R. 1997. "A Vision for Africa," address at the world economic forum, southern Africa economic summit, May 21, 1997, Harare.

———. 1991. J.H. Heinz Company foundation distinguished lecture, University of Pittsburgh, Soldiers and Sailors Memorial Hall, December 6.

Nash, A. 1999. "Mandela's Democracy," *Monthly Review*, Volume 50, Number 11.

Mbeki, T. 2003. Responses to Parliamentary Questions in the National Assembly, 5 May, Parliament, Cape Town.

McKeown, T. 1983. "Hegemonic Stability Theory and 19th Century Tariff Level in Europe," *International Organization*, Volume 37, Number 1.

Michie, J. and V. Padayachee. 1998. "Three Years After Apartheid: Growth, Employment and Redistribution?" *Cambridge Journal of Economics*, Volume 22, Number 5.

Milner, H. 1998. "International Political Economy: Beyond Hegemonic Stability," *Foreign Policy*, Number 110, special edition. Spring.

Minowa, M. 2001. "Japanese Capitalism in Crisis: A Regulationist Interpretation," (A book Review) in *Asia-Pacific Development Journal*, Volume 8, Number 1.

Moodie, T.D., *et al*. 1988. "Migrancy and Male Sexuality on the South African Gold Mines," *Journal of Southern African Studies*, Volume 14, Number 2, pp. 228–256.

Moll, T. 1991. "Growth through Redistribution: A Dangerous Fantasy," *The South African Journal of Economics,* Volume 59, Number 3.

Mphephu, N.F. (undated) "Rehabilitation of Tailing Dams on the Central Rand, Johannesburg," Center for Applied Mining and Exploration Geology, University of the Witwatersrand.

Murray, C. 1995. A Bed Called Home: A Book Review, *Journal of the Royal Anthropological Institute*, Volume 1; Number 2.

Naidoo, R. 2003. "The Union Movement in South Africa's Transition, 1994–2003, National Labour Economic and Development Institute (NALEDI), Unpublished paper.

———. 2000. "The Impact of Socio-economic restructuring on the Working Class and the Challenges Facing Them," paper presented at the Harold Wolpe Forum, University of Cape Town, August 17.

Nerys, J. 2000. "The Campaign against British Banks Involvement in Apartheid South Africa," *African Affairs*, Volume 99, Number 396.

Netshitenzhe, J. 2000. "National Democratic Revolution and Class," *African Communist,* Number 154. Second Quarter, South African Communist Party, Johannesburg.

Nkomo, S. 1985. "Migrant Labour Economic Theory and National Development Policy: The Case of South Africa and Lesotho," Ph.D. Thesis, (unpublished), University of Delaware.

O'Meara, D. 1975. "The 1946 African Mineworkers' Strike," *Journal of Commonwealth and Comparative Politics*, Volume 12, Number 2.

Pogue, T. E. 2000. "An Overview of Producer Services in the Mining Industry in South Africa," Development Policy Research Unit, Working Paper Number 00/35, University of Cape Town.

Sally, R. 1994. "Multinational Enterprises, Political Economy and Industrial Theory," *Review of International Political Economy*, Volume 1, Number 1.

Segal, N. and S. Malherbe. 2000. "A perspective on the South African Mining Industry in the 21st Century," The Graduate School of Business, University of Cape Town.

Simon, J. *et al*, 2001. "Estimating the Impacts of AIDS on Business in South Africa," paper presented at the Boston University African Studies Seminar, April 10.

South African Communist Party. 1997. "Economic Policy in the Alliance: A Central Committee Discussion Document," South African Communist Party, Johannesburg.

Southall, R. 1998. "The Centralization and Fragmentation of South Africa's Dominant Party System," *African Affairs*, Volume 97, pp. 443–469.

———. 1986. "Migrants and Trade Unions in South Africa Today," *Canadian Journal of African Studies*, Volume 20, Number 5.

Strange, S. 1987. "The Persistent Myth of Lost Hegemony," *International Organization*, Volume 41, Number 4.

———. 1985. "Protectionism and World Politics," *International Organization*, Volume 39, Number 2.

Taylor, D. 1987. "Migrant Labour in the Mining Industry: A Future Perspective," *South Africa Journal of Labour Relations*, Volume 11, Number 2.

The Economist. 2001. "Jobless and Joyless: A Survey of South Africa," January 24.

Tickel, A. and J. Peck. 1992. "Accumulation, Regulation and the Geographics of post-Fordism: Missing Links in Regulationist Research," *Progress in Human Geography*, Volume 16, Number 2.

Tshitereke, C. 2002. "Securing Democracy: Party Finance and Party Donations—the South African Challenge," Institute for Security Studies Paper Number 63, Pretoria.

———. 1999. "Archaic Labour Agreements need Attention," in *Crossings*, Volume 3, Number 1, Southern African Migration Project, Queen's University, Kingston.

———. 1998. *Debate on the Contract Labour Migrant System in South Africa—1990–1998*, (unpublished), Masters Thesis, University of Stellenbosch.

Van Rensberg, T. 1999. "A Critical Assessment of Primary Listings of South African Companies in Offshore Stock Exchanges," paper presented to the TIPS Annual Forum at Glenburn Lodge, Muldersdrift, September 19–22.

Viner, J. 1948. "Power versus Plenty," *World Politics*, Volume 1, Number 1.

Wade, R. 1992. "East Asia's Economic Success: Conflicting Perspectives, Partial Insights, Shaky Evidence," *World Politics: A Quarterly Journal of International Relations*, Volume 44.

Walters, S. and J.W. Prinsloo. 2002. "The Impact of Offshore Listing on the South African Economy," *South African Reserve Bank Quarterly Bulletin*, September.

Waltz, K. 2000. "Structural Realism after the Cold War," *International Security*, Volume 25, Number 1.

Webster, E. and E. Glenn. 1999. "Lessons for South Africa: Unions, Democracy, and Economic Liberalization, *Working USA*—September/October.

Weeks, J. 1998. "Stuck in Low GEAR? Macroeconomic Policy in South Africa, 1996–1998," *Cambridge Journal of Economics*, Volume 23.

Whiteside, A. and C. Patel. 1985. "Agreements Concerning the Employment of Foreign Black Labour," *International Migration for Employment*, International Labour Office, Geneva.

Williams, P. 1999. "Reflections on the 'New' South Africa," *African Affairs*, Volume 98, Number 392.

Williamson, J. 2000. "What should the World Bank think about the Washington Consensus?" *The World Bank Research Observer*, Volume 15, Number 2. The World Bank, Washington.

Wilson, F. 2001. "Minerals and Migrants: How the Mining Industry has Shaped South Africa," *Daedalus*, Journal of the American Academy of Arts and Sciences, Winter.

Wilson, F. 1996. "Human Capital Formation and the Labour Market in South Africa," *American Economic Review*, Volume. 82.

Index